As I Was Saying...

For Paula
All beautiful you are, my darling; there is no flaw in you.
Song of Songs; 4:7, NIV

My thanks to Matt Schepeler, my brother in the Lord and publisher of The Exponent in Brooklyn, Michigan. My weekly column has been a seedbed for the entries that have become this book. Thanks Matt, for your encouragement and your kind permissions to retain rights to my work.

Contents:

The Basics; Always the Basics   1

From childhood, you have learned   5

And they shall be one   26

The joy of the full quiver   45

And all that is in the world   92

I will build my church   124

Bread, by the sweat of your face   147

Wanderers in the wilderness   199

As I ponder upon my bed   236

The basics; always the basics

101.

Whenever I encounter that number, my reaction can usually be summed up with a deep groan of despair. In academic circles, 101 signifies the beginning of a long journey. It identifies the portal, the first step, the entry-level primer. Any course of study usually finds its starting point flagged by this number, such as US History, 101. Or, Introduction to Ceramics: Studio Art 101. Looking back over my life, I couldn't give anything but a wild estimate of the number of 101 classes that have been part of my education.

Since receiving new life in Christ back in what my children believe were the dark ages (also known as 1980), there has continued to be an unending series of "101" lessons in my life. I am sure that while the Lord never demands perfection from us while in this earthly life, he is daily looking for progress in our walk with him. Progress involves, like driving, a series of turns and corrections. I would see myself as somewhat an expert in that field, having made some pretty intricate maneuvers on the road of my life. Sometimes I left the roadway completely.

I spent my youth and early college years as a member of the Christian-as-nice-person denomination. You may have been one, or perhaps have met such a practitioner in your lifetime. The religion is simple enough: live a life that gives a nod to God, while proudly working for the prize of heaven by doing good and living clean. There was no need to have any real relationship with Jesus, the Son of God, and trusting his work alone for my salvation. The focus was upon self, which gave huge strokes to my ego while padding my spiritual resume. What a great, "feel good, little god" religion!

Not to appear overly proud while working myself upward, it did become necessary to mention Jesus on occasion. Sometimes a bow coupled with pointing to heaven had its place as well. Understated, with just the right touch of humility for the spotlight. After all, Jesus' approval could be valuable as "bonus points" on my eventual entrance-into-heaven exam. In those years, I figured I was well past the 101 stage of being a Christian, when actually I hadn't even taken a chair in the first session of the remedial class yet.

The Lord used a long string of happenings to bring me to the truth about him, and then myself. Among many events, there were the deaths of close friends, the dashing of career dreams, and most profoundly, the unmistakable leading of God's Spirit to trust solely in Jesus Christ for my salvation. Gradually he broke apart all my "righteousnesses," and shortly after coming to faith in him alone, I was once again in the classroom—this time in preparation for a life of vocational ministry. It was all new: new purposes, newly married, and a completely new path. I was as green as they come, yet the Lord had given me a simple, unquenchable thirst for three things:

1) Know him.
2) Appropriate his word for daily living.
3) Help others experience what they too were created for: Relationship with Him.

In order to prepare you for what lies ahead, you will do well to understand this: I am hardwired for order, contemplation, and structure. I am drawn to those who excel in being focused, academic and precise. I would delight to have such routines and traits, but they are at best only fleeting qualities in this life of mine. You will, however, see vestiges of my personal quest in the pages that follow.

I must leave an "out" even as I confess my sin of obsession for structure. I realize that not every area of my sojourn on earth can be categorized and linear. I would tend to think that perhaps this unevenness of human experience is a universal truth, and not just my personal reality. Those areas that I can manage, I tend to micromanage. Other situations that come at me (often referred to as life) I deal with on a case-by-case, moment-by-moment basis. It's probably much the same with you.

This flexing with the days I am given tends to come out in my writing, for I am prone to write about it all. You might find it hard to categorize this compilation because of that scope. As life unfolded, this book appeared: through experiences, parenting, vocational ministry, community involvement, citizen concern, personal struggles, outreach, and learning how to live an examined life before my Lord.

My "style" in approaching these facets of life is equally uneven, so hang on. To avoid the niche for these pages as simply "reflective" or "devotional," I've worked at avoiding stained glass, pastoral voicing. Often times I employ humor, for without it I would only descend into gradual madness in my world. Some light moments help to remind me that I often need to lighten up. In other sections, there is nothing I can find to be either amusing or light. Life isn't always laughs and good times. That's when my conservative, wound-too-tight prophet's voice rings in. We all need some deeper moments to draw us deeper into Him, especially in our amusement-as-priority culture.

> **The good news is, God's Word is always at work, even when my tiny thoughts and halting words clutter the view.**

As part of my ministry for the past several years, I've had the privilege to write a weekly column for my local paper. The invitation to contribute seemed to me as an open door, so I walked through. I was impressed with two ways that the Lord desired to use me in that very public arena.

First, as a Christian, a ready-made platform was presented to me as a location from which to encourage other believers. I could not overlook that opportunity. We can all grow weary in our walk, and building one another up certainly has scriptural backing.

Second, there was an opportunity among the readership for pre-evangelism; "sowing seed" by simply relating God's word to everyday life. Where else could I offer an encouraging invitation to thousands, to just consider one's life from a new perspective? Less threatening than walking into a church, I felt some would at least read and ponder, if I were sensitive to their biases and avoided the stereotypical rant or mush that would lead to them simply voting "no" by turning the page. My hope for these pages is likewise still twofold.

This is the practical encouragement I can offer you for your walk with the Lord. Life in our Savior is multifaceted, and something He has impressed upon me may be just what you need for your present day and situation.

This could also be a tool that God can use in the life of that friend or relation that you desire to introduce to our Lord. Maybe it will be a conversation starter that opens the door for spiritual things. Perhaps it will help to knock down some stereotypes that present Christians as being plastic, milquetoast, or Teflon. That contrary to popular myth, we exist beyond and above the clichés and steeples marking our days. Maybe it will mirror your heart, to demonstrate that Christians are indeed real people, with real joys and struggles.

The good news is, God's Word is always at work, even when my tiny thoughts and halting words clutter the view. Perhaps I write first for myself, to bring some semblance of order, and contemplation, and structure to my world. I pray that as you read, your perspective will be lifted as well. I trust you will be encouraged and in some real ways grow in hope, for I continually point to Him, the only true source of hope in this life, and for the life to come.

And, as promised, some 101 lessons that the Teacher has imparted to me.

From childhood, you have learned...

Do not speak against one another, brethren. He who speaks against a brother or judges his brother, speaks against the law and judges the law; but if you judge the law, you are not a doer of the law but a judge of it. There is only one Lawgiver and Judge, the One who is able to save and to destroy; but who are you who judge your neighbor?

James 4:11-12; NASU

My first bust was for smoking in the seventh grade. It was a pretty cut and dried case. The evidence was placed before me—an eyewitness account. My expected actions would be a thorough confession, followed by a period of contrite living, say perhaps a century. The contrite part would in all actuality last only until I arrived home. Once there, I would be summarily executed by my folks who had raised their boy better than that. I pause to inform any younger readers that in the Stone Age School days, if there were an offense worthy of punishment there, God help you when you got home to the real deal.

It was my first memorable crime. It was humiliating because my best friend's parents were the eye witnesses. My soon-to-be ex-best friend also took the liberty to broadcast the crime details to my peers. I was in the spotlight with nowhere to hide.

A teacher in our area had probably felt like that in the accusation she recently faced. From teacher to flushed-out felon, all by her inclusion in a list posted by the State's Department of Education. Troubling news, considering she had not committed any felony, let alone misdemeanor. Setting the record straight was the only way she could go back to her career of educating children, so that they hopefully in the end might not become deviants and felons.

A word of wisdom reminds me that a rush to judgment can destroy others. Proverbs 18:13 states that "He who gives an answer before he hears; it is folly and shame to him." How many times have I gone looking for a rope rather than a balance when

5

the accusations come? Even Christ Himself was executed through trumped-up charges.

I know first impressions are often quite mistaken. It's human nature to receive dirt rather than gold about others—especially if I'm a bit biased toward them already. A certain senator that maybe I'm not particularly fond of was once highlighted in the news for his weekly role in mentoring a student through a reading program. Nuts. The guy does have a heart in there somewhere. And so it goes. Senators. Teachers. Seventh grade boys...

Back to my crime. Whatever became of me on that fateful November day? I was exonerated. My rap sheet was cleared. Cleared for mistaken eyewitness accounts. I was where they said I was, and with whom they saw me. The one I was walking with knew the true truth, and set the record straight for everyone. The narrow stick in my mouth? Not a Marlboro, Lucky Strike or even the real-man unfiltered Camel. It had been a straw. A white drinking straw, like countless others that I had a habit of chewing on after indulging at the local burger pit.

I had a lesson in life reinforced that day, and days like today when I read the teacher's story. Not everything is as it appears. Sure, there are folks that are truly guilty. Matter of fact, everyone is guilty of something. As I once heard, "Why do people lie when the truth is bad enough?" Yet in my thirst for justice, coupled with cynicism that assumes the worst, my wisest approach is still to reach for the scale. And reaching for a word of wisdom can only help me.

I'd guess it's probably the same for you.

When the Spirit of truth comes, he will guide you into all truth. He will not speak on his own but will tell you what he has heard. He will tell you about the future. He will bring me glory by telling you whatever he receives from me.   John 16:13-14; NLT

Guides are a necessary part of this life. Whether we are taking in new terrain in our own county or trekking a thousand miles from home, guides are indispensable and worth their weight in gold. Today we have electronic maps and global positioning devices to keep us on the right path. In earlier days, there may have been crude maps, but the best guide was the living, breathing kind that had been over the trail before. You couldn't go wrong with someone who knew the path that lay ahead. Couple trust and preparation with a good guide, and you could travel anywhere you needed to go, sure to not stray and surer that your destination would quickly loom before you. The element of trust was the critical sticking point. A guide could not be viewed as a person simply offering another opinion to consider over which way to go. Either the guide was in charge, or the party was open to drift according to popular consensus or baseless hunches. Anyone here remember the Donner expedition?

I have had many guided adventures through this life of mine, but none compare to the simple days of youth and my touring of the neighboring woods, hills and ravines on a simple contraption called the Trail 70. It was a smallish motorcycle designed by a sadistic engineer who wanted to combine the weight of a Buick, the pickup speed of a moped, and the maneuverability of a wheelbarrow, all in one package. And to make it doubly fun, it was equipped for not only the guide-driver, but also for a hapless victim known henceforth as the passenger. That would be me.

My first guide was Dad. He intended to give me a series of tutorials about the safe use of the 70, so I'd be up to speed (so to speak) when I was big enough to launch out on my own. As we approached Dead Man's Hill, I was aware of it only because of the immediate shift in our orientation to earth. You see, the passenger's view was largely limited to scrutinizing the backside of the driver. Due to some ergonomic oversights, most of my time as the passenger was spent concentrating on how much skin I'd left on either the exhaust system or the drive chain since my feet rode on pegs scant millimeters away from these features. The manly way to ride was not by clinging wildly to the guide-driver, either. I was to hang on to the underside of the seat, the edge of which had been honed to a razor-like finish by an obviously disgruntled assembly worker who hadn't been able to bump to a better shift. Anyway, about midway up the mountain (everything over twenty feet high is a mountain when you're just over four feet tall), Dad up

7

shifted because we were basically bogging down in third gear. Immediately upon said up shift, I found myself being propelled through space as the bike's front wheel headed heavenward. My last glimpse of good ol' Dad was as he raced wildly down the hill beside the bike, having the presence of mind after a few hundred yards to let off the throttle and heave to a stop. I lay there feigning death, hoping at least to be carried home, but it was of little use. I extracted myself from the ruts and sand and took my seat, once again the passenger. This is perhaps my first memory of concentrated fervent prayer and deal making with God: "Gracious Lord, if you will allow me to survive this and get home to Mom, I'll go to Africa…"

My next memorable encounter with my guide comes courtesy of Mom's vision to make me a pianist. The teacher lived a short distance away, unfortunately near the head of one of the trails that wound through our neck of the woods. Why bother driving junior to lessons with the Chevy Nomad, when someone could just whiz him over on the bike in a safe, convenient manner? That someone would be my older brother, Jeffrey. He was very particular in keeping all the codes of the older brother handbook, and an opportunity to abuse his younger sibling like this was as enticing as shooting a duck in a barrel. I came out of the house, a helpless patsy on my way to sure death aboard Jeff's Transit Authority. It was a dark afternoon and the clouds looked ominous as I climbed on. Complicating the matter was the fact that I had to hang on to my red satchel, the carrier of my tormented paper renditions of Chopin, Beethoven and the like. Remember, holding onto the guide/driver was not an option, and the older brother code stepped the rule up a notch by ensuring that if younger even touched older, there would be swift retribution in the works. I slid rearward and almost off the seat. From this perch, I braced for a deeply textured mud stripe up my back, as the rain came down and we peeled off on the knobby-tired executioner.

The trip over was mercifully quick and event-free. Jeff would spend the half-hour zipping around the trails while I took my place at the keyboard and tried to hammer out mazurkas, nocturnes, and etudes, all the while brooding over the impending trip back home.

After the lesson was over, which never seemed to take longer than three days, I would be dismissed and wait outside for a good hour 'til Jeff remembered he had a kid brother to torture some more. And there he would be, urging me to hurry up and get on and don't touch him or else and then we'd be off like greased lightning, round two. Jeff always made sure our trip home included a drive-by to egg on the neighbor's rabid timber wolves for a pursuit. He would accelerate just quickly enough to leave only the tiniest threads of my JC Penny plain pockets in the drooling jaws of certain death. Steven Spielberg must have gotten his Jurassic Park "T-Rex in the rear view mirror" scene by observing my brother's bait-and-run game from a secure location.

This day, the final few yards of our journey took us through our side yard, resplendent with stately maples and cherry trees. Due to my stylin' horn rims, the rain had left me quite impeded visually, sort of like that grim scene in "Lord of the Flies" where Piggy gets his. My guide veered and took a short cut under the biggest maple tree. Now normally, you would think a word like "duck" could be uttered. It's not a long word; it has deep meaning and promotes immediate response, especially among younger brothers. But no, this day the word "duck" was not in vogue. As my guide bent down, the last thing I saw, blurred and rapidly approaching, was a sodden branch with my name on it. My trusty satchel took the brunt of it, and together we were swept off the bike like sheet music from a stand. Thankfully, my mud-encrusted backside, courtesy of the guide's careful steering through every slough from pianoland to home, allowed me to slide to a gentle stop, although the resultant wedgie almost required a surgical procedure. My satchel would never recover from its injuries.

I never did learn the art of driving the bike. When I became old enough to be my own guide, I had various encounters with immovable objects ranging from rocks to fences. I just wasn't that good at being a guide, and it left me a little edgy at really letting others be my guide as well. I still twitch like a dog whenever someone yells "Honda!" For years after "The 70" was out of my life, I would study the scars on my ankles and remember. This too came to a close after that particular posture for ankle inspection became a

As I Was Saying . . .

guaranteed run up to a particularly nasty charley horse.

Lately, I spied a bumper sticker that at one time was very popular. It read, "God is my co-pilot." I've reflected back on my days of being guided as a passenger. There is no way that simple trails and motorbikes can compare to the difficulties on the road of life. The idea of God splitting duty with me in the guide-seat of life is hard for me to imagine, even absurd. I don't want to sound like I'm splitting hairs, but that erroneous thinking goes against what God's Word says about the role of the Holy Spirit leading in my life. The faulty idea that God is somehow an equal to me, sitting there folding maps, pouring coffee, and offering suggestions of what I might want to consider for my route is ridiculous. Either he is God and I am his servant, or I have created another god for my life that is no god at all. How convenient to have a god that always wants to go my way. And how deadly. The Holy Spirit is more than my backup advisor. He knows the Lord's will, and he delights to reveal that will to me. The key is my obedience to Him, and my continual receptiveness to His rule in my life. Obviously, he is not present to debate courses with me as an equal. My guide knows the trail, knows what lies ahead, and is fully prepared to lead me if I will trust him fully.

I've had some rough guides over the years. I suppose we all have. I've also gotten into one dead end after another trying to be my own guide. The guide I now follow is trustworthy, but still daily I must choose to trust and follow him. Maybe you're in need of such a guide for your life as well. Or maybe your issue is more of trusting this One you have started with. In either case, you will do well to stick with the guide who has your best interests in view, knows the destination, and is willing to take you by the hand and lead you home.

Simon Peter said to them, "I am going fishing." They said to him, "We will also come with you." They went out and got into the boat; and that night they caught nothing.　　　John 21:3; NASU

John recorded this scene with Peter and six other disciples, in an

10

end-of-gospel event that closely followed the days of the cross and empty tomb.

It seems remarkably out of place to read and discover here that the disciples are back at their old haunts, doing once again the things that had occupied their pre-Jesus days. The gospel clearly states that they had recently seen their risen Lord. Why back to the boats? Why such an anticlimactical response to resurrection from this inner band? Why a return to quiet waters and men after fish, rather than to the teeming cities, fishing for men?

Tonight, as I sit and mull over Peter's call and response in chapter 21, I recognize that there are many factors that can lead any disciple to abdicate a position appointed by the Lord. There are the obvious ones: personal failure through unchecked and unrepentant sin; unbridled pride and ambition that self-propels one on a path toward "success" but away from the Lord's will; getting one's focus on others instead of on the Lord; or a false spirituality, making one believe he or she can operate apart from and above other disciples in a supposed moral superiority or special privilege from "knowing" the Lord. Some of these causes may be at work here in this story from the lakeshore, or found through other gospel accounts that spotlight the disciples as they travel together, contemplating what they felt to be their bright futures.

In John's gospel, Peter especially may also be struggling with the gnawing reality that he has failed miserably in his faith, though he had been quick with lip-service loyalty in fairer days. The self-disappointment and guilt is perhaps coupled with a real world dose of fear, because the countryside must yet be crawling with those who seek out the followers of this Jesus, whose body has disappeared. So I struggle within my meditation, wanting to gain some access and insight into the mind of Peter, for in his response there might be a key to understanding myself and my response to Jesus. Why is there such a struggle to walk as Jesus directs? Why is it so easy to drop my eyes and enter the dark fog of discouragement and unbelief? Can I too come to terms with the times that I am disappointed with Jesus' call, wanting to resist the path he has for me to walk? And what about those nagging trials I bring upon my life when I choose my misaligned goals and personal ambitions over the Lord's directive?

Peter is taught by the Lord one last lesson in this final story of John's gospel. Better, taught once again (and this time he will understand) that the important traits of a disciple are an undying love for Jesus, and a personal steadfastness for Him. The paths will vary, the persecutions and failures will ebb and flow, but the disciple must be found faithful to the task appointed, whether great or small. And so in the evening, while sorting this out for myself, my mind flashed back, to a time when this lesson was first given to me, but not understood...

The call had gone out from our church musical director that there would be a youth choir forming to present music at services and special occasions. My twelve-year-old frame could barely contain the excitement, for I fancied myself to be quite a vocalist. Some singers look back to Pavarotti or Sinatra as their motivating examples. The inspirational spark in my singing career? Mr. Don Ho.

I was well versed with Mr. Ho's smash hit "Tiny Bubbles," which I would break into while the family was a captive audience in the Chevy Nomad station wagon. This was the family car, and we toured extensively in it from Michigan to Florida. To while away the hours, my brother and I would invent games, like "torment the brother," "annoy the brother," and my personal favorite, "whip the brother into an aggravated froth." The older brother especially loved being serenaded by younger brother when mom was watching them from the visor makeup mirror so he couldn't reach over and pummel younger brother into a literal back seat pulp. I wonder yet today how mom has had any vision left after drilling holes in our skulls with her eyes through that well-placed mirror.

Besides the bubble song, my repertoire contained a smattering of Hank Williams tunes such as "Your Cheatin' Heart," the Johnny Cash classic "Jackson" (incidentally my runaway hit due to our proximity to a city of the same moniker, although I didn't realize there was another Jackson down south) and everyone's favorite, Roger Miller's "King of the Road." It occurs to me in hindsight that my entire youth was spent singing about love gone bad, liquor, stogies and wild flaming romance, things I had no concept of, but that's the price you pay for entertaining the crowds with the tunes they demand. How I ever ended up in the pastorate is a miracle of its own—I should be hopping freight trains in the Pacific Northwest or doing gigs in a smoky bar in Arkansas—but for the grace of God and a girlfriend-now-wife whose Baptist roots put me on the straight and kinda narrow...

Anyway, along came the day for the youth choir tryouts. The fireplace reception room in the church became the audition stage, and one by one we were called in, a secretary closing the door behind. The music director, a tall, fiercely red man, sat at the piano. He was not a humorous sort of person, and I keenly remember him as having the distinct look of someone who never enjoyed good gastrointestinal health. He was very intense in his musicianship and especially performance at the organ, from whose perch he would conduct the adult choir by a series of articulated head motions, swift elevated hand gestures, and huge pantomime expressions. One classic hymn arrangement after another, I would sit enthralled. It was as close as I got to opera and theatre until introduced to Gilbert and Sullivan some years later.

The song we youth were auditioning with had not been disclosed to us prior to the day. In preparation, I had been feverishly singing through the whole gamut of my personal favorites, and had even been trying to warble a little more robustly during congregational worship in the weeks leading up to the audition. The director sat at the massive upright piano, and announced that I would be required to sing the chorus of that great hymn of faith, "How Great Thou Art." He began his introduction with great flair, as only a professional who has played that same introduction about a billion times can do. My tiny mind raced as the vocal entry measure loomed ever closer...How Great Thou Art? Are you kidding? How Great Thou Art? How could it be? All this nervous energy and practice for nothing! I had been asked to sing a song—the prize song—from my church catalogue of favorites. It was a done deal; I was in before the first, "Then sings my soul..." would leave my lips. A star was born. I would be singing the lead tenor quicker than you could utter, "Wow, that's really an amazing kid singing right there, uh huh."

About an hour after my show-stealing performance, all of the

13

As I Was Saying . . .

auditions were at an end. The director shut off the lights, closed the audition room door, and bunkered down in his office for "the tally." We kids milled around, and I did my best to try to stop my buddies from messing up things, but you know how immature some twelve year olds can be. The moms hovered a lot and chased us back outside every time we'd come in to see if the selections had been made. Finally, the red man emerged, entered the church narthex and hastily posted his list on the bulletin board over the water cooler. Then he was off to organ recital or whatever it is musical directors do when the youth choir has been selected.

The better share of my buddies made the cut, even the ones who had auditioned at threat of bodily injury from their moms. Several had figured they could still throw the test once sequestered in the mom-free zone behind that closed audition door, but strangely, they still were chosen. Most of the girls made it, too. They giggled and whispered and got very dramatic about the whole thing. There was a lot of weeping and some real backstage Miss World theatrics by those who weren't in, and I suppose they are still in therapy today. Beside the "in" list, the assigned practice times were given, along with rules for attendance, conduct, dress code, and a short treatise on the proper care for one's vocal chords. The only item I really noticed missing amid all the postings was one thing—my name.

Moments later the secretary drew me aside, and inquired as to whether I would consider the job of running the lights for the youth choir. It required knowledge of reading music so as to get the blue light on just at the chorus and fade the yellow during the last syllable of phrase four and other technical stuff like that. I told her I would do it, and I did—though I am sure that there were times in performance where the director must have heard another voice, somewhat distant, adding a distinct flavor to the sound even as the colored lights blazed and dimmed in synchronized splendor.

Whatever the personal disappointments, like Peter and the disciples on that lake, it is good to hear the call and respond to Jesus as he lifts the fog and funk of failure and disillusionment. The call of the Lord is sure, and those who love him will find restoration and further command. He provides all we need, he accompanies us on

14

our journey, and we cannot be detracted by the world or his other disciples' paths. He has chosen us for a particular walk and obedience; it is our duty to stay to our individual task at hand.

Peter, turning around, saw the disciple whom Jesus loved following them... So Peter seeing him said to Jesus, "Lord, and what about this man?"

Jesus said to him, "If I want him to remain until I come, what is that to you? You follow Me!" John 21:20a-22; NASU

Do I love Jesus? If so, I will be found doing what he wills; not what suits me as desirable, familiar or comfortable. And if perchance His will involves singing, so be it.

But it's good to know; someone had better heed the master's call and go run the lightshow for all it's worth.

"Why do you look at the speck that is in your brother's eye, but do not notice the log that is in your own eye? Or how can you say to your brother, 'Let me take the speck out of your eye,' and behold, the log is in your own eye? You hypocrite, first take the log out of your own eye, and then you will see clearly to take the speck out of your brother's eye." Matthew 7:3-5; NASU

When I was a kid, absolutely eons ago according to popular household belief, I enjoyed a lot of unstructured time with my young friends. Our world was only as big as the blocks that composed the immediate neighborhood. When the new guys moved in from Canada, we were stunned to learn they spoke English and played baseball—both rather well. Our farthest jaunts were the all day fishing trips to the river that formed the farthest western boundary of our world. It was perhaps a mile ride, but it seemingly went on forever, especially to a "husky" kid on a fifty pound bike bearing an equivalent weight in poles, buckets, lunch and of course, BB gun. The gun was purely for protection of the party, just in case any pesky wolves or bears decided to show their mangy hides. Granted, none had been spotted in this region of southern Michigan for perhaps the last hundred and fifty years, but we were sure it was just a matter of time. Any unsuspecting he-man boys who stupidly left their rifle at home would get what they deserved. It wouldn't be happening to us.

There was, however, an overarching standard procedure in all our youthful recreations. Whether we were at the fishing hole, shooting hoops, on the ball field, or riding horses, kid protocol demanded that we would constantly establish and reestablish who was top dog. The exact system by which this played itself out would be somewhat difficult for the casual observer to decipher. Let me try to explain a bit:

Perhaps it would be the first fish of the day, whereby the master fisherman would deride the rest of the troupe for their lack of skills and

> **My careful study and teaching of his word merits nothing if I am not willing to apply it to myself first...**

technique. This self-honor would usually be short lived. Fish would pile up from every pole, and the prized position of angler par excellence would flop back and forth between us, like the bluegills on our stringer, until it was time to head home in the fading light.

While shooting hoops, the taunt exchange would occur during endless rounds of horse, which quickly sorted out those who could or could not perform a left-handed layup or the newly popular sky-hook. In my many endless summers, I don't ever recall having the bragging rights in that arena. My prowess with a basketball was the stuff that would spawn a whole new genre in film—the nerd movie—a few years hence. I couldn't jump, the dribbling was equally pathetic, and my shooting was a pure exercise in futility every time. At my buddies' driveway court, their mom would feign hysterics every time they placed that huge orange ball into my hands. As I lined up my specialty move, subtly yet derisively called the "nothing but air" shot by the guys, the speed at which she would get their garage door up was yet another source of my personal chagrin. I ask you, who ever decided you had to have windows in garage doors, anyway? Sheesh. One lousy accident and they label you a miscreant for life. No, there was never a top dog title for me on that concrete proving ground.

Over on the diamond, my odds at owning the bragging rights improved somewhat. There, the one-upmanship would surface with a swing and a miss, uncorking a tirade from the batter about just how poor the pitching was that would drive him in desperation to swing at such lousy offerings. This would be countered by the pitcher, usually capping his equally disdainful comments with some line involving your mother and her far superior batting skills compared to yours, you wimp. Then I'd usually draw the bean ball, whereupon I'd lie in the dirt for a few minutes before actually remembering my name. Surviving one of those babies typically gave me top dog honors at least through the weekend. Additionally, headshots were our normal cue for a change in activity, so we'd drop the mitts and bats and be off to ride horses, or some other form of recreation. The "what" didn't matter, as long as we could rag on each other, try to assert our dominance, and keep a sharp eye out for the next opportunity for me to receive a fresh blow to my noggin. It was my true skill set.

Jesus' words to his disciples remind me of how very little has changed in this adult world I now inhabit. My careful study and teaching of his word merits nothing if I am not willing to apply it to myself first, correcting my incredibly skewed vision. How often I need to be reminded that the standard for my life is God: total perfection; absolute holiness; unadulterated light. I will always fall short, continually needing his grace, forgiveness, and restoration. When I look at others for the pride of comparison, running them down to build me up, it is nothing but a game of top dog where I continually lose for all my supposed winning. I may impress myself for a king of the hill title, but the one whose opinion counts was the King of another hill, where he went to die so that I would not be destroyed. How much of the playground shuffle for position still invades my world today.

When I can clear out the logs—the vision killers in my own life—maybe I'll then have the vision to help others see their way to things far beyond what I would accomplish. That's a goal my lord would certainly agree with. Maybe it could be a goal for you, too.

Of course, just for the record, no one will ever beat out my trophy carp, taken with a Zebco 202 and 4 lb. test line from the boundary river back in the late summer of '71. Why, I remember it like it was yesterday…

The best-equipped army cannot save a king, nor is great strength enough to save a warrior. Don't count on your warhorse to give you victory—for all its strength, it cannot save you. We depend on the LORD alone to save us. Only he can help us, protecting us like a shield. In him our hearts rejoice, for we are trusting in his holy name.

Psalm 33:16-18, 20-21; NLT

I learned pretty early on not to trust in my warhorse.

In the prehistoric days of my youth, many things were far different from today. Summer vacation lasted at least twice as long. I had six or seven times the energy I have now. Candy bars were better, ice cream was richer, and hot dogs had a certain snap when I bit into them. My kids tell me that the reason things were different then was that the earth's crust was still cooling, and I got a lot more exercise, what with having to run away from all those pesky dinosaurs. They go on to explain that the hot dog thing was due to the red hots being full of gross byproducts that constituted the "snap" element, and now (thankfully) there are laws against that. Ah, my wife's kids. They discover a few Upton Sinclair references in US Literature class and suddenly they're experts on everything. They're a riot to live with. Wait 'til they want to drive—then we'll see who's laughing. "Yeah, I'll let you drive…drive me over to the drive in, for hot dogs." Then they'll retort, "What's a drive-in?" See, I even anticipate my going down in flames with conversations that haven't taken place yet…

But back to my youth, which certainly was glorious in its day. Another thing that was far different then was that little gem called television. I remember shows that were full of adventure and moral value; viewing devoid of butchery, profanity, risqué situations or anything that would constitute poor taste. Kind of a direct opposite from most of today's broadcasting, to be sure. My brother and I would sit enthralled over a Roy Rogers movie or the latest installment of Gunsmoke or the really stylin' Bonanza (in color, too!) Then we would get to the serious bit of reenacting all our favorite episodes. It was rough being the younger brother, to be sure. He would be Marshal Matt Dillon; I would be Festus (though I often had to double up on parts and fill in as Doc Adams to pull yet another slug out of the lawman). Then he would be the nimble Little Joe, and I would be his portly brother, Hoss. Then we would shift again, he becoming Roy Rogers, and I would be...ahem...well, you get my drift. The cowboy boots and hats were always handy, and I had few summer nights when my hands didn't bear the manly stink of spent caps. The trusty six-shooter would have center stage in my life until supplanted by the Daisy Air Rifle, some years later. Then, of course, there was the other manly issue—having the right horse.

At home, we had horses. Real horses. There was Princess, an Appaloosa, huge and towering over me, at least 30 or 40 hands to my young eyes, easy. She was good to ride, tolerant to a point with cap guns going off in her ears, and in every way a fine horse, except for the wimpy name. Princess. Yeesh. "Here comes Deadeye John to round up the rotten-no-good-for-nuthin' gang on his trusty steed...Princess." You probably see how that wasn't working for me. I always drew her in the horse raffle, because older brothers have first picks. And, as you will find out, our pony pool was pretty slim pickin's to boot. The only other ride was the Shetland, who went by the name Duke. Not that it mattered. You could've called him Glue Factory and not gotten a raised hair from him. Blend equal parts of distain, detachment, and spite, and you pretty much had this horse pegged on the personality inventory. Even The Horse Whisperer would've chambered a round and started humming Goodbye Old Paint after about twenty minutes with this case.

Duke probably had some rare Shetland brain fever early in pony-hood that left him unaccountable for his own actions. He was nearly impossible to saddle. Just the sound made by getting out the tack would send him to the far reaches of the pasture. After doing battle out there and finally getting a lead on him, you then faced the daunting task of dragging him back to the barn to saddle up. To appreciate this, try pulling a '69 Bonneville stalled in first gear approximately 400 yards. Uphill. With three feet of rope. Once the saddle was on, and the cowboy was on, we would immediately prepare for the "swipe." This was the dismount technique Duke preferred to use on his annoying riders. He would start out real casual-like, then ease ever closer to the nearest section of fence. Once there, he would launch himself against the fence, grinding himself along it, hoping to scrape off rider, saddle, and any other trace of human contact. If the swipe proved to be unsuccessful and he found himself in the open, there was the sure-fire method of the "drop and roll." His pace would slow almost imperceptibly, as if he were resigned to an afternoon of chasing down rustlers and heading off the stampede before it reached the orphanage. Then, he would drop on his front legs, and immediately start the roll. The rider, Marshal Matt Dillon, Festus, or whomever, had approximately .06 seconds to extract himself from the stirrups and jump clear, else become another nameless victim of life in the wild west.

Once, when we were mending fences, I watched him eat my granddad's glasses. Picked 'em right off a gatepost and crunched them down. I have issues, my friend, deep horse issues.

I was almost ready to trust in horses the day I learned we were to get a third one for our pasture. I was sure this would be the one. A tough horse, with a tough name like Bullet or Hombre. This would be the horse that would leap at my whistle, charge in and take control when the dirty-skunk gang was just about ready to send me off to Boot Hill. Yeah, a tough horse. Maybe one-eyed, too. Deadeye John and Hombre, his one-eyed steed. It was sheer poetry in my ear. Soon the day came, and I was introduced to our new colt, Missy Sue… Just hog tie me and drag me through a cactus desert. Such is the outcome of setting oneself up to trust in horses.

Scripture gives me plenty of warning about not placing my trust in the symbols of power that this world embraces. There will always be tougher horses, mightier armies, more powerful rulers, and better-prepared warriors. The power plays here on earth go on in an endless parade. God's Word encourages to focus on the one who ultimately has all power, and might, and control over all men and nations.

It's also good for me to remember that I am to rejoice in this knowledge at all times. He is there, keeping me eternally secure when the world scrapes me off my feet, when I feel "rolled over" by events around me, or when it seems like there is one endless wave of good-for-nuthin' gangs darkening the days. Of him it is written, *And I saw heaven opened, and behold, a white horse, and He who sat on it is called Faithful and True, and in righteousness He judges and wages war. His eyes are a flame of fire, and on His head are many diadems; and He has a name written on Him which no one knows except Himself. He is clothed with a robe dipped in blood, and His name is called The Word of God. And the armies which are in heaven, clothed in fine linen, white and clean, were following Him on white horses. From His mouth comes a sharp sword, so that with it He may strike down the nations, and He will rule them with a rod of iron; and He treads the wine press of the fierce wrath of God, the Almighty. And on His robe and on His thigh He has a name written, "KING OF KINGS, AND LORD OF LORDS."* (Revelation 19:11-16; NASU)

It is comforting for me to know, that in the end it will still be as it was in my youth. The hero will still be making his entrance on a fine horse.

A fine, white horse.

Be on guard. Stand true to what you believe. Be courageous. Be strong.

1 Cor. 16:13, NLT.

A sad but common observation we share is that of viewing many lives that go down in flaming ruin. Lest we get smug and judgmental, it's sobering to note that age, education, family, position, and faith or absence of faith are no concrete markers of success or failure across the landscape of life. Those who "don't have a chance" rise to lives of character and contribution. Those with every advantage self-destruct through amazing and bewildering choices.

Observation is for me a reality check. To keep my feet from slipping, I focus on what I believe, and why I believe. To stray into unexamined, random living would be a set-up for disaster. Life, family, reputation, career and example as a disciple of Christ can be destroyed in a minute of unguarded action. I must remain vigilant, and labor to eliminate my blind spots. I learned this lesson from my old friend, Buck.

When I was twelve years young, life was good. Raised by parents who knew the value of responsibility, I had a host of animals to care for. It was the usual collection. There was the dog that responded to every spoken word as if hearing only one—"jump!" There was the ever-changing parade of tomcats that dragged home prey bigger than me on a nightly basis. There were rabbits, which I fed with eyedroppers, and who later fed us, though I was told it was chicken. There were the horses, of which I have written, who grudgingly tolerated my intrusions into their pastureland world. Above all these, there was my older brother, who filled in to make my life interesting any time the pets were having a slow day.

On a warm spring afternoon, when my brother had just finished experimenting on me concerning the effect of a firecracker in an glass olive jar held by human flesh, we looked up to the roar of dad's El Camino bouncing down the gravel road. Into the side yard with a swirl of dust, he backed up to the pasture gate. We sprinted over as dad was coaxing a bewildered looking animal off the tailgate. He explained that our ewes needed a "friend," and we were introduced to our newest pet, a ram named Buck. I was to learn in the coming days that the animal had been purchased at the local livestock auction—special edition deranged animal sale.

Some brief weeks later, I was retiring from evening chores at the horse barn when Buck made his move. I had noticed a lack of bonding in our relationship, but hadn't felt the time was right to broach the subject with my new squinty-eyed friend. I approached the small gate to exit the livestock yard and make my way to the house for yet another chicken dinner.

Years later, I try to calculate the velocity that had to be achieved to launch a husky, fully clad male juvenile completely through a latched gate. NASA would've been proud of ol' Buck. I lay there, counting stars and trying to focus back on his Clint Eastwoodesque squint. I had let my guard down, and the resultant blindsiding left me with marks I would bear for days to come.

Life, like Buck, can blindside me if I drop my guard. I continually learn from this Word of Life that every human's path is fraught with snares and dangers. Not merely as an occupation, but first by my being a believer, I am to encourage others to consider the dangers and guard their heart. The Word says, "Gently instruct those who oppose the truth. Perhaps God will change those people's hearts, and they will learn the truth. Then they will come to their senses and escape from the devil's trap. For they have been held captive by him to do whatever he wants." (2 Tim. 2:25-26, NLT) For my particular calling, Paul again champions vigilance, "Otherwise, I fear that after preaching to others I myself might be disqualified." (1 Cor. 9:27b, NLT)

It's true. We have an enemy that never rests. Life can often knock us off our feet. There's no sense in setting ourselves up to be willingly blindsided. It pays to know the guidebook for life, and the author who gives us a heads up to approaching danger. Be careful out there. Guard your heart. Watch your backside. The life you save from flaming ruin may be your own.

And, it wouldn't hurt to read the fine print over at the livestock auction, either.

Don't you realize that in a race everyone runs, but only one person gets the prize? So run to win! All athletes are disciplined in their training. They do it to win a prize that will fade away, but we do it for an eternal prize. So I run with purpose in every step. I am not just shadowboxing. I discipline my body like an athlete, training it to do what it should. Otherwise, I fear that after preaching to others I myself might be disqualified.

1 Corinthians 9:24-27; NLT

Cross country is a running sport developed by sadistic miscreants, with the main goal being to simply inflict pain on the body. My CC days are long past, but the memories are burned in somewhere between summer baseball and spring track recollections. The more pleasant reminiscences include fall running camp at Lake Michigan's Dunes (sandbur, anyone?), blizzards at several invitational meets ("Hey guys, check out Masters with the dopey hypothermia stare!"), and the constant scourge of shin splints, which Webster's 11th defines as "Injury to and inflammation of the tibial and toe extensor muscles or their fasciae caused by repeated minimal traumas (such as running)."

"Minimal traumas," my eye. Shin splints feel like every bone south of Mr. Kneecap will in short order explode through your skin. The coach was sympathetic as he applied another mile of athletic tape (from the makers of Nair®) and chanted his mantra: "Ice it down; run it off." During the run, Coach would maneuver between key junctions of the course, where he was always good for some pick-me-up phrases to get the motivation flowing. "It's a long way from your heart." "The faster you run, the faster you can lie down." "Dig in!" "Tie the rope! Don't fall behind!" "Attack the hill! Get up there!" "Pick it up! GO! GO! GO!"

Then he would usually slip into some illustrative and borderline-derogatory commentary, juxtaposing the everyday running speed of his grandparent with that of my own current pace. Shortly, gratefully, I would lumber out of earshot, heading on a path into the woods, across some farmer's field, up a cliff, or into a bog; all great possibilities in the ever changing legs of the awesome 3 mile gauntlet we called "the course."

Running cross country was a lonely sport. It was not unusual for the spectator count to be tallied on one hand; the weather of fall's madness often kept even the stalwart away unless they had been tapped for stopwatch duty. I pitied the one stuck recording my time, as in the early years my race was better clocked with a calendar than a sweep hand. Still, the finish was all important, and finish I did, along with a fledgling team that eventually grew in stamina and speed, actually becoming contenders in our latter high school years.

The finish. How important it was, and still is. Finishing races, and finishing the race of life.

Finally they returned by ship to Antioch of Syria, where their journey had begun. The believers there had entrusted them to the grace of God to do the work they had now completed. Upon arriving in Antioch, they called the church together and reported everything God had done through them and how he had opened the door of faith to the Gentiles, too. And they stayed there with the believers a long time. Acts 14:26-28; NLT

The anticipation of seeing the believers in Antioch again must have kept Paul and Barnabas moving ahead when the journey they were on got tough and long. I can imagine that on that day, there was a crowd gathered to cheer the two missionaries as they returned to that city in which the faithful were first given the name, "Christian." The Word here is an encouragement as it states that they had "completed" that which God had called them to do. There was no glory in starting off. Many do that, year after year. What mattered was the finish, and they kept at it until that race had been run.

This story in Acts reminds me that while I often think of this Christian life as a single race, it is actually composed of several "races" that the Lord orchestrates. Though Paul and Barnabas stayed a long time, enjoying wonderful fellowship and camaraderie that surrounded their days back in Antioch, it was not the "end" of the race for these two runners. Soon there would be a new commissioning, new travel orders, and new priorities that would send Paul and Barnabas out again. The next leg would be run separately, accomplishing more through their painful division than could have ever been realized had they chosen to stay as one. Another starting line, another race, another finish awaiting.

May God find His children faithful in all our running; and may the thought of the final finish line propel us forward in all our "races" big and small. And may He never be in need of a runner, as long as we have breath to expel on this course here below. Dig in. Attack the hill. Tie the rope. Don't fall behind. You can rest when you finish. The Coach will not approve resting, while the race is on. Run to win.

Finishing is better than starting. Patience is better than pride.

Ecclesiastes 7:8; NLT

And they shall be one...

On the third day there was a wedding in Cana of Galilee, and the mother of Jesus was there; and both Jesus and His disciples were invited to the wedding.

John 2:1-2; NASU

As in Cana then, many preparations still surround a wedding today. Not so much preparation is always made toward building a solid marriage, but I ask you, who really has time for that, when after all, there's a wedding to plan?

I have my share of weddings to officiate, and they are preceded by several counsel sessions, reading assignments and discussions. The goal is practical and not academic: assist the couple in establishing a foundation for marriage upon biblical principles that will guide and preserve them until "death do us part." If I had to narrow down to the central idea behind this counsel, I believe the term "selfless sacrifice" would be my summation. If a couple can envision the big picture as they come together—no longer living for self but for the promotion and care of the other—they are indeed standing under a very sturdy biblical umbrella that will weather life well. The fitting illustration of this is a unity candle, which is often a part of today's wedding ceremonies. The couple comes together, each holding a candle representing their individual lives, or "self." After together igniting the unity candle from their individual flames, they turn and extinguish their personal candles of "self." These candles of "self" are to remain extinguished; they have committed now to one selfless light, guide, and focus.

And as Jesus has modeled so plainly for us, death to self is a beautiful thing.

The Lord, for all his miracles and lessons, never was recorded as saying too much about marriage. There are his illustrations of marriage in connection to readiness, his return, and the church, but not much about the actual marriage of husband and wife in this world. His few recorded comments are in effect warnings; these directed toward the religious-yet-clueless who had selfishly misapplied and loopholed God's law as to provide them an easy exit from marriage for any reason real or contrived.

And He answered and said, "Have you not read that He who created them from the beginning MADE THEM MALE AND FEMALE, and said, "FOR THIS REASON A MAN SHALL LEAVE HIS FATHER AND MOTHER AND BE JOINED TO HIS WIFE, AND THE TWO SHALL BECOME ONE FLESH"? " So they are no longer two, but one flesh. What therefore God has joined together, let no man separate." Matthew 19:4-6; NASU

It is sobering for me to remember, while living in this age of continued loopholing, that marriage is God's provision for man and woman, being the first among all institutions given to His beloved humanity. There extends today, as in Cana times, the similar core efforts to dilute marriage, redefine it, and finally strip away any semblance to the original biblical model once delivered.

Nothing new under the sun.

I would be quick to point out that in all the posturing of the evangelical community and the vocal defense of marriage, it would be good for us to do a bit of soul searching and house cleaning in regard to the sanctity of marriage—not others' marriages, mind you, but our very own. That is, if what I say does not add up in what I am practicing (publicly or privately, for God knows the hidden man), then it should not alarm or concern me that mankind mocks and dismisses the "church voice" that demonstrably has become just hollow and duplicitous rhetoric. Such do and say dishonesty is everywhere these days, from national leaders to local shakers, from company boardrooms to shop floors, and sadly enough, from John Q. Churchgoer. Bottom line: our evangelical track record for modeling biblical marriages is found desperately wanting. In time, all is discovered, and it has added up to the church exposed as deficient in the marriage-God's-way arena, among countless other sins of omission and commission. In the lingo of the streets, it's fair to say, "Put up, or shut up."

The remedy for us is plainly told truth. If your marriage isn't holding a candle to the clear teaching of that book you claim God gave you, or even to the marriage of the not-yet-believer next door, what would it take for you to die to self and do it God's way? How about this for a reason: Simply to practice what you say you believe. Here's another: To obey your Lord and follow His ways, to be found pleasing in His sight.

Of course, I have heard all the excuses. "They" don't treat me right. "They" started it. "I" want to be happy. "I" am not fulfilled. "I" deserve better. Sometimes in counsel I must query as to their understanding of where the focus should be in a biblical marriage, whether on "I" or on "you." That usually puts an abrupt end to sessions. Sure enough, most want a sympathetic ear and a changing mate, not radical biblical change starting with "I". Heaven forbid "I" be the first, and lead out to model dying to self. It's a standoff of biblical proportions. Compounding the problem, if the marriage began without Christ at the center, how difficult it is to dig down and begin on the new, sure foundation.

Two don't walk together unless they agree. I read that somewhere…

Pretty heady stuff for us all, here as I ponder this in the springtime. Maybe we all need the sharpening, at this season when so many thoughts turn to the "I do's" here in our world.

For believers, it is a fair question to ask, "What does the world see when they look at our marriage?" It's true no matter your doctrinal slant or denominational marker: someone is always watching and learning from you, about whether your faith adds up.

And for all contemplating such a step as marriage in your future, I close in question as well.

Is Jesus invited to the wedding?

And better yet, is he receiving the more important invite into your marriage?

And the LORD God said, "It is not good for the man to be alone. I will make a companion who will help him."

Genesis 2:18

Today was going to be a common day, just like so many of the others that come and go. The morning began with a 6 am chirp of the alarm, punctuated by the aroma of my Mr. Scorchy brewing another pot of caffeinated splendor upon its automatic timer cue. Only today, something was wrong—terribly wrong. The other side of the bed was empty.

There have been other occasions where this has happened. By virtue of bringing several children into this marriage, my wife has often earned a full night away after delivering a child. I have no problem with twenty-four hours of down time after that particular feat. Yes, I've been there for most of the blessed events, and no, I have never had the help of an anesthetic, thank you very much.

It's just that usually I'm the one away. School. Seminars. Camps. Mission trips. Outfitter store field research sabbaticals. And of course, endless meetings and the daily office grind. It was an uneasy feeling as I arose and began my investigation. The apprehension amplified as I discovered my Darling deposited on one of the couches in the living room. Darling was ill; fever, chills, sore throat, ache. Samuel, preschooler, joined us seconds later, also feeling puny and not afraid to share his misery. I experienced immediate vertigo as the grim reality set in. This was not going to be a running-a-half-hour-late day. This was not even going to be a quick morning at the office and then home for the remainder kind of day. Today, there would be no office routine, no study routine, no calls and computer and mail and pastoral duties. Today, I would simply have to take "off." I steeled myself and drew a deep breath. Like it or not, today I would become the stay-at-home dad.

Things went remarkably well for about the first ten minutes. Samuel dissected a pop tart across most of the dining room table, chairs and floor while I struggled to make tea for Darling, pack three lunches, put cereal, milk, juice, toast and yogurt out for the gang, and watch my coffee go cold (mug) and stale (pot) while the noise of the risen household gradually increased in pitch. Two bathrooms are no match for the 6:30-7:10 rush, and I found myself wondering how long the new copper pipes would hold up before eventually eroding away under such a volume of water coursing through them. The steady slosh and gurgle emanating from captive supply lines within the walls and drain lines under foot had me nearly convinced that my windowless kitchen post had become the galley aboard the submarine USS MILDEW, nearing its dive limits and preparing for the rivets to start popping out. I hope they can get Tom Selleck to take my role in the made for TV movie...

Thankfully the stay at home dad had no time for such meandering thoughts, for I was snapped back to reality by the need to make phone calls to cancel busses and forewarn the school that Samuel was out for the day. Then there was the lengthy lecture and rolling eyes from daughters concerning specific things that should have been included or excluded from their nondescript brown paper bag lunches. Not only could I not tell them exactly what I packed, but I was so far in the weeds by now that if I were actually sitting with them when they finally opened it up at lunchtime, I would probably be equally surprised and/or disgusted. Who knows? It's bologna or peanut butter or tuna or something and I'm just a stay at home dad, not a short order cook for cryin' out loud...

Samuel put an exclamation point on the girls' departure for the bus stop by foregoing all his rules of common etiquette and advanced potty training. The ensuing few minutes of what came next is best left out of print so as to not offend the sensitive or repel the squeamish. There are things that should just not happen to stay at home dads, and I don't think my nose will ever work right again. Egad.

It was now a leisurely 7:30 am and time for the stay at home gang to start their schoolwork. This particular day for Isaac and Hope would have a certain "work at your own pace" tenor to it, as my skills at simultaneously teaching two different grades of classes, while entertaining I'm-sick-and-have-a-toxic-sludge-odor-about-me-boy are, shall I say, somewhat underdeveloped.

The laundry was not done. Come to think of it, the laundry at my castle is never done. The machines run all the time, like a pacemaker or an atomic clock. If they for some reason should be shut off, you know something's not right. My mind raced as I envisioned Darling being ill for several days. When they break, I can jump right in and fix either the lousy washer or dryer—just don't ask me how they're supposed to be operated in the day to day. I had to come up with a plan. Then it hit me. After midnight, I would sneak off to MegaStuff Mart and just load up on one color and size of sweatshirts and pants. Thirty, maybe forty pair. Whisking away all the other clothes in the household, we would all wear something that required no sorting, no special handling, no hangers, and no hassle. I mentioned this plan to the dining room table students, who were trying to avoid getting too much pop tart residue on their paperwork. Hope never looked up, but bluntly said that we'd all look like gangsters, and Mom wouldn't like it. I should've expected that response from my wife's daughter. Isaac laughed and said that Mom would never stand for it. Rats! She'd gotten to him too. Gotta take that boy camping or something...

So I did the laundry, though I think it may be more like "did it in." I didn't know some bozo had snuck my good pen back into the pocket of my white shirt. Oh well, I'll still be doing MegaStuff Mart tonight—"whites madness sale," after I haul out a really full dumpster to the curb for pickup.

Darling languished on the couch. It was 10:30, and I was still in my sweats. Aptly named item, to be sure.

The afternoon rolled by a little calmer, with naptime for Sam and schoolwork finishing up before the girls came in off the bus. I destroyed a sweeper by running over some large wet object in the hall, so I was assured of a little shop time when I got caught up with the housework next century. Yippee. Supper was well underway, I having invented a new dish called Super Burrito Casserole. It is quite simple and the reader may well want to replicate it at home. Open your refrigerator. Empty the contents into a large casserole dish. Top with burrito wraps and cheese, then bake it until the handy dinner bell/smoke alarm combo signals that it's time to dig in. My kids would eat a hubcap if it had cheese on it. Probably yours would, too.

I would've loved to have sampled some myself, but it was now time for me to don my chauffer's cap and start the evening shuttle service for the girls. Work. Practice. Pep band. Study group. Starting now, and upon the hour from 5:30 to 9:30 pm, I would be privileged to pick up and reshuffle everyone to the next activity. Then there would be the final drive home. Then there would be getting everyone settled down for last minute homework, bed, and of course another final onslaught on the township water system.

31

As I Was Saying . . .

After locking up, getting ready for bed was a breeze for me, as I had never gotten out of my jammie/sweats all day. I set the alarm and tried to focus on simple tasks, like remembering my name. I made Darling a final cup of tea. The paper sat unread. My personal "routine" work for the day had never gotten started. All I could do is sit and type this, slowly and deliberately.

I imagine that over the course of these 25 years together, we've pretty much settled into our routines, roles, and responses to life and one another. There have been other times of illness and interruption, but we always seem to flex and go with it. Oftentimes, as when kids come along, our routines have been totally rewritten. Sometimes, like in sick days, the routines just encounter bumps on the road of normalcy.

I take comfort in knowing God has brought us together, to fulfill one another in His particular relational math where one plus one equals one.

I also take comfort in knowing that God, unlike me in my feeble attempts to "cover the bases" in times of flux, never tires, takes a sick day, or abandons His post. He is the tireless one who is always there, always fulfilling His work in my life even when I press blindly on, forgetting his presence and benefits.

Darling is feeling much better now, and I'm ready to call it a night. All I need is a little sleep. Trouble is, I've got a slightly sore throat, and I'm feeling a little chilly…

In the same way, you husbands must give honor to your wives. Treat your wife with understanding as you live together. She may be weaker than you are, but she is your equal partner in God's gift of new life. Treat her as you should so your prayers will not be hindered.

1 Peter 3:7; NLT

What's in an anniversary? There are so many happenings that transpire in one year alone, how can you begin to recount events when the multiple years pile on? Five? Ten? Twenty? I will be quick to admit that I don't know it all. In this swirl of just two decades in

32

ministry, all around me I have witnessed couples who have remained strong well past their fiftieth wedding anniversaries. For some, death brings too quickly to an end what has been the strongest of bonds. Others have found Christ, a God-centered remarriage, and have begun again on a sure foundation that with His grace will prayerfully last a lifetime.

What I offer today is some advice about what I have learned about marriage. I think of this writing as proverbs from my book of "John." Though the humorous things may communicate well in print, I need to assure you that they are indeed no stranger to the usual character of our actual life together. Not all things are funny all the time, but we have learned to seize every opportunity to laugh often and long. So read, and drink in, and hopefully learn from one yet an amateur, enjoying a day that marks our twenty-fifth together as husband and wife.

• Remember the dates for her anniversary and her birthday. You may be content with observing them, but she wants to celebrate! Every other date can be fudged a bit, but never these two. This is for your mental health when she starts bringing those children into the marriage. There is only so much memory a guy can expend on dates. Where would we keep the spark plug numbers and 2-cycle mix ratios if our brain was cluttered with, "Junior's preschool graduation?" Buy a day planner, let her fill it in, and read it second only to Holy Writ. It will keep you from harm, my friend. Speaking of birthdays, never get her a card with a numeric reference to the birthday. Never utter the number. If queried from her, say, "Gosh, honey, I don't know. You look as young as the day we met. Why do people get so hung up over the birthday number thing?" Learn, little grasshopper, learn.

• Whenever she says, "Do you know what day today is?" feign a seizure or throat obstruction, unless you are darn well sure the next thing out of your mouth is what she's expecting to hear.

• Smell good, and shave. Wear gloves when you are working at guy things. I've tried that "Just lettin' you know you're with a man" phrase, and believe me, it does not work.

• Speaking of work, work at being cuter and not quite so annoying.

- Learn as a couple to compromise. She wants you to take her shopping; you want to watch a ballgame. Compromise, and take her shopping. Wasn't that easy?
- Guard her, care for her, provide for her, honor and keep her.
- Try to keep your manly manliness in check. Jane doesn't always want Tarzan running amok and chest thumping about everything. Go out in the workshop and build something. Use some of that testosterone to get the yard in order, bucko.
- Be patient with her. She has been patient in working with you for so long now. Look at how far she's helped you to progress. Now, just hearing the newspaper being rolled up makes you move. You don't need any further lessons in her patience running out, do you?
- Pick up your stuff. Even your mother told you that about a zillion times. You don't want her telling mom on you. Do you? Huh?
- Learn to speak and demonstrate to your children that your wife is of first importance. They are indeed special, but there is a time in every growing child's life when they need to understand a basic truth. (and now, a free "Dad" speech: clip and save!) "Mom and Dad were together a long time before you came along. We intend to be together a long time after you are on your own. Don't ever do anything to try and cause division between us, or it will not go well for you."
- Learn prudence. When you walk in the door from a busy yet productive day at work, and it's dinner time and the smoke alarm is firing off and her kids are running berserk like the heathens that they are and the television in blaring out a theme song with an "absorbent and yellow and porous is he" lyric and the youngest child is missing pants and there is obviously a classmate relational crisis being talked out from the middle schooler and something resembling a thrift shop clothing store explosion is leading from the laundry room and down the hallway, do not—I repeat—do not ask, "Hey Hon. So…how's it goin'?"
- Always, always date your wife. My honeymoon hasn't ended. Who ended yours?
- Fix stuff. My woman goes nuts when I fix stuff. If you're no good at fixing stuff, make sure you don't touch her stuff. Women go even

more nuts if you break their stuff. There's a good "going nuts" and a very bad "going nuts." Be aware; aim for the good one.

• Get geared up for a lot of listening. Wives love to be listened to. Us guys can use up all our words just grabbing a coffee at the drive thru and maybe pumping a tank of gas. Just remember, when you get home, she's ready with a lot of pent up conversation that needs to be released, or it could be a stormy night. Learn empathy-laden phrases like, "Uh Huh." "Really?" "What else?" and the granddaddy of 'em all, "What do you want to talk about tonight?" Once she recovers from hearing this, and if the fall wasn't too severe, you're in for the talking of a lifetime. But persevere; the post-talk is usually quite good.

• Pray together.
• Laugh together.
• Grow together.
• Minister to others, together.
• Love her as Christ loves the church. I believe, the last time I checked, that he willingly laid down his life for her. If you haven't started yet, start today and lay down your life—your ways, your demands, your rights, your very self—and prefer her in all your ways.
• Above all, choose wisely. Find the wife God wants you to find.

The man who finds a wife finds a treasure, and he receives favor from the LORD.

Proverbs 18:22; NLT

In the same way, you husbands must give honor to your wives. Treat her with understanding as you live together...

1 Peter 3:7a; NLT

I'm trying to get better. Honest, I am.

It comes as no surprise that as a man, and a Midwestern, southern Michigan male to boot, I have certain characteristics that set me apart from the woman in my world. But perhaps these distinctions are more than geographically or culturally linked. Maybe they go far deeper, to the very way that this guy, and guys the world over and throughout the ages are hardwired.

I would venture to say that this distinction of the sexes is in fact a basic part of my inherent makeup, given to me by my creator and resident in me despite any theory, training or "progressive" thought that says it 'tain't so. In other words, I do what I do and I am what I am because, well… I'm a man. It's not sophisticated, but hey, it sure beats, "I dunno."

But I'm trying to get better. Honest, I am.

This quest for dwelling in understanding with my fairer-of-the-sexes darling is not entirely of my own initiative, but it is undeniably self-serving in the end. I have a strong liking for being with my wife, having regular meals, and avoiding spending nights outside, the latter most chiefly in cold weather. I find that things are so much better at the Masters' Estate when I am practicing understanding, that it is now becoming more and more a part of whom I am. I say whom because this too demonstrates my desire to please her through poised speech; refraining from the improper and barbaric use of "who," which would betray my lack of understanding. (When I self-analyze and contrast this with my use of 'tain't in the earlier paragraph, I'm back to the sad realization that I am a man torn by the complexities of life with a woman while yet itching to retain my identity as a manly man.)

This is not to say I'm getting in touch with my feminine side. I will poke anyone in the eye that even uses the term "feminine" in the same sentence with the words "John," "pastor," or any other that puts that shadow over my path. Well, maybe not literally a poke in the eye, but I can give out a pretty leveling smoldering look… The point is, there's no feminine side lurking here. Nope. None. Look, I got shop rags, a shop vac, and wrenches for Christmas. Note the liberal use of the word "shop" in that last sentence. Twice. And close together, too. Shop is a manly term, not to be confused with that distinctly feminine homophone "shopping." I'm rebuilding my tractor engine this winter. I have an infected finger. I didn't shower yesterday. So don't throw that "feminine side" thing my way. I laugh a big, loud, manly laugh at the very insinuation that my growth in understanding would ever smack of feminine overtones. I'm just being...understanding. It's a biblical command, so don't scoff.

I was so understanding, that four of us went to the musical "White Christmas" at a distant theater last month. It closely followed the movie, but they couldn't recreate the WWII battle scenes on stage. They can do "snow" during the finale; you'd think they could come up with some cannon roar and a little smoke. Hey, I know, it was probably not a guy that did the stage adaptation. I may have tapped my toe occasionally and hummed during the theme sing-along at the end, but when we got over to Greek Town, my buddy and I made sure to have a lot of flaming cheese, hollering, "Opa!" almost as loud as the manly waiters who sweated profusely and sported patchy eyebrows. We could relax in that place. The Greeks know all about how to care for manly men.

Entering the New Year, and not wanting to lapse into negligence in my understanding, I scored really big points this past week by taking darling to the ballet. Tchaikovsky's "The Sleeping Beauty" was being performed by the Moscow Festival Ballet, and my college buddy had obtained four free tickets from a radio call-in contest. After a little phone counseling with him over manly traits and their link to radio station listening choices, I accepted the offer. Darling was beside herself with joy. I was filled with dread and anxiety for what awaited... would all the horror stories be true?

Saturday night came, and there, amid a packed house at The Ford Center for the Performing Arts, I learned many things. First, Tchaikovsky did not base his ballet on the Disney classic, but strangely, vice versa. Second, they do not serve snacks, period. Third, when the curtain finally falls and you extract yourself from your seat to go, you have to come back because there are two more lengthy scenes before it's over. Fourth, there are mystery audience members appointed to clap randomly at something that happens on stage. All others are then to pick up and join in. If you violate protocol and try to be the clap initiator, people will not clap, but will stare a hole in your very soul. Fifth, ballet writers weren't any good with words, so the dancers never talk. Nor do the pantomime extras. If you drift off for even a few minutes, you're so far in the weeds plot-wise that you'll never recover upon coming out of

As I Was Saying . . .

your siesta. The female you're escorting will not be understanding, and will pinch your thigh menacingly if you ask for a little synopsis post-nap. Lastly, the whole tights and tutu thing is a little unnerving for a Midwestern guy who thinks that even short pants on any man looks goofy. I'll bet if the Greeks wrote ballet, they'd have some words, sensible trousers for the cast, and snacks for everyone. But what do I know; I'm just a guy who's trying to be understanding.

I wondered, would darling acquiesce, and attempt to understand my world by venturing with me to say, Monster Truck Mayhem this spring? She responds by telling me my Dakota is a monstrosity of a truck already, and there's plenty of mayhem in her world without going out and paying good money to look for more. She also tells me the vacuum swallowed a rug and she's sure it's ruined unless her man can fix it. She finishes by tossing in that we're having meatloaf for supper. I'd pursue the debate, but anyone knows I can fix that thing, meatloaf sounds good, and besides, the nights are turning awfully chilly now...

And so this evening, as I sipped my herbal tea and mulled over the on-line parts catalogue for my tractor engine, I asked myself the hard question. Am I destined to be, forever, just another hapless manly man? Rubbing my crocheted slippers together under my chair, I pondered afresh the nagging thought: Am I getting anywhere in my understanding of this feminine side? Then it hit me, and I almost dropped my fancy, caramelized cookie. I turned off the Rachmaninoff CD and just sat, staring at my teacup. Egad. I'd said it. The phrase. The non-utterable had been uttered, by me. Feminine side.

I'm trying to get better. Honest, I am.

So God created people in his own image; God patterned them after himself; male and female he created them...Then God looked over all he had made, and he saw that it was excellent in every way. Genesis 1:27,31a; NLT

Amen, God.

Amen.

38

And they shall be one . . . .

Anyone who listens to my teaching and follows it is wise, like a person who builds a house on solid rock. Though the rain comes in torrents and the floodwaters rise and the winds beat against that house, it won't collapse because it is built on bedrock.

Matthew 7:24-25, NLT

The village where I minister is awash with news concerning rainwater runoff problems and the steps being taken to fix them. It's no laughing matter when you are submerged; take it from a survivor. The pine scent air freshener attached to my rear-view mirror is hardly keeping the odor at bay. I'm fighting a losing battle with a car-sized case of mildew. I too have been through the flood.

Our anniversary, an annual event, came around a few weeks back. It is much easier for me to remember this date now that I am older. Unlike my wife, I wasn't very good with numbers and reading a calendar when I was first married, as I hadn't had that unit in school yet. (I might add at this point that it is never wise to joke about marrying an older woman in a public forum such as a newspaper column, sermon or address. It results in tiny welts about one's head and shoulders, and uncomfortable night lodgings next to the mower where there is limited entertainment and no snacks.)

Anyway, my anniversary plans for us were spectacular, beyond my usually meager stabs at being romantic and thoughtful. That one year I pulled up to the speaker, giving her a smoldering glance and saying, "C'mon honey, it's our anniversary—go ahead and supersize it," comes to mind as one of those meager stabs. This year, her role was to simply be gorgeous by four-thirty. I was taking her on a mystery outing. We left on what was to be (cue Gilligan's Isle music) a three-hour date. A three hour-date...

After the book store and the coffee shop prelude, where I had a calming double espresso, and she had something carmel-orange-chocolate-cream—that might've actually had a trace of ol' Joe in it somewhere, I drove my date to her mystery dinner destination. The table was reserved, requested a week earlier by yours truly. The hostess gave me a stare that indicated she remembered my call. So granted, I had been a little short with her on the phone when she acted as if she didn't know my name, or what "my usual table" meant. Sheesh. You don't get to a place for a couple of years and they act like you've never existed...

Dinner was fantastic. We had great, unhurried service, wonderful courses, and best of all, time to ourselves. As we ordered dessert, it started to lightly rain. By the time dessert came to the table, it was getting hard to see across the street. When coffee arrived, there were objects floating down the sidewalk. We lingered, well past my three-hour expectation. As nice as the table was, I figured we wouldn't want to spend the night. Something about kids and home also came up. Talk about a mood killer. We phoned to make sure things were just the normal unbridled chaos there, and then arose from dinner.

There's always a situation that arises to test your manly manliness, and mine for the day was fast approaching. Over the entrance to the restaurant was an elegant maroon canvas. Beyond this was purely a wall of water, accompanied by a passing stream about calf-high. This is the point where manly men make their tiny-headed moves. I instructed my wife that I would be getting the car and driving up close, so she could simply step into the awaiting vehicle without getting a drop on her. She was sweet and I'm sure she was thinking, "I wonder if his policy's paid up?" but she relented and let me step off into the maelstrom.

If anyone reading this doubt's our Lord's sense of humor, let me assure you it is fully intact. Just for grins, as I was trying to keep my footing and resigning myself to the fact that my hair was not going to be right, there was the simultaneous flash and roar of lightning and thunder. My reaction made me glad that my clothing was already soaked. For a fitting capstone on my blind sprint to municipal parking lot "B", hail the size of quarters cascaded down upon my drenched noggin. I made it to the car, messed with the keyless entry code for a record four attempts, and threw myself into the seat with a sound reminiscent of a fully clad well-fed man, totally soaked and sitting down on a vinyl seat in a rapid fashion. I circled the block to our rendezvous point.

"That was quick," she said.

"No problem," I replied.

Our drive home was extraordinary due to the flooded roads.

Wipers beat madly while the defroster vainly tried to clear condensation from the windshield. Intersections grew deeper and deeper, until at the last major crossroads, we found ourselves driving into a seeming lake. Common sense swelled through the brain of the manly man, and I decided to bond even deeper with her by revealing in words my master plan to get us through safely and sanely.

"Hold on," I said.

We got home, though someone sitting in close proximity to me was not overly thrilled with getting wet feet while sitting inside the car. Though the car started fine the next day, I thought it best to do a complete tune up. This resulted in the car not starting for two days as I figured out what I had done to disable it. It's my old motto, "If it works, I can fix that." Anyway, the resultant damage to the vehicle is now mainly the moldering smell. I don't know if that will ever be fixed.

The passage from Matthew I began this story with speaks about the importance of preparing for life's floods. While natural disasters are always with us, Jesus is speaking of those storms that can destroy us within. There is no "if" to Jesus' caution: the spiritual "floods" will come, unpredictable yet as sure as the floods that sweep over these streets I travel. His point is that my preparation is not complete by just hearing his words. As his teaching in that section of Matthew (often referred to as the Sermon on the Mount) draws to a close, the focus is on obeying his commands. To hear and not heed him is akin to my ignoring a siren warning, to take cover from an incoming storm. Action saves the day, as much in spiritual storms as in the physical ones.

My main girlfriend, coincidentally also my wife, accepted my offer to go out to eat again last night. We like date nights, and find no reason to end them just because we're married and statistically should be beyond the "love" thing by now. Our outing was compliments of an anniversary gift card to one of our "romantical" dinner spots, my favorite kind of payment. It started to rain as soon as we backed out the driveway. Dinner was accompanied by a downpour we saw and heard from our atrium room table. I couldn't help but notice my hands shook a little. But this time the rain quit, and we made our way home on streets cleansed from the showers. Still, the mildew smell reminded me that I'd best keep my wits about me, because the floods can come up awfully fast. A good lesson for life, the reminder of which could linger for weeks or months to come.

"For I know the plans that I have for you," declares the LORD, "plans for welfare and not for calamity, to give you a future and a hope." Jeremiah 29:11; NASU

I have a date with destiny, and am now carrying the appointment card to prove it. A year from now, given that everything in life is normal, planned and uneventful, I will return to my ophthalmologist for yet another eye exam. His business being good, and my eyes being somewhere just above "flying mammal" quality, I needed to book my exam this far out in order to guarantee a space in the chair. At this point other plans for next year, whatever they are, will have to fit in around this date. It's a lot of pressure to live with, I know. The calendars all have to be marked, and I'll be sure and add it to my flat black day planner when I buy the next version along about September. I probably should labor at keeping my health up as well. I wouldn't want to be charged for a missed appointment due to "failure to show" or anything like that.

In the chapter I've begun this story with, Jeremiah encouraged the captives that they had an appointment with better days just down the road, when seventy years had passed by. I wonder if that was the encouragement they needed to keep going. I also wonder how effective a counsel like that would be in my life or yours. How would I respond if someone I trusted would say to me, "Hey, cheer up! Y'know, I have it on good source that things are going to be getting pretty good for you in just another seventy years!"? I suppose my first reaction would be to give them a poke, but that's not in keeping with my image and the proper decorum for a pastor. Maybe I'd get away with kicking them in the shins under the table, and making it look like an accident, though.

I take great pains with detailing and listing my plans, but somehow I always chafe at the timetable of the Lord's plans for my life. Though I'm quick to "Amen" the idea that His plans are always best, it seems like I am often looking furtively for a plan "B" that better suits me.

While I'm on the topic of plans, I have some quick tips for any dads who may be pressed into child care while their spouse takes off on a trip for say, New York City with the older children. That's right. My wife gets to take off in resplendent pleasure, chaperoning a group of mild mannered senior high band students on board cushy coach busses and within dignified high rise hotels, while I get left at home with five others, including her three younger ones, one of which is dubious in reputation for yet being even housebroken.

Fearing a backlash of unfounded comparisons, let me start by saying that I know in advance what biased people may think. I've totaled up literally months of being away, what with seminary classes, mission trips and mental health junkets to secluded woodsy locations, often involving firearms and spotty bathing. She has about an hour and ten minutes weekly for the grocery run. Is it fair? No, but such is the burden I bear in life and ministry. So do I begrudge her going? No, absolutely not. It just seems to me that her other younger children would also benefit immensely from accompanying their mother on this cultural excursion. Admittedly, I would have to bear up under the load, probably lapsing into a deep funk at the lonely house; quiet, peaceful, and beaver den-like for those precious days that they gave me a break—er, I mean, that they journeyed into America. Such is my willing spirit of self-sacrifice. But seeing plainly that that's not happening at this late date, I have developed a plan to help me cope with what's coming. Here's where the dads can start taking notes.

Laundry will be a breeze, what with all of those sweat suits I purchased when she was ill last time. One size and one color means no sorting, no lengthy closet deliberations over what to wear, no mess, no fuss, and no hassle. Cold water, no bleach, dryer to drawer, or pile them on the floor. The motto for the five-year old? "Roll 'em up, tuck 'em in!" Yes, and I like the idea of school uniforms, too, but I would suppose that's a whole 'nother story.

Cooking will be equally painless. Local establishments that specialize in all-you-can-possibly-hold-down-for-one-price will experi-

43

ence an upswing in sales. Upon her return, should she protest at my free spending ways, I am not above lying and telling her that the left-rear-burner-sauté-motor-overload-bearing-switch-control-arm on the stove went out, and I just got it replaced before she got home. Since I always have a spot of grease somewhere on me and my clothing, I think it may be convincing. As my back up distraction, I will also have pizza waiting for them.

Bath time is a non-issue, since baths will be a non-issue. April will be here soon enough, and the hose and the kiddy pool are but scant weeks away. Should the girl protest, I'll tell her it's "medieval days reenactment month" and she gets to be the princess, encouraging her subjects to be brave while waiting for their rescue from the evil witch who has rendered her castle waterless under a horrible spell. She'll buy it.

For entertainment, we're going to stick with a few of my all time favorites, such as "health night," where everyone turns in right after dinner, and "don't wake up the crawlspace monster," where I tell a really creepy story about what happened at the neighbor's when their kids made too much noise last night. Throw in a couple of videos and some Benadryl, and I think we're set for entertainment all around.

Yes, five days will blaze by so quickly, it will probably seem like no more than, say, seventy years.

The joy of the full quiver...

The laws of the Lord are true; each one is fair. They are more desirable than gold, even the finest gold.

Psalm 19:9b-10a; NLT

I think a little vacation is in order. The spot I've picked out is Murfreesboro, Arkansas, home of the Crater of Diamonds State Park. I figure that with all of the kids and their mother digging away, we could finance the trip, an occasional meal, and perhaps strike it rich with a monster gem. Coincidentally, it'll probably help pay for the marriage counseling and my resultant medical bills if I follow through with the plan.

I've done some reading about the 1896 Klondike gold rush. The Yukon saw many who struck it rich, and countless others who struck out or even perished in their quest for fortune amid the unforgiving wilderness. My reading was prompted by a friend who returned from an Alaska trip full of tales. I was fascinated to hear a bit of the history, and then to read more of that scramble for elusive wealth.

I have had a taste of mining in my past as well. As a child, my grandfather introduced me to our local caves, home not to diamonds or gold, but a band of horse robbers according to legend. The caves my brother and I entered there would have held perhaps a miniature pony, but no self respecting horse thief would've made a living grabbing those.

I remember touring Kentucky's Mammoth Cave as a lad, and being slightly ruffled when they cut out the lights in the main cavern. The skeleton of the Indian who died there while mining gypsum added to the weight of evidence convincing me that spelunking was not going on my hobby list. My body type was the other factor. Something about the mental image of dying like a cork in a bottle alone in a dark, constricted passage really leaves a lasting impression on a kid. Thanks, mom and dad, for that trip.

Canoeing some of Michigan's rivers can be another form of mining, though the Petoskey stones are often abundant and easy pick-

45

ings from virtually every shallow. I would caution you to not to be overly zealous in packing your canoe with these treasures. An encounter with rapids will result in an immediate yet frenzied sinking of your vessel. Looking back, I believe that's why they call it "rapids." It is difficult in and of itself to unload a fully submerged canoe of its Petoskey ballast. Add to the mix that A) your lunch has been ferried away, B) you are thigh deep in fast water, and C) your glasses are irretrievably lost, leaving you to the elements with vision that uncorrected is just slightly below that of a wombat's, and you see how quickly the problem compounds. Heed the voice of experience. Stupid rocks.

The copper pit mines out on Lake Superior's Isle Royale add to my encounters with treasure seeking. These vertical shafts made by Native Americans are found at several locations around the island. The Minong Mine, developed in "modern" years by European descendants, was more robust and productive, but it too reached a point where labor outweighed the diminishing returns. Still today, the ruins of what was once a thriving treasure hunt are still visible for the backpacker who takes that trail.

I was introduced to pit mining here in Michigan by a good friend many years ago. This mining consisted of digging up old privy spots in search of bottles and other discarded objects that found their way into the hole. It was always interesting to see the array of objects brought to light. Besides glass, there was pottery, clay pipes, china dolls, coins, and the occasional wildcard of cast iron toys or strangely preserved leather shoes. My friend dug as a source of income; I went along just because it was so interesting to see those time capsules opened up. It was a blast. All you needed was a map, a few tools, permissions, and a current tetanus shot.

Now, there is a treasure that occupies me, not simply due to profession, but because of my quest to know the One who has created this world down to the smallest detail of gemstone and mineral. This treasure is in effect a "map" to discovery, though it is not written in secret codes or clever puzzles reserved only for those with special knowledge or inside information. The Word, that truly does consume me in my quest, is much like the gem fields and gold veins that litter our world. Much of it is plainly on the surface, there in the open and clearly detected. Other riches take a bit more digging, but in this Word there is never a dead shaft; I always find treasure useful for my life. Within its pages, I find encouragement to spend my time in God's diamond field, such as this passage: *Joyful is the person who finds wisdom, the one who gains understanding. For wisdom is more profitable than silver, and her wages are better than gold. Wisdom is more precious than rubies; nothing you desire can compare with her* (Prov. 3:13-15; NLT).

There may be some fun and reward in earthly treasure seeking, but it's good for me to remember that the precious gold this world scrambles to uncover and possess will one day be pavement under my feet. And that's truth that, so to speak, I can take to the bank.

It's good I have that treasure to consume me, because from the feedback I've received from the home front, it doesn't look like traveling to Murfreesboro is going to pan out for me this year.

Then Jesus spoke to the crowds and to His disciples, saying: "The scribes and the Pharisees have seated themselves in the chair of Moses; therefore all that they tell you, do and observe, but do not do according to their deeds; for they say things and do not do them. They tie up heavy burdens and lay them on men's shoulders, but they themselves are unwilling to move them with so much as a finger."

Matthew 23:1-4; NASU

What's in your backpack? It seems like a fair question for me to ask, especially as each September rolls in and children everywhere prepare for their fully laden return to the classroom. We even have a designation of a national Backpack Safety Month; a time to focus upon the proper loading, wearing and general etiquette surrounding school backpacks. Our culture has bid adieu to my era of the simple pencil box. Supplies for grade school alone now rival an outfitting for an Everest ascent. In keeping with the illustration, most parents would welcome a Sherpa with an oxygen tank when the tab for the necessities is tallied up as well.

As I indicated, when I was a school-aged kid, backpacks for school were rare. Guys were expected to tough it out by carrying all their stuff at their side, excepting the pencil in the shirt pocket, and your seat pocket for anything else deemed necessary for the day. Granted, there were no hand-held calculators, no laptops (or PC's!), no cell phones, blackberries, iPods, or electronic devices. Still, textbooks were always hard cover, and the minimum weight per volume was a federally mandated twelve pounds. As I recall, every class required at least three texts, which you consulted every day. It was very important for us guys to carry our books at our side, in one arm—never clutched in front of you, two-handed against your chest. This would have been a dead giveaway that you were not manly, and the resultant torture in gym class and probable corporal punishment by the gym guy (whom we swore was once featured on the post office wall) were enough to convince us to suck it up and keep the books at our side. Death by arm constriction was preferable to being thought of, even remotely, as unmanly. Most of my upper body strength and a good deal of my limp I owe beyond a doubt to the manly art of book carrying.

Life today has gotten far more complex. Not only are my children educated in the art of backpack loading, weight distribution and selectivity, but I too have come a long way in my personal acceptance of the fact that I can't carry it all at my side. While the kids have stylin' packs with straps and Velcro and specialty pockets, all in cool colors and graphics, I have graduated to a plain black men's bag. This soft-sided leather friend is my support system for every minute spent away from home. It contains all the essentials and a few extras to keep me productive, effective and flexible in the event my schedule suddenly changes. If I find myself taking an unexpected trip, or dealing with a prolonged day away from home, I usually can cover nicely with the contents of my bag.

Lately however, I've been a little disillusioned with the burden of the pack. The inclusions of a list-making, task-focused male have resulted in a bag that has gradually grown to a staggering weight. Day planner. Cell phone. Directory. Camera. Sunglasses. Bible. Books. Notepads. Calculator. Laptop. Pens, pencils and markers.

Wallet. Keys. Miscellaneous reading and correspondence... Something has to give, and I don't want it to be my back.

I am struck with the similarity of this earthly "burden of the pack" with the scripture starting this story that speaks of encumbering spiritual burdens. Left to man's meddling, the freedom that I have in the Lord can quickly be weighted down by those that would love to load my back with invented rules, regulations, and restrictions. For the Christian, please don't feel led to believe that I have abandoned the faith and am a profligate walking in unrestrained licentiousness (that's a church word that means recklessness or decadence, which I will admit to only in the arenas of caffeine and chocolate). No, I am far from that.

This Word I would live by has much to say about three approaches to life in Christ: license, liberty, or legalism. Only one is sanctioned and commended in the sight of God. Just by reading and meditating upon the book of Romans, I walk away in liberty, amazed with grace. If I do not comprehend this grace, I will err exceedingly toward one of the other two graceless extremes.

My past has been a tapestry of varied experiences. Most remembrances are positive; others are remembered, but not fondly. In life, it has been important for me to reflect on all of my experiences, so that from good or bad, I can glean something of true and lasting merit. It's good for me to sort out the backpack of faith and make sure the contents are truly what the Lord would have me to carry. My life evaluations have led me to these "aha!" moments of clearer thinking, especially concerning the burdens I needn't carry any more. What a joy to lay some things down, never to pick them up again.

It could be that you are in need of a little burden lifting as well. Maybe it's time to sort through your bag of "burden" and see what can be pitched and never missed. For the Christian, the necessities left will be a joy to carry; they will not be a burden, but a balance that truly reflects the Lord's working in your life. This is the instruction and warning the Lord gives us in this passage from Matthew.

So here's to lighter packs for us all. Whether child or adult, we could all enjoy a better posture by leaving the trappings behind and carrying only the essentials we need. I've been working hard at sorting out the pack and discarding the nonessentials. It works for backpacks and men's bags; it works for life in the Spirit too. I invite you to grow with me. Unpacking and sorting may take a little time, but maybe along with our kids, we'll be walking a little taller real soon.

Fathers, don't aggravate your children. If you do, they will become discouraged and quit trying.

Colossians 3:21, NLT

The shocking truth was discovered years ago. A personality inventory revealed that I am a… beaver. My inner beaver likes the quiet, the work in the den, the focus in silent industry upon my studies, the unhurried perusal of books, and the quest to capture my tiny thoughts of God and life before they flit away. However, far from a monastic retreat and continual contemplation, ministry is active in the steady tide of lives and life. Still, I crave that environment that feeds the beaver.

A recent at-home beaver feeding was rudely interrupted by a series of eerie, cat-in-distress sounds emanating from an upstairs bedroom. Clearly, something was dying a prolonged and agonizing death by garrote or the iron maiden. Sensing the danger, I sprang into action. Paula doesn't think hollering for her is exactly springing into action, but it seemed fitting, as I didn't want to unleash my manly manliness without first checking the facts with headquarters. Her response to me roughly translated was, "False alarm, Tarzan." It seems that Kelsie, daughter number three, had been given the privilege in school band of stepping up from the clarinet to the bass clarinet. It was nothing more than practice that I was hearing.

The learning curve is essential to life. Learners abound in our home, for such diverse skills as driving, French horn, guitar, piano, computer, pottery, reading, fishing, cooking, trying not to get on mommy's nerves, potty, Spanish, and yes, bass clarinet. This then is my bias, even from an avowed old beaver in my world of young otters: to let my learners learn. I wonder how many people have abandoned some interest simply because there was no encouragement from others when the practice began. As I age, my concern for the learner grows at many levels: the family, the society, the congregation. That concern is to help others focus on their inner development of character, discipline, and drive to contribute to their world, even as the skills they practice outwardly emerge. If they are indeed a delight to God, perhaps I will find it in me to approve them as well, and see that they have an arena to contribute in. I might even thank Kelsie's band instructor for giving her this new challenge. OK, I said might...

In my not-too-distant past, I sat in tears while attending a Montreal Symphony Orchestra performance of Bedrich Smetana's Má Vlast. It was flawless; visually and audibly passionate and effortless. Yet I knew: the hours, the years, the sacrifice, the focus. But as I write today, I realize I am moved even more profoundly by the flawed performances of the learners. Perhaps their heart is even more obvious amid their labored efforts.

So I press on, still a learner, granting patience and asking patience. And I am assured that other like-minded souls are sitting somewhere, enduring the sounds of cats-in-distress for the good of a learner. Yes, I crave the quiet of the beaver den, but that's why God created the early morning hours.

Practice on, Kelsie. Practice on.

Direct your children onto the right path, and when they are older, they will not leave it.

Proverbs 22:6; NLT

Solomon had it easy. After all, as a parent he never had to endure driver's training with his children.

Now granted, receiving one's driver's license is a huge rite of passage in this culture, and I would never take that opportunity away from my wife's kids. Actually, I would love to take it away from virtually everyone, but that's a rabbit trail and actually not relevant to my thoughts today. (Note to self: future topic for book.) Anyway, we've been through driver's training five times already, and if my math is accurate, that leaves three to go. As with other parenting issues, this milestone for the teens became much easier for me to bear, once my mind was completely shot.

License in hand, some of our young drivers have been raring to go; they had a fevered eagerness to get behind the wheel, inventing opportunities to drive when the normal jaunts had been exhausted.

"Here's your groceries, Mom. Hey, Dad! Do you need anything from the store?"

"Mom, we're going up for ice cream. Again."

"Hey guys! Need anything from the end of the driveway? I'm just gonna take a spin out to the mailbox..."

Others in our nest, an insurance agent's dream, were more reticent to spread their wings and head for the open road. Theirs was a more gradual parental nudge into life on the streets, rather than a frantic attempt on my part to hide the keys and pull the coil wire.

Likewise, my driving attitude is itself more on the reserved side. I don't enjoy driving, finding it an annoyance and a distraction from better things I could be doing. One of my favored authors is A.W. Tozer, who at his midlife gave up driving and was summarily reliant on public transportation or chauffeured service in the discharge of his speaking and ministerial duties. I wonder when I could get that introduced into my pastoral compensation package?

I've not seen a "wild streak" in my kid's driving habits. That is no surprise, as if they would floor it and swerve wildly with the grumpy bald guy in tow. Some have been more cautious than others, but I'm not naming names as that's all a matter of public record anyway.

As for me, I never had any desire to be wild behind the wheel. First, I have an older brother who obeyed the older brother code to the letter, encouraging me to explore passive restraint systems before they were the law, and likewise prompting me to develop a prayer stance from the floorboards while pulling several g's in rapid succession on various hairpin turns in a neighboring park. Second, I was duly impressed with my granddad's tales of driving the Model A at "fifteen miles an hour and not one mile an hour faster," a directive he had received from his grandfather and was sworn to under threat of physical violence. My wife has taken to calling me "Charles" now, especially when I am searching for a parking space so as to not get "dinged" by a careless door. I consider it a great honor to be associated with his name, and her derisive tone and continued use of his name when commenting on my highway speed or signaling prowess only makes me slow down more, and long for the day when she can switch from "Charles" to "A.W." when addressing me.

As a third and final entry to my cautionary driving stance, most any vehicle I've ever owned would not have survived any operational practices even bordering on "wild." Most of them have been a wild enough ride in their advanced state of wear and tear. Duct tape and straight 30 weight oil can only nurse it out for so long. Looking back, most of them never even held up to cautious driving, especially as one last Michigan winter usually assured their total demise.

As it is for driving, so it goes with all of life and our children. You can train them, encourage them, test them and set the rules for life before them, but in the end, when at the wheel, they make the choices. We can hope, pray, and promote every sign of life and growth in the Lord, but I know God has no grandkids; each must decide for themselves who it is that they will serve. Like driving, some poor choices lend themselves to minor corrections. Others are indeed life altering.

I have to believe that when and if my kids look back, the example I set for them to follow will be far more important than any or all of the words that I spoke. On the road of life, I hope to leave a clear path to follow.

As life goes, maybe we'll bump into each other sometime. If you'd like, perhaps there will be a chance for a quick run for coffee. Just remember, if you don't mind, I'd like to read, while you drive.

"...what man is there among you who, when his son asks for a loaf, will give him a stone? Or if he asks for a fish, he will not give him a snake, will he? If you then, being evil, know how to give good

As I Was Saying . . .

gifts to your children, how much more will your Father who is in heaven give what is good to those who ask Him!"
Matthew 7:9-11; NASU

I've never had a knack for picking out the perfect gift. It's best I admit this up front, for the many who reside with me would only be too happy to verify this statement if queried. Yes, I won't try to pretty it up: I am gifting-impaired.

Now, so as not to appear oafish, I do know a handful of the really big landmines in gift-giving to avoid. You know, things such as the anniversary vacuum cleaner or the Christmas frying pan. I'm not totally out of it, but I have had my lesser moments. Over the past years, I have committed gift blunders that included wrapping up and giving deodorant, socks, John Wayne movies, and even 2-liter sodas to my significant other, the one I on occasion introduce as my wife with all those children from her first marriage. Upon retrospect, these were probably not the best things to proffer as presents. Retrospect, that is, coupled with a series of tiny painful welts from well-aimed pinches to sensitive areas. I blame this gift-blundering on 1) being male, 2) my parents (just because that's trendy today) and 3) impaired thinking because the store is closing and I slip quite naturally into panic- grab- gift- mode.

Am I cured of this impediment? Obviously not. This past Christmas season I was caught at home extolling the virtues of perhaps buying Pump-Mart gift cards as practical presents that truly would keep giving well past the twenty-fifth of December. Taking me aside, she first reminded me that I alone am the point man for all vehicle fueling of the Masters fleet. Secondly, she was quite clear that while occasionally acceptable, she would not appreciate push-button cappuccino to any large, endearing extent. Together, we explored options, settled on suitable alternatives, and produced for me a tiny scrap of paper she called a shopping list. She was happy, and I scored big points on the relational scale—though I have to admit that she is still one expensive date, even after all these years. That lone tiny box under the tree for her would've bought a wallet full of Pump-Mart gift cards. But hey, what do I know?

54

I come to the passage of scripture that starts this story, and find in the Lord's words a truth reflected, albeit imperfectly, in my life. Yes, it is natural for earthly fathers to want to give good gifts to their loved ones. It is not always played out that way in the reality of this life, but the premise is a sound one. The Creator once wired us for beneficence, but the fall has marred the generations, giving us a mixed breed of fathers that span the range from brutes to saints. I was blessed; many were not.

In God's economy, fathers take their cue from the Heavenly Father, who in love sought us, in order to gift us. They take their cue from Jesus, who loved his bride the church enough to die for her. In fact, Jesus' words here are either a confirmation or an accusation, depending upon one's spiritual state. "This is how the relationship is designed," Jesus in effect states. His underlying message bleeds through, "What I describe is indeed your reality in your fatherly response to your children… isn't it?"

I too am reminded that the Father's loving response does not need to be pried from his fingers as if he were reluctant to impart his blessing to me. I cannot always understand that which I am given; often I might be tempted to believe (by my earthly limited perspective) that his loving best for me is harsh or uncaring. Still, I have trusted him for all my eternity, and I can trust that even the "harder" gifts he gives me now are for my good, my growth, and my continued reliance upon him.

So I continue on, learning, growing, failing, and rebounding. Have I gotten the reality of the passage tied up deep in my heart? Not as good as it will be tomorrow, but certainly better than I got it yesterday. You can ask the many who reside with me—they'll give you the unvarnished truth. After all, if they were to ask me for a twenty tonight, I would respond with a father's heart of love. That heart may only produce a five, but after all, I am a fallen creature, and my gifting impaired syndrome may still require years for the development of a cure.

Pay attention, my child, to what I say. Listen carefully. Don't lose sight of my words. Let them penetrate deep within your heart, for

55

they bring life and radiant health to anyone who discovers their meaning. Above all else, guard your heart, for it affects everything you do. Avoid all perverse talk; stay far from corrupt speech. Look straight ahead, and fix your eyes on what lies before you. Mark out a straight path for your feet; then stick to the path and stay safe. Don't get sidetracked; keep your feet from following evil.

Proverbs 4:20-27; NLT

Like you, I encounter year after year that season of impending graduations, baccalaureates and ceaseless piles of shaved ham and potato salad. For those completing this first gate in education, I offer some maxims: things I wish I had understood as my high school years ended. Most were realized some time later. A few came much later, and almost too late.

• Your graduation ceremony is the last time you will ever be together with everyone from your class. Getting your entire class together again will not occur. Ever.

• The great majority of your closest friends will begin a rapid fade from your life. People including yourself will move on and out to new challenges, new geography, and new acquaintances.

• Many things you probably consider as very important right now—cars, music, clothes and entertainment—will seem strangely trivial when you begin managing your own family, living and work issues.

• I, like countless others now in middle age, have no idea where or if my high school diploma even exists. I can however, tell you every name of every teacher that made up my K-12 experience, along with memories of each. Many are good friends to this day.

• The world is a much larger place than your high school, and it will not be particularly enamored with you just because you have graduated. There is now a much bigger pool you are swimming in. If you are resolved to build success in your life, you will have to dig in deeper and work harder.

• There are even more novel and numerous opportunities to ship-wreck yourself once you are out on your own. The consequences of one foolish event can close numerous doors to your future, immediately and permanently.

• I have known countless people who have had lucrative careers and are miserable beyond words. When God directs your career plans, He will provide all you need. Do not become one of the walk-ing dead, pulling the cart in pursuit of the wrong carrot.

• Your parents, teachers and other adult influences will for the most part grow infinitely wiser in the next few years. The change of course has everything to do with you and very little to do with them.

• Regardless of what you have come to believe through media, you are not invulnerable, and the world can be a dangerous place. Your life is worth more than a crapshoot of worthless acquaintanc-es, illicit behaviors, and being found at the wrong place at the wrong time.

• If you are relieved that your educational days are finally set aside; that you can leave off learning, close the books, and get on with your life, it will not go well for you.

• Things you can never fully regain include personal purity, an upright reputation, and a clean conscience. These things are price-less, though many discard them like common trash.

• You will be amazed at how quickly the time flies by. Don't suc-cumb to being part of the "if only" crowd. It is your life to live; be responsible and take charge of your own discipline.

• If the Lord is not the center of your life, not much else really mat-ters in the end, after all. I have seen the rich and poor live beside me; neither carries one lump of gold or clay out of this world.

• The wealthiest and most successful people I know are those who honor the Lord, following His Word. They for the most part live quiet lives, influence their world one life at a time, and are at peace with themselves.

• With all of its struggles, challenges, and hurdles, life is still a precious and beautiful gift. Years from now, perhaps you too will pause and look back on what the experiences of your life have taught. I pray that you have much the Lord shows to you; that which can in turn be of profitable advice to the ones who will come behind you.

...And God has given us this task of reconciling people to him. For God was in Christ, reconciling the world to Himself, no longer counting people's sins against them. And he gave us this wonderful message of reconciliation. So we are Christ's ambassadors; God is making his appeal through us.

2 Corinthians 5:18b-20a; NLT

I'm thinking about revoking Isaac's ambassadorship until he gets with the system I have devised for our recycling operation at the Masters' Estate. Now granted, his role as my ambassador is fairly fluid. When he's a model 10 year old, I am perfectly content to call him my son and link him with my last name. In other times of brain-lock and his more age appropriate antics, I tend to link him verbally with his maternal parent. That of course has repercussions of its own, which in all discretion shall remain unmentioned in this family friendly book. You'd think I'd learn.

The recycling incident I am about to impart has become one more example of the struggle I face, to live as an ambassador of Christ in this world. Even with the charge to represent Christ in my life, I would readily choose my own kingship instead of service for Him. It is in reality a struggle for every believer, and perhaps it will be helpful to share my story today.

Recycling is near to my heart. I am awestruck by the volume of waste that this family produces. Low maintenance guys like me are always boggled by just the sheer number of shampoo bottles they go through. When was the last decade I even used that stuff? And milk jugs? Why so many milk jugs? Are we unaware that humans can drink water, too? I do some bemoaning to my wife, who listens without any noticeable compassion, and then promptly asks me to haul my stack of newspapers and magazines away from my chair before they spontaneously combust. I explain that these are not refuse; these are useful. They are the grist for ideas and thinking and articles and books and sermons...I pause here and give you my word: she can look right through me, especially when I make a really well reasoned male-frame-of-mind point that she has not even the slightest intention of entertaining. As I grudgingly carry the news stack toward the door, I am swept up in a vision of this mountain of debris that could one day be labeled, "Masters' Landfill." So, given the plain and standing biblical charge that I am here, among other things, to tend and keep this earth garden and not turn it into one enormous blighted heap, I have been trying to do my part in recycling. The trusty Dakota is now turned into a Fresh Kills barge every six weeks or so, as I transport a full truck bed of recyclables to my area collection point.

The recycle system at home is basic: different containers in a corner of the shop hold newspaper, plastic, glass and tin. That's it. No computer codes, passwords, multi-spectrum analyzers, or DNA samples. Put the paper in the box for paper. Put the plastic in the plastics can...you get the drift. As Thor, the eminent lord and master of my estate, I have ordained the system and deemed it good. Now the charge, given to Ambassador Isaac, is simply to carry out Thor's policy and procedure. This involves his conveying our daily collection of recyclables from the house to the shop, where they are sorted into their appropriate receptacles.

After my return from yet another mission trip to Guatemala, I took a moment to wander into the shop for the first time in nearly three weeks. Thor and Isaac had made the Dakota pilgrimage prior to my travels, so the bins had all been emptied and all was set for orderly business while I journeyed in Central America. When the shop lights came on, I thought I had been transported to an actual landfill. Gone was my simple and foolproof system of sorting our recyclables. Heaps of plastic, glass, and tin cans were everywhere; jumbled in the bins, beside the bins, under the bench, upon the floor. I summoned Isaac to the shop, and trying to keep my Thorish composure, inquired as to what in heaven's name had happened out here.

Now ten-year-old boys, who don't have a clue most of the time for why they do anything, incredibly have developed a strategy to help them over the really rough inquisitions they will face. The line of counter-attack they employ consists of offering—in rapid-fire succession—a litany of reasons/excuses until the parental unit, authority figure, or officer in charge feels that the right one has been proffered. Isaac's list went something like this:

"It was cold out."

"The lighting isn't very good out here."

"It was Hope. Hope did it. I told her she'd get in trouble."

"My friends wanted to help. We hurried so we could have more time to play."

"You weren't here. I was going to straighten it up before you got back."

"The bins got full and I didn't change the bags."

I am reminded of how many times I fail in my ambassadorship to the Lord. My stubborn streak of independence rears up often, leading me to disregard my Lord and his word for my life. I should know better. There are few things more self-destructive than a self-made man who honestly believes it. Hasn't my Lord told me, "Apart from Me you can do nothing" (John 15:5b)? When will I finally let that truth sink in?

I am also reminded of these things he gives me in His Word:

"A pupil is not above his teacher; but everyone, after he has been fully trained, will be like his teacher."   Luke 6:40; NASU

Whatever you do, do your work heartily, as for the Lord rather than for men, knowing that from the Lord you will receive the reward of the inheritance. It is the Lord Christ whom you serve.

Colossians 3:23-24; NASU

For we must all appear before the judgment seat of Christ, so that each one may be recompensed for his deeds in the body,

The joy of the full quiver . . . .

according to what he has done, whether good or bad.
2 Corinthians 5:10; NASU

"Why do you call Me, "Lord, Lord,' and do not do what I say?"
Luke 6:46; NASU

Perhaps it's not just a characteristic of ten-year-old boys to try to escape the neglect of "ambassadorship" by any excuse that presents itself. Whether it's FEMA, the Walter Reed Army Medical Center, or my life in the midst of Jackson County, there seems always to be a breakdown in the chain of command. The servants are prone to forget their servanthood, figuring the big guy is away, or the system given them to follow is just not suited to them, or it's really someone else's job to see that the job gets done. And after all, there are so many other pressing things that we'd all rather be doing…

We got the mess in the shop straightened out, and I regaled Isaac with tales of some of my ten-year-old escapades. As an aside, Dad, once again I'm sorry for tearing apart a perfectly good push mower way back then.

I'd volunteer some more examples and ideas about ambassadorship, but time is of the essence now. Thor has some straightening up to do in the living room, and he's to have it done before supper tonight. No excuse will fly with his fair wife, either. And after all, I can handle it. It's not like I'm ten years old, for cryin' out loud…

But the LORD said to Samuel, "Do not look at his appearance or at the height of his stature, because I have rejected him; for God sees not as man sees, for man looks at the outward appearance, but the LORD looks at the heart."
1 Samuel 16:7; NASU

The tension had been building around our house for several weeks. I had noticed it because I am particularly in tune to the human condition and the presence of relational stresses. My wife would almost agree, but rephrase slightly to emphasize that I <u>am</u>

the relational stress. Whenever she's hitting a low point, I pick up on it immediately, like a coon dog on a scent trail. So sensitive I am to the subtle barometric changes in our communicative air. That sensitivity is also aided by slight physical cues I often receive when walking in the door. Such hints as being cornered and nearly throttled by a woman who needs to talk—now—also go a long way in picking up on the ol' marital radar that a storm is brewing. Yes indeed, I usually put it all together, so don't call me clueless. Then, when I deduce that a stress point is present, I can usually help her out through some careful admonition of her children, a little date time, and some quiet conversation. Add to that my sincere contrition for what I did this time, toss in a milk chocolate or two, and we're on our way to wifely wellness again.

Being pretty level emotionally, but still a sensitive guy, my rare funks are best handled by cutting out all the relational mumbo jumbo and just getting to the chocolate. But please—being a manly man and all—I prefer to stick to the dark variety. The darker the better. Lately I have discovered that if I come home somewhat moody, I can have a small round of dark chocolate offered to me every night. So, being morose and melancholy has its upside—sweet!

But this week, as nearly unique as it was in my life, the tension was not about her, or more thankfully, me. The looming cloud I had sensed had nothing to do with darling at all. The "stressed" this time was son Isaac, and his anxiety was due to two little words penciled in on the household calendar's Saturday lineup: Isaac's tryouts.

The community youth football league had been a topic of conversation for several months, and true to my word, Isaac was registered, sports-physical'd, and slated to appear at the local field for his tryouts. The much-anticipated player draft would then be held, and teams would form to begin their practices. I asked him if he was nervous because of his impending agent contracts, product endorsements, concerns for playing clean in a doping environment, or competing under the officiating of scoundrels that might be bought off to throw key games for the shameless profiteering of the sports gambling industry.

"No," he replied. "I just don't want to drop the ball when they throw it to me."

Saturday came, and we arrived to be greeted by a host of other nine to eleven year olds, a large contingent of parents, several coaches with clipboards, and a really hefty sack of footballs. Being a lousy spectator, I brought a book, a bible, a notepad and a pen. I also brought a pad for the bleacher seat, obviously designed by a sadistic doctor whose sole purpose in life was to promote fiber-glass chaffing and lower back surgeries.

I observed as Isaac and fifty other boys participated in free play with the balls, often referred to as chaos by adults who have lived anywhere near male children for more than ten minutes. The coaches and other helpful adults milled around for a bit, sorting out the boys' registrations by age, weight and height. Then suddenly, a whistle blew, and they were off on the main event—tryouts. My mind for some strange reason flashed to cartoon scenes from Rudolph, as the Reindeer Games were being held. I can't explain it—such are the distractions that swirl in my head.

The boys were quickly placed into groupings based on their obvi-ous physical similarities. The first competition was a forty yard dash, where heat after heat queued up by lanes and then hurled themselves down the track on command. It was especially poignant as the diehard football moms raced down the bleachers with sports drinks for their sons to consume as soon as they crossed the finish line. After all, forty yards can dry out a ten year old pretty quickly, especially on an overcast morning with an air temperature of fifty-six degrees. I felt the lesser for sitting there, sports-drinkless for my son. But, I nursed my steaming Guatemalan Antigua coffee, and the guilty feeling soon passed.

Following the dashes, there was throwing, catching and kicking to be observed. It was enlightening to see that Isaac was holding his own very well. Granted, at that level there weren't really any stand outs. And there shouldn't be. As the organizer had explained to us, this is the league that exists to give the boys some essential skills of the game. Everybody is selected, and everybody plays every game. In the years to come, these boys may have the oppor-tunity to try out for teams where they have to make the cut, but for now, all are welcome, all are safe, all are on the team.

In the scripture starting this story, the prophet Samuel thought Eliab was going to be the "quarterback" for the team, Israel. God was clear in His pronouncement that the reigning Saul was to be sacked. Samuel, wanting to be a good scout for the Lord, had determined that a new leader must certainly be one of prominence, stature, and rugged good looks. After all, he would be leading the team, serving as the king of God's nation! God changed the rules for the "draft" in this one brief verse. His "tryouts" would have nothing to do with the outward man, but everything to do with that which is hidden; that which was and is of immeasurable worth. David had already been selected to become his new starter.

I am reminded that I do not choose the lineup for Christ's team, either. Like Samuel, I must go with God's endorsements, and not get sidetracked into thinking Christ's team members must have a certain "look" to warrant my acceptance of them as team members. He is the manager; I must leave those decisions to Him and concentrate instead upon my role on the team. And like Samuel, I must be open to "recruiting" for my Lord wherever and with whoever He chooses to send.

Isaac really had it right in his summation of what was truly important for his tryout day. Like him, it's of utmost importance that I stay focused and do my best to not drop the ball.

And it happened that He was reclining at the table in his house, and many tax collectors and sinners were dining with Jesus and His disciples; for there were many of them, and they were following Him. When the scribes of the Pharisees saw that He was eating with the sinners and tax collectors, they said to His disciples, "Why is He eating and drinking with tax collectors and sinners?" And hearing this, Jesus said to them, "It is not those who are healthy who need a physician, but those who are sick; I did not come to call the righteous, but sinners" (Mark 2:15-17; NASU).

In this season of tryouts and the sorting of the teams, it is helpful to remember that the Lord Jesus bids all to come and be a part of His winning lineup. The playing field is level and the selection is not based upon the outward appearance. Indeed, the Lord's players, through their individual response to His call, find themselves upon His team. The selection hinges upon the heart, and all who will come to Him are at once as readily accepted as the most seasoned veteran upon His team.

The self-assured, who cling to their talents and measure their worthiness by comparison to "lesser" others, will find there is no spot open to them on Christ's roster. Indeed, they are suited to play for the opposition.

So maybe I'll see you at one of the upcoming games. I'll be the one with the book, the bible, the notepad and the pen. There will probably be a camera, too. The steam you'll see will be coming off my Guatemalan Antigua coffee. But the bag next to me will hold a cool sports drink. After all, when a boy plays hard, he needs that.

After he's done, Isaac and I will talk about the game, and how well he's doing, and what a great thing it is to be part of the football squad.

And no doubt I'll be talking with him about Samuel, David, Matthew and Jesus—and that other team that we're privileged to play on, where all are welcome, all are safe, and all are on the team.

Once a religious leader asked Jesus this question: "Good Teacher, what should I do to inherit eternal life?"

Luke 18:18; NLT

The commands of God are always a hot topic for us pastors. There's a lot of press energy expended upon them, especially if it involves public displays or large monuments trailer'd across the USA for courthouse lawn demonstrations. There seems to be a lot of disagreement over the Ten Commandments, from every walk of life within our country. Disagreement over whether we really want to have them open before us as a type of guide or standard in the national life. Disagreement over their role in the historical establishment of our laws. Disagreement over their viability and validity as religious guidelines to act as a foundation stone for secular society. This uneasiness is not contrived, for the commandments can cause an uncomfortable squirm among those who don't want

As I Was Saying . . .

to be reminded that there is indeed a God, and He has spoken very clearly to us. There can also be a lot of mishandling of the ten by followers of Christ who have yet to grasp the role of the commands in the life of a believer.

Similarly, there is a struggle in my world among my wife's children to grasp fully the rules of life for their world. To help them and all of us caught in the parenting phase of life (roughly 75 years in duration) I have taken to writing out my ten commandments for kids in the hope that now, finally, they will get it. Feel free to post it or trailer it around the nation as you feel led.

1.   Thou shalt not linger in the bathroom. Hot water does not grow on trees. Tissue does, but don't get smart with me. The line in the hallway is now six deep, and they are itching to come and use MY bathroom. I know where the shut off valve is located, and I'm not afraid to use it.

2.   Thou shalt not touch the thermostats. God gave us feeling so we know when to put on more clothes or change into lighter clothes. There are also wonderful conveniences in the house called windows. Open them when you are hot, and close them when you are cold. Electricity does not grow on trees. One exception: If you are 6 years old or under, when Mom is cold, you will be under the mandatory sweater rule.

3.   Thou shalt turn off the lights. The switch on your wall has two functions—learn the second one. You cannot look like you've been to the tanner by staying in front of this type of bulb, although I'm thinking of tanning something if you don't shut it off. By the way, I just checked and sure enough, the electricity is still not growing on trees.

4.   Thou shalt not frequent the kitchen. Unlike the food joints you visit at all hours of the day and night, the kitchen is not a wellspring of unending food. While mealtimes are regular and bountiful, heading for the fridge before the table is even cleared is officially off limits. The stove is not the altar of eternal flame, and having to install grease fittings on the fridge door to keep the hinges from overheating was the last straw. Have an apple and go turn off some lights. Apples grow on trees.

5.   Thou shalt do laundry once a week. The laundry depart-

ment, due to the proximity of the washer to my pillowed head, is strictly off limits after my bedtime. Wearing an article once does not constitute a "dirty" article. For males, an amendment is made to that last rule to allow a sniff test from the maternal figure of the home. You shall measure soap products carefully, as the neighbor gets ruffled when she sees bubbles rising up through our lawn.

6. Thou shalt not tarry over the television, computer or other media devices. Kids who linger are clinically shown to have brains that fall right out of their heads. Brains do not grow on trees, but books are made out of paper, which fortunately for you, does. Reading books about electronics is strictly forbidden.

7. Thou shalt be ready on time for everything. Your alarm clock is furnished within your room and board package. There is no way your alarm chooses not to go off. Revving the engine costs me money, and I never know if it is wise to shut the car off again and put wear on the starter, which would be a doozy to replace. Just be on time. I will not lie in the road in the early morning and feign a leg injury to hold the school bus for you. Ever again.

8. Thou shalt keep the silence of the beaver den. Any music with lyrics has the ban. Allowable music will always have "string quartet" in the title. Most conversation is profitless, so keep it down. Quiet hours are in effect whenever you're home. Talk time is a wonderful part of why you get to ride the school bus.

9. Thou shalt do your chores. Saving up the garbage for Thursday night is pushing for plague to develop. Same with the compost bucket. Sure, it's not pleasant, but the opossums and Mama Skunk sure would miss you if you didn't show up right after dark with "treats."

10. Thou shalt not ask for money. There is none. Money does not grow on trees. Maybe it did, but our tree died a quick, ugly death years ago. Search the sofa, or go look for some cans. If that fails, go hit up your working siblings—they need the laugh.

Now that this great tool for communication has been delivered, I feel that all of my issues with the kids will be quickly resolved. After all, I've spelled out the heart problems, covering every detail and every conceivable thing I need them to know. I'm sure you agree, it's about rules and not relationships with the kids, right?

Wrong.

Then what about the Ten Commandments? Is there a parallel in this rules-versus-relationship illustration I've offered? I can only present this counsel.

In what is often called The Sermon on the Mount (Matthew's Gospel, chapters five through seven), Jesus gives a series of statements (chapter 5) bookended with, "You have heard...But I say." In these sayings, the Lord goes to the heart of several of the commandments, revealing that His followers will have a deeper standard and motivation for living that will come from a right relationship to God through the Christ, Jesus of Nazareth. God's people will be known for emulating the One who is the fulfillment of the law, not for the keeping of finely drawn lines and mechanical rules (Mt. 5:17). In simpler terms, they will serve the Lord in a deep and full way out of love, not out of a rote guidebook kept in their heads. They will go far beyond the tersely worded commands of Exodus twenty.

The real issue is that of law keeping versus heart love. The first legislates and prescribes activity on the external front; the second goes beyond the "code" to the very heart, fulfilling the deeper law of love. The first is driven by an ominous shadow of punishment; the second is driven by a desire to please and not disappoint the object of our deepest affection, the Lord Jesus. The first can claim smugly that the law, at a shallow face value, has been kept. The second claims nothing but humility, love for Christ and others, and an open desire to be constantly drawn deeper into the well of grace and an examined walk before God.

I can be comfortable with my rule sheet. My religion, like my life, can be very comfortable if I am content just to fulfill the letter of the law. The problem surfaces when I leave off grace for code keeping. If I never go beyond the letter of the law to the heart issue, I wear the shoes of the rich young ruler in the Luke 18 passage that began my story. "Don't tell me about my need for following God from the heart—just give me some things to do that I can work at and feel good about. It gives me a standard of comparison so I can know at any time if I am good enough, and who is bad. It helps me to keep my eyes off Christ and His higher call, and upon myself and my self-wrought righteousness. It keeps me focused on religion, and not relationship."

And that is the dead stuff that even hearty proponents of the Ten Commandments can hold dear to, while yet trying to win others to their cause.

Rules are great. Rules built on God's Word can be a blessing. But for the believer, the real issue comes down to relationship with Christ, not rules. That relationship is what is desperately needed within my home, my community, and my effective witness everywhere. The world apart from Christ watches, to see if my life adds up to what I say I believe. Do I present Him, and relationship with Him, or a chiseled set of "relation-less" rules? The jury is still out, weighing the evidence and deliberating toward a final decision.

My understanding of rules and relationship should not be difficult. Once, in Eden, mankind chose poorly. Through Christ, we all have the invitation for choosing relationship with God again. Come to think of it, it all started with something that grew on a tree...

Fathers, do not provoke your children to anger, but bring them up in the discipline and instruction of the Lord.

Ephesians 6:4; NASU

It's probably one of the best guy routines I have going. I'm not exactly a news junkie, but I do like to know what's happening on the block. With a couple of newspapers and a journal or two, you'd think that I would have my fill of all things good and bad around the county, nation and world. But, I also enjoy the guy routine, and so I do it—nightly when possible.

All that is necessary is a healthy snack (anything slathered in peanut butter or covered in dark chocolate), a working remote, several oversized pillows, and the tube. Fifteen or twenty minutes of viewing pretty much gets me up to speed, and I am then content to find something else to do. Simple. Effective. To the point.

As pleasant a guy routine as that is, my repose was interrupted this week by the intrusion of son number three, sometimes more affectionately referred to as Isaac. At age ten, he's prone to inter-rupt my news time. It's not that he wants to hone his conversation starters about the crisis in the Mid East, either. He's much more mercenary than that. His concerns center more on the Mid Section. That's right—it's just about securing a snack. After all, there's a lot of free time between the three main meals for a growing young man to fill, literally.

I was doing some remote control exercises—forward search, reverse search, mute/volume, review—while biding my time in anticipation of the news to roll around at the top of the hour. Isaac is enthralled with my savvy remote handling; as fluid as some men are with goose guns, impact drivers, or a pitching wedge. What happened next was a jolt that caused me to lose my composure, my grip on the remote, and my focus for the upcoming top stories.

I had landed upon an Elvis movie in my channel surfing. Don't ask me which one—that would be for somebody who really knows their blue suede shoe history. He was there, in Technicolor splen-dor, sporting a garish red marching band uniform and belting out a swing rendition of "When The Saints Go Marching In." The support-ing cast, made up of myriad adoring females, supplied harmony and huge frozen smiles as the jazzy little number went on and on.

Isaac was mesmerized. "What's this show?" he inquired.

"Some old Elvis movie," I said.

And then, another great "Aha" moment in my life made its arrival. The snacking ten year old turned to me and asked, "Uh, dad...who's Elvis?"

Thus the sons of Israel did as Joshua commanded, and took up twelve stones from the middle of the Jordan, just as the LORD spoke to Joshua, according to the number of the tribes of the sons of Israel; and they carried them over with them to the lodging place and put them down there. Then Joshua set up twelve stones in the middle of the Jordan at the place where the feet of the priests who carried the ark of the covenant were standing, and they are there to this day...Those twelve stones which they had taken from the Jordan, Joshua set up at Gilgal. He said to the sons of Israel, "When your children ask their fathers in time to come, saying, "What are these stones?' then you shall inform your children, say-

ing, "Israel crossed this Jordan on dry ground.' "For the LORD your God dried up the waters of the Jordan before you until you had crossed, just as the LORD your God had done to the Red Sea, which He dried up before us until we had crossed; that all the peoples of the earth may know that the hand of the LORD is mighty, so that you may fear the LORD your God forever" (Joshua 4:8-9, 20-24; NASU).

God had a plan for the children, and he primed His people to be ready with the right answer when the little ones would ask. It seems so unfitting to note that just one book of the Bible later, the children wouldn't have a clue about their God.

Then Joshua the son of Nun, the servant of the LORD, died at the age of one hundred and ten. And they buried him in the territory of his inheritance in Timnath-heres, in the hill country of Ephraim, north of Mount Gaash. All that generation also were gathered to their fathers; and there arose another generation after them who did not know the LORD, nor yet the work which He had done for Israel (Judges 2:8-10; NASU).

I was struck with Isaac's question, because it reminded me anew about the importance of teaching my child about his Heavenly Father. Like the new whiteboards in our church classrooms, these kids are indeed the "blank slates" that I cover with either the important information of eternity or the trivial fleeting nonsense of life divorced from their Creator.

Isaac had no idea who "the king" was. No reference point. No history. No exposure.

I cannot err like the Hebrew fathers and "assume" that Isaac knows the Lord. Assumptions won't get it done. He may not need to know much about Elvis, the King of Graceland, but he sure needs to know of Jesus, the King of Grace.

Now you followed my teaching, conduct, purpose, faith, patience, love, perseverance, persecutions, and sufferings, such as happened to me at Antioch, at Iconium and at Lystra; what persecutions I endured, and out of them all the Lord rescued me! Indeed, all who desire to live godly in Christ Jesus will be persecuted. But evil men and impostors will proceed from bad to worse, deceiving and being deceived. You, however, continue in the

As I Was Saying . . .

things you have learned and become convinced of, knowing from whom you have learned them, and that from childhood you have known the sacred writings which are able to give you the wisdom that leads to salvation through faith which is in Christ Jesus (2 Timothy 3:10-15; NASU).

Paul hit it squarely in his "advice" to Timothy. You've got a foundation; don't waver from it or the evil men and imposters will eat you alive.

Here's to making sure the young ones in our charge get that foundation, and a fighting chance in the same arena that holds our days.

They will thank you one day. The Lord himself will commend us. And I'll add my gratitude as well:

"Thank yuh. Thank yuh very much."

What can you point to that is new? How do you know it didn't already exist long ago? We don't remember what happened in those former times. And in future generations, no one will remember what we are doing now.   Ecclesiastes 1:10-11; NLT

Way back in 1492, Columbus made an important "discovery." It probably wasn't too earth shattering for the folks who had been in these regions for centuries, but the fallout sure has been. Leif Erikson gets the short stick in comparison to Christopher C., but who among us really has the time and luxury to sit round and debate whom discovered what, and when? After all, we're all busy making our own discoveries, and time is short.

I'm not the sharpest knife in the drawer, but over the years I think I've made some reasonably important discoveries. These truths may have been common knowledge in past times, but I have no solid proof to document that. For now, I'll assume that I'm the discoverer, and stand in line to receive my accolades and medals of recognition. So, for perhaps the first time in print, I bring you just a tiny sampling of the many "firsts" that I've discovered:

• Nothing makes a child so concerned with their GPA, homework, and study for impending pop quizzes as does the mention of chores after dinner.

• "New" does not necessarily mean "Improved."

• Everything takes longer when you absolutely need to be on time for an important appointment.

• Unless you stand at the toaster and raptly observe the process, the release mechanism will fail to deploy and your toast will be incinerated every time.

• A cat will not come when it is called; it will show up after you are so agitated that you wouldn't let it in if it was the last mouser on God's green earth.

• A dog will come immediately when you call a cat; it will act as if it's been twenty years since you've seen each other, though you let him out the same door about two minutes ago.

• There is no piece of furniture so well made that a pack of 40-pound kids can't destroy it in one afternoon. Keeping legs on couches would require a direct intervening miracle from the Lord.

• For every additional channel one can receive on television, there is an exponential increase in the odds that there is nothing on that is worth watching.

• At two o'clock in the morning, when struck at the right angle and appropriate velocity, I can move a bed approximately four inches with my big toe.

• In between the closing of the dinner prayer and my quick retreat to the kitchen for a glass of water, the remaining family of nine can consume an entire four-pound meatloaf.

In my desire to pass on this wisdom acquired from years of simply being alive, it is important to know that space alone prohibits me from naming every key insight I have had over the course of my life. There is one discovery however, which stands far above all others.

A life that is lived in the presence of God will certainly yield new discoveries every day. *What this means is that those who become Christians become new persons. They are not the same anymore, for the old life is gone. A new life has begun!* (2 Cor. 5:17; NLT)

As I Was Saying . . .

There is nothing in life that is to remain the same after God is given first place. Nothing.

Relationships. Priorities. Motivation. Work Ethic. Compassion. Security. Self-esteem. Care. Conservation. Stewardship. Values. Empathy. Identity. Origin. Future. While the writer of Ecclesiastes can truthfully note that the commonalities of this life are continually rediscovered by succeeding generations, the real discoveries at the heart of man can only come from knowledge of his Creator. Even the commonplace becomes uncommon in the life of one who is born anew.

One day, I have the promise to experience all things being recreated as amazingly "new." This newness will encompass every aspect of my life, forever. *And the one sitting on the throne said, "Look, I am making everything new!" And then he said to me, "Write this down, for what I tell you is trustworthy and true."* (Rev. 21:5) While anticipating this "one day," I still press to discover the new things of life in him today. There is no discovery by clinging to the dead ways and that which is no longer true of me. The writer of Ecclesiastes is right. Apart from God, everyone plods as he or she has always plodded, in the trench of lifeless living, toward the same deadly and dismal godless end. With God, life is a continual discovery. It is the life we are meant to live. And after all, everyone enjoys a little discovery now and then. Just ask Christopher or Leif.

Or John, discoverer of the Great Toaster Axiom; October, 2007.

After everyone was full, Jesus told his disciples, "Now gather the leftovers, so that nothing is wasted."　　　　　John 6:12, NLT

You will hear it if you listen very intently. It is a droning sound, similar to a pump motor kicking on and off in a steady rhythm. Often linked to specific times, it most frequently occurs from late afternoon to early evening. It is the groan of scattered children throughout the land, whining their distain. They have discovered that the dinner table is featuring... leftovers.

Waste is a big part of my world. In a throwaway society, I'm not supposed to let waste bother me, but it does. Similarly, greed gives birth to waste, where the conquest for the next possession becomes the focus, not the thankful use and care of what one already possesses. Likewise, hoarding is a form of both waste and greed. Stockpiles are amassed and clung to, held so tightly and improperly that they erode in value, spoiled for any use by anyone.

If you were to live in connection to the community in which I minister, you might well be a part of a cleanup crew after the checkered flag has been waved at our local speedway. I have served such time. Clean up inside the big oval is a dicey business for me, and for those I've raised. After all, I realize that we can't take it with us, but do they have to leave so much of it behind for us to deal with? After our last volunteer stint to benefit the school, our problem became what to do with all the good stuff left behind which obviously was not waste. A collection of handleless axes, leaky bottle jacks, zip-top soft-sided approved race coolers, and other abandoned items occupied shelf space in my shop for weeks. After all, what's the sense in wasting all of that?

At times I am compelled to labor at ridding my personal space of unnecessary possessions. There is a fine line here, as I am married to, well, a woman. The woman in my world has a strong urge to line her nest with pictures, full shelves and various displays of knickknack. This is a correct spelling so don't bother seeking to undermine my reporting on grounds of mere mechanics. To be fair, note that I once tried to get in touch with my feminine side. My shop inbox received a request from the homeowner for a shelf installation in the honeymoon suite. I was obliged to do this, as I have borne witness to rooms where the homeowner has cut loose with a hammer. Machine Gun Kelly would've been proud of the carnage. Upon completion of the job, and with the homeowner away on shopping detail, I took the initiative to set up a tasteful display on the shelf. I felt this would help me to bond with her in her world and interests. The shop rag, WD-40, cordless recharger, and peanut jar were quickly relegated back to the shop upon her return, as was I. So much for my feminine side. I really labored over the feng shui with the shop rag, too.

I'm working on my list of vacation projects, and this has required several trips to the cellar to retrieve paint cans and the like. Some of the hoarded stuff, put there for future use, has turned into science experiments gone horribly wrong. Even with the hazmat suit on, I still developed a rash after prying open that last one. How long has it been since the hardware clerk mixed that up, anyway? I'll have to inquire about warranties and a refund when I get back in the office. It has occurred to me that if the homeland security department gets wind of my cellar, there'll be a new front in our war on bioterrorism, and yours truly may be writing from a smaller, cell-ish space in the near future.

I also have for sale a boat anchor. It strongly resembles a five-gallon bucket of dried up wallboard compound, but if you can overlook that little detail, have I got a deal for you.

In this consumer culture, which I blame my parents for allowing me to be born into, I'm supposed to be discontented with my current stuff. Scrapping my stuff is encouraged; the new stuff I'm to clamor for is flaunted from every network and billboard. I am not to consider myself complete and whole without the current fashions. I am to look down on myself until I raise the bar by acquiring the new model, even if it breaks the bank or spirals me down in uncontrolled credit debt.

The problem is not with things, but the demands upon me by a lifestyle that takes its meaning from possessions. I want my impact in this world and the memories people have of me to go beyond my things. I hope I'm never fondly remembered because of all my stuff.

I recall the true-life story of a friend now with the Lord. In his days, he had once been a first responder, ambulance crew. One call had him playing referee in the front room as the relatives of the deceased practically came to blows over dividing the stuff. The coroner hadn't even arrived yet. My friend told me that after that incident, he loved his dog even more.

I have many friends who have downsized and opted to get rid of much of their stuff for reasons of stress, security, and sheer upkeep. Many of these friends have found their real purpose for living in the One who has created them, and their freedom over the material things of life is freedom indeed.

Clamoring for stuff. Wasting. Hoarding. Keeping and losing. I find my picture next to each offense. These are all real and tangible problems of this physical life that I hold. Likewise, each is an illustration of their counterpart in the deep world of spiritual life. Wasting of time, talents and treasures. Coveting attitudes toward spiritual gifts. Hoarding the Christian life and message, starving self and others as the seed and branch rot. Jesus reminded the disciples that all things, physical or miracle-wrought, have a need to be used as they are intended, for the benefit of self and others, and to the glory of God.

Not that I was ever in need, for I have learned how to be content with whatever I have. I know how to live on almost nothing or with everything. I have learned the secret of living in every situation, whether it is with a full stomach or empty, with plenty or little. For I can do everything through Christ, who gives me strength.
Philippians 4:11-13, NLT

Yep, it's leftovers for supper tonight. And I will pray with my family, and thank my God.

He comforts us in all our troubles so that we can comfort others. When they are troubled, we will be able to give them the same comfort God has given us. 2 Corinthians 1:4; NLT

At this season of reflection on His appearing, I remember this.

Many years ago, I had an acquaintance who suffered with a debilitating disease. The effects were numerous, one being a frequent rosy flush to patches of her skin. This was the visible reminder of the pain she would quietly bear. It seemed my words always fell short in conveying to her my heart and empathy for what was endured each day.

I recall this story now, writing in the season of Advent. And like my faltering attempts to share with her, I sense that same inability to convey in words all that my heart encounters. Through all I experience of the Christ of Christmas, it remains impossible for me to ignore the shadow of the cross over the scene of the manger. It is all encompassing; the cradle-to-empty-grave divine act that I pray to understand more fully. The basic tenet is amazing: God sent his son to know suffering, in order to rescue the insufferable who were not asking for any rescue, thank you very much. To try framing this in words during the festive "holiday" season is risky business. Few welcome sober truth and deeper reflection. It sucks the life out of amusement and commerce that now mark this Xmas culture.

Suffering is a dark friend in this world. Those who do not embrace suffering have no business offering words of counsel. They are blind guides, theoreticians in a vacuum of isolation, untouched by that for which they present their clichés in ignorance:

"You'll get over it."

"C'mon, snap out of it."

"It can't be that bad."

"I know exactly how you feel."

The apostle Paul knew firsthand of the need to own and grow through our deeper sufferings. While he disclosed to us much of his harrowing travels, tortures, imprisonments, and ceaseless concerns for the churches he nurtured, there came a time for him to pause in silence. A personal suffering existed that was so intense, though alluded to, Paul leaves off disclosing its exact makeup. This veiling is indeed God's wisdom; all who walk in that shadowland of suffering may find common ground in Paul's thorn. There is hope, for perhaps the apostle carried that which is their particular burden as well: *...I was given a thorn in my flesh, a messenger from Satan to torment me and keep me from being proud. Three different times I begged the Lord to take it away. Each time he said, "My grace is all you need. My power works best in weakness." So now I am glad to boast about my weaknesses, so that the power of Christ can work through me* (2 Corinthians 12:7b-9; NLT).

The dark friend, meant for driving one away from the God of all comforts, instead accomplishes the opposite for individuals who remain fixed upon their savior. In Christ, those who suffer discover that it is a path they travel, and not an effort of lonely trailblazing through uncharted territory. One has been there before, and that One will accompany, encourage, protect and deliver, until they are safely home at last. *This High Priest of ours understands our weaknesses, for he faced all of the same testings we do, yet he did not sin. So let us come boldly to the throne of our gracious God. There we will receive his mercy, and we will find grace to help us when we need it most* (Hebrews 4:15-16; NLT).

The big picture, which I find so improper to divorce from this season, is bound up in the fact that the Son came to earth, appointed to suffer. We as fallen creatures were all justly condemned, destined to be separated forever from our Creator. God in compassion chose to come for us, the offenders, when we were hopeless and powerless to relieve our guilty standing before him. The only acceptable sacrifice, perfect, sinless and *Suffering is a dark friend in this world. Those who do not embrace suffering have no business offering words of counsel. They are blind guides, theoreticians in a vacuum of isolation . . .* innocent, would be provided by the offended, God Himself. *But God showed his great love for us by sending Christ to die for us while we were still sinners* (Romans 5:8; NLT).

Through Christ, we are spared from the ultimate, eternal sting of suffering; that of never living eternally in His presence, experiencing our fullness of joy. By God's grace, Jesus took our suffering to himself. *Yes, by God's grace, Jesus tasted death for everyone. God, for whom and through whom everything was made, chose to bring many children into glory. And it was only right that he should make Jesus, through his suffering, a perfect leader, fit to bring them into their salvation* (Hebrews 2:9b-10; NLT).Through Him, the darkness of suffering is destroyed ultimately, though for a season we must endure earthly sufferings presently. As the scripture that begins my story indicates, it remains a part of our mission to help each other in all our various testings. Everyone needs encouragement to remain focused on the finish line when the long shadows and dark days come. *Yet what we suffer now is nothing compared to the glory he will reveal to us later* (Romans 8:18; NLT).

As I Was Saying . . .

It is a good thing for me to reflect on his suffering at the cross, even in this season of wonder at the manger. I find this discipline a mooring post in the undercurrent of suffering that washes through life. It brings stability to my thought, my ministry, my perspective, and my days. *My suffering was good for me, for it taught me to pay attention to your decrees* (Psalm 119:71; NLT).

If I did not experience chronic pain, I might callously dismiss it in others.

If a child of mine did not have special needs, I might never enter into others' worlds, who also live in that reality.

If I did not experience firsthand the sufferings of the third world, I might remain absorbed in petty problems here in my North American bubble, rather than reaching out and trying to make a difference for them.

If I had not struggled with the issues of a large family, they and I could have missed the faith lesson of seeing the Lord provide our needs.

If I would not endure hardness in ministry, I would not have the privilege of seeing the Lord grow my faith and his church.

If He had not come, appointed to suffer, all my present sufferings would be without remedy, for the end of all things would only be the beginning of my eternal, multiplied sorrows.

And finally, what of my suffering friend? One day in a visit with her, I had one of my daughters in tow, perhaps a little over three years old at that time. My drive time pondering over words to say hadn't helped much. Nothing really seemed to flow that was going to be helpful and pastoral and caring and encouraging and spirit led. It seemed like in our history of so much time and so many visits, everything about her suffering had been said. In the awkward silence, my daughter got up from her play, and in childish innocence stood staring at my friend. And there, as the woman now paused in her rocking, I witnessed the manifest comfort of Christ. Very simply, the child touched one of the inflamed patches on the woman's arm. Bending her head down, she placed a tiny kiss on the spot, and quietly said, "I get owies, too." She then turned and went back to her child's play. I stood, too dumb to speak, realizing that Christ had already clearly spoken.

In this season of Advent, have you experienced his appearing? Have you claimed his suffering for your healing? Then go, and see that you bring others to him for the healing they are dying to receive.

It is for this reason, and none other, that he has appeared.

———————————

Two things I asked of You, Do not refuse me before I die: Keep deception and lies far from me, Give me neither poverty nor riches; Feed me with the food that is my portion, That I not be full and deny You and say, "Who is the LORD?" Or that I not be in want and steal, And profane the name of my God.

Proverbs 30:7-9; NASU

The rituals of observing a birthday at the Masters Ranch are rooted deep in tradition, running quickly now toward the twenty-five year mark. My wife and I had no experience in orchestrating these milestone celebrations until child number one needed party number one. We were so inept that the obligatory ice cream remained in the freezer until sometime the following week. Our folks never said a thing, but I can only imagine what they were thinking... We have improved somewhat since that inaugural, due to the fact that children numbers two-through-eight arrived and there has been ample opportunity for us to experiment with and hone these events.

With a family that size, you'd better have a plan, a calendar, and one very dependable oven. The plus side is, we get to eat cake often. A lot of cake.

When the children reach a certain age, dad also includes breakfast out as an opener for their birthday celebration. "A certain age" is dad-code for being toilet trained. Nothing ruins the ol' biscuits and sausage gravy like a full diaper. Believe me; I learned that one hands-on, just prior to the implementation of the "certain age" rule.

When the child is of age to know some of the local breakfast haunts, they are also invited to name the place where our table for two will be spread. Each has their own preferences, ranging from

81

the no-frills diner to the glad-I-brought-the-debit-card restaurant. The boys seem to follow my lead, tending to favor the plain and hearty working man cafés, while the girls tend more toward their mother's refinement and delicate sensibilities. I'm not complaining—it's a big part of my answer for why I married her and not anyone else. Given my shortcomings, I would imagine she's still mulling over her answer to that very same question.

Megan is truly following in her mom's footsteps. For her recent birthday morning, she chose a restaurant quite a drive away. As we were seated, the hostess presented us with menus that in sheer bulk rivaled phone books for a small town. Surrounded by our heady atmosphere and fidgeting slightly with a delicate coffee cup that was not intended to ever fit a guy's hand, I casually inquired of her what delectable item she was contemplating to order for our celebration. This after all was one of those "special" ages, and I was ready to shoot the works to help her realize this was indeed, a big day. Belgian Waffles? Crêpes Suzette? What would her choice be?

"I'm getting the oatmeal," she stated.

"Oatmeal?"

"Yes, oatmeal. It's yummy and I like it!"

So we both went for it, and enjoyed ourselves immensely, talking about driving and school and friends and well...anything she wanted to talk about. I don't even recall if it was "good" oatmeal or "so-so" oatmeal. I was occupied with her. The breakfast came, and it was consumed as an item quite detached from our pleasant conversation.

Now as they were traveling along, He entered a village; and a woman named Martha welcomed Him into her home. She had a sister called Mary, who was seated at the Lord's feet, listening to His word. But Martha was distracted with all her preparations; and she came up to Him and said, "Lord, do You not care that my sister has left me to do all the serving alone? Then tell her to help me." But the Lord answered and said to her, "Martha, Martha, you are worried and bothered about so many things; but only one thing is necessary, for Mary has chosen the good part, which shall not be taken away from her" (Luke 10:38-42; NASU).

I was reminded of this tale from the Lord's life as Megan and I shared the simplest of meals that morning. With all that surrounded us, and the possibilities of that menu, it could have been very easy to focus on the food, and miss each other in the meal. Megan brought me back to the point of what was of first importance: the friendship, not the food. Jesus brought that lesson home to one very distracted Martha, who had lost track of her guest in the focus on her preparations for Him.

It happens often, still.

More than once I have choked down a meal just to get it over with and dismiss myself from the presence of distracted diners. There's nothing quite as unpleasant at mealtime as a main course of strife, with a heaping side of discord. Even a filet mignon tastes like wallboard in that atmosphere. It's much better, as the Lord demonstrates, for us to focus on one another and be content with setting out the simple things. How fitting: the presence of comfort foods, and the presence of the God of all comforts.

Scripture likewise offers a pair of proverbs stressing the importance of the fellowship over the feast. *Better is a dish of vegetables where love is, than a fattened ox served with hatred* (Proverbs 15:17; NASU). *Better is a dry morsel and quietness with it, than a house full of feasting with strife* (Proverbs 17:1; NASU).

Paula and I are experiencing the rebirth of this simplicity in our dates. One of the dangers of marriage is that of forgetting to date, and we have taken to planning out our calendars to include regular times to slip away for an hour alone, together. Rather than "formal" or expense-laden escapes, we have settled upon a handful of quiet places, where we can share a chocolate "anything" and some good coffee. What could be simpler? More delightful? Our quest is clear: Forget the fuss; it's you I want to spend time with!

This understanding of cherishing simplicity is applicable to my life as a worshipper as well. After all, Martha was missing out on God in the house, because of her distracted stirring of pots in the adjacent room! God forbid that I emerge from "worship" having completed all types of chores, tasks, and rituals, but never having truly worshipped. How careful I need to be, to enter with a heart of undistracted devotion! Entering into the "house of worship" with a mindset to "see" or "be seen" as part of the "show" should hold no place in a believer's life. I do not disparage the ministries and ministers that come together for our times of corporate worship. But even while desiring to bring excellence to God in our worship, I cannot forget this truth: simple acts of worship guided by His Spirit will always stand as excellent gifts of worship to present to Him.

Am I learning from the examples of scripture, and my daughter-dad date? I admit I often run to distraction, but I'm trying to temper being perfectionist-hospitable with the clear need to keep fellowship the priority. In worship, I am focusing more on just being in the presence of the Lord; working at anchoring on Him, and not getting swept away in the "busyness" that the Lord's Day can easily run to. How encouraging it is, in both the big and little things of life, to find joy in the excellence of simplicity. How refreshing it is for me to know that God, who has authored all this unfathomable complexity surrounding me, desires to have nothing more than a simple, uncomplicated and undistracted relationship with his child.

May we all grasp the truth of this, in spirit and in practice.

So eat your oatmeal. It's good for your heart, in more ways than one.

Don't long for "the good old days." This is not wise.
Ecclesiastes 7:10, NLT

Just as sure as the seasons change, all things follow suite, and not always for the best. I read much about schools revising dress codes to help stifle some forms of exhibitionism, rampant vandalism at local parks, and the growth in gang participation coming to a city near you. I had no time for such foolishness when I was a kid. Of course, in those times (that's late Iron Age for you history buffs), my parents ran the show, my schools had their full support, and there was a multitude of adults to make sure I stayed on the right page socially, intellectually, physically and spiritually. Then too, I had Bean Creek.

From early elementary through junior high, the last June day of the school year went roughly like this: Bell rings, mom drives, we unload, mom waves goodbye, and I am on retreat with the grandparents seemingly until fall. It strikes me odd now, as I had often been referred to as a perfect child by my mom. Maybe "perfect" and "removed-from-premises" somehow merge in meaning, but at any rate, I was off to my private summer camp on Bean Creek.

I know it's shocking to the modern reader to consider it, but my summer days were often unscheduled yet always carefully supervised. Little wonder that I never committed a felony, a petty crime, or so much as tore up anything. I was taught and then held to the expectation that I would do what was right. There was that one downed-tree-over-the-creek incident, but that was accidental, and I was a strong swimmer even for a chunky kid…

Fishing was the pastime of choice, though there was plenty of swimming, hiking, .22 target practice, barn exploring, gardening and rock collecting to fill in the days. There was also steady work, mowing with the reel mower. If you aren't familiar with this tool, ask your elders to describe it for you. This activity was twice blessed: the yard was maintained, and I got an excellent night's sleep. The occasional trips to town were tolerated in order to lavish choremoney on lures, ammo or the newest copies of Outdoor Life or Field &Stream magazines. As an aside, Snickers bars were much bigger back then, but Coke was a 6-ounce dark green bottle, and you'd better nurse it out, because you got one. Baths and haircuts were both bi-weekly and short. I tell you truthfully that we once shot, cleaned and roasted a woodchuck just because we wanted to try it. Once.

All too soon, summer was gone, and the necessary return to academia whisked me away from the Bean Creek. I remember my summers as a time for exploration and fun. A time when things were good and right. A season when adults had the time, responsibility was rewarded, and we were all on the same page.

Different winds blow today. Electronics are the new playgrounds. Nuclear families are the exception, as are involved grandparents. Schools are overwhelmed with the unfitting task of being the chief socializing element in many children's lives. Sports, once a primary play tool in my life to build character, can now turn into the serious work of adults bent on professionalizing the sand lot for junior's ride to fame. Childhood summers now carry a meaning far removed from my Bean Creek days. Or worse, no meaning at all. The Word I read tells me not to long for the former days. It's hard to not sit, reminisce and lapse into grumbling about "how it used to be." Maybe it's the same for you. Yet, because of His perfect track record in every other area, I'm relying on God's Word to be correct in this warning as well.

When I consider the days of my youth, the same headlines were being printed, whether appalling dress or tearing things up or running with the pack. The difference was in how the adults in my world worked together. There was strong disincentive and positive alternatives to keep me from straying too far afield. There were wonderful rewards for playing by the rules. Anything of value in my life is largely due to the previous generation fulfilling their time-intensive duty to model biblical values for me, and hold me to the same.

To avoid my lapsing into sappy moralizing and a maudlin, soap-box appeal, let me simply state my story's point: The key is not more stuff for my kids' lives, but more of my time invested in their lives. The Word is absolutely on the mark: it's about living life now, and living it for others, not self. I can invest my time to build and model a strong marriage. I can invest my time to get proactive with my kids, my schools, and my community. I can invest my time to impact the new generations that always need godly direction. "Longing for the good old days" simply excuses me to dig the bunker, build the fence, widen the moat, and turn inward to reductionist, selfish tendencies. A generation absorbed with longing for "what was" has really missed the lesson of having once been there. Life lessons are to be transferred, not just rehearsed in the mind. And that takes time.

And on a hot June day with summer now arriving, I wonder if my kids will one day reflect on some good old days that they fondly remember, but choose not to "long after" because there is still much work for them to do for the generation they bear.

Tomorrow, if you phone the office, please leave a message. I

won't be in. I have an appointment with a boy and a creek.
Maybe I'll see you there.

---

*Man's steps are ordained by the LORD, How then can man
understand his way?* Proverbs 20:24; NASU

It's official. My kids are ruined.

Some time ago I read a news article about parents doing anything to make their kids' dreams come true. It confirms this truth: I
am a dream killer.

Slain dream number one: no big Spring Breaks for my kids to
"discover life" south of Michigan. Emily, who is too snide for her
age and obviously takes after her mother's side, summarized her
last break for friends returning from Florida, Aruba, and other
places that dream-caressed teens flock to. Slipping into her best
bumpkin accent, she exclaimed, "Ah just staid ho-um an' scu-
reened up thuh cahm-post pi-uhl fo' muh paw." I failed to find
humor in her soliloquy, as the compost pile was indeed a mess and
needed some tendin'—er—serious attention that may have included screening out the big chunks. A perfectly wholesome springtime ritual that any teen and her dad would bond over. We sure
did.

Slain dream number two: Megan once announced her plans to
be a ballerina and a doctor. Rather than packing my bags, cashing
out and living out of the back of the Dakota so we could shuttle
between exclusive medical schools and the nearest orchestra hall,
I told her to get her homework done and quit draining the water
heater nightly or we'd all need a doctor for our hypothermia. And
besides, we as Christians were not supposed to enjoy dancing or
anything that involved leotards or especially men in tights.

Slain dream number three: Isaac figures he is going to have to
fend for himself soon, as double digit birthdays are upon him. He
announces that his career path will be that of serving as a police-
man, a fireman and a pastor. I figure he threw in the last one just
to mess with my head. Surprisingly, the three he's selected are

quite similar in scope and function, so I congratulate him with a pep talk on his upcoming college education costs and the importance of grade points, scholarships and completing household chores with a generally good attitude. He grins, grabs a snack and goes back to what sounds like some type of casual demolition project in his room, seemingly non-plussed by his impending pedagogic hurdles.

> **But still, as the dream killer, I think I'm on to something . . .**

And so it goes through the ranks of these ruined kids—all eight of 'em except Samuel who at his current age is unconcerned with anything but helping us realize he needs to have his way and why are we so clueless?

But still, as the dream killer, I think I'm on to something. Being a family requires sacrifice, but as much as I love my family, it's not my children that I worship. The main issue for us all is who is ulti-mately in charge. Indulgence and the feeding of a spirit of entitle-ment have hell to pay in the end. For parents whose kids call the dance, it must be a crushing day when the monster they have fed turns to devour them. So much for the mantra, "anything for junior's happiness..."

"And now a word to you fathers. Don't make your children angry by the way you treat them. Rather, bring them up with the disci-pline and instruction approved by the Lord."(Eph. 6:4, NLT) My kids' success by God's standards is my parental goal. Yes, some fleeting happiness might be found in chasing dreams. But the call is to guide them toward real joy, only found by living out God's pur-poses for their lives.

And you never know. For some, maybe God has chosen ballet.

Again and again they said, "Everything he does is wonderful. He even heals those who are deaf and mute." Mark 7:37, NLT

Miracles are a touchy subject, even in the faith that claims resur-rection and amid my vocation that often seeks claim to them. The world is lousy with hucksters tossing away crutches for tossed dollars. The quest for a shazaam! moment of instantaneous healing, from AIDS to fallen arches, has led many to discover sickening truth: those who claim to know God and direct Him in the miraculous often operate under a cloak of greed.

The plain-yet-flawed logic for those in need of a miracle (and honestly, who does not need one?) is simple enough. Good God + bad situation = response that meets my personal criteria. Speediness in God's supply is also a decisive factor. Should the order not be filled by heaven now, God will be bypassed in the explanation should things turn out suitably at a later date. In effect, God is hostage to His creatures' demands and stopwatches, or else...

It's my conviction that miracles do occur. Yet God is not my cosmic Santa Claus, jumping to fulfill my "git" list as if He hasn't a clue to what is needful in my life until I spell it out for Him. And God is not ruled by the clock. Neither quickness nor lengthiness are true gauges for the miraculous. I've observed that those who will not see Him in the gradual unfolding of the miraculous will likewise look past Him when the unusual falls suddenly.

What then have I come to know? Perhaps a story will suffice.

He came into the world while I was laboring for his Creator in South America. I might as well have been on the moon, so helpless was I as his mother labored. Over a static-filled connection in a village where the telephone was a new marvel in 2002, I got the news from Michigan. Not my expectation, and certainly not my timetable. He, my eighth surviving child, had arrived. The Sunday night after I first held him, I struggled to breathe life into him while the professionals raced. Then he was ushered off in flight, clinging to life as my wife and I followed dumbly and earth-bound, the helicopter lights our guiding star, fading in the east like our hope.

For days we lived in the fragile cocoon of the children's hospital, answering questions and nodding affirmatively, trying to appear composed as the tests, reports, and medical practitioners kept coming.

In a place and time so focused upon health, life, and death, I remember reflecting over some of the short, meaningful lives I'd known. I also remembered several in the category of having lived long, miserable lives. God began prompting me to pray in ways I never had. Much more than simply desiring for Samuel's life, Paula and I asked that if God were to allow Samuel to live, that his living would be for God's purposes, and simply not for an accumulation of years. People asked us how we felt. We could answer that we were concerned, but not anxious. It was one of those times in a God-worshipper's life where there is a tangible feeling of being spiritually, emotionally and physically lifted and carried by Him.

Incredibly, Samuel survived. His underlying medical conditions would be diagnosed, yet the developmental hurdles he will face are still being discovered. There have been additional hospitalizations due to the chronic nature of his illness, but he presses on even as his fourth birthday looms.

At home, I have kept a 3x5 card in my desk for nearly three years. It contains the words of Mark 7:31-37, the story of Jesus miraculously healing the mute. I have used it as a basis for prayer concerning Samuel since the day I wrote it out. You see, one hurdle Samuel faces is speech. There was no cooing as an infant, no experimenting with sounds, no imitation, nothing. When he finally did begin to vocalize, it was with agonized labors and seeming months between recognizable sounds. Single words may or may not sound like what they're intended to be. "Mama" is heard more frequently. "Dada" has never been heard, and I've had my doubts that it will ever come. How ironic: a preacher with a kid that can't talk.

Just last month I enjoyed a rare Saturday morning off. The quiet beaver life is never better than Saturday morning, because the otters could seemingly stay passed out until noon. I was at my desk, reading, praying, writing…a day without a day planner, though there was an appointment to be kept that I had desired for nearly three years.

Samuel was stirring, as he has his father's constitution and equally enjoys his breakfast with gusto. As I worked at my desk, just a few feet from his room, I heard him start to quietly call, "Mama, Mama" as he is now apt to do upon rising. I stayed at my desk, confident that the infant monitor in our bedroom would be piping his call to my wife, and equally confident that she would still be passed out in otter repose, unresponsive to field artillery let alone the tiny speaker poised at her head. Still, I stayed at my desk and my studies, even when Samuel grew quiet. Then it came. Calmly. Distinctly.

"Dada!"

The only time I'd ever jumped quicker was the time I'd shut off the wrong circuit and began to detach the wiring on our garbage disposal. That was painful—this was joy. It was the call I'd longed to hear, now repeated again and again as I ran to his room, embracing a son now calling for his father.

My heart grows in a deeper understanding of how much our heavenly Father desires for His children to call out His Name. *Seek the Lord while you can find Him. Call on Him now while He is near.* (Isa. 55:6, NLT)

My devotion to God has not hinged upon the gift of this word Samuel has spoken; yet I find in it my quiet confidence that God always grants those things that support His will for my life, and that occasionally my requests do align with God's ways. *Because he bends down and listens, I will pray as long as I have breath!* (Ps. 116:2, NLT)

My son has called out my name. I now pray that he too will one day delight to call on his Heavenly Father. Maybe his speech won't be particularly smooth, but God even used Moses once he learned to deal with his impediment. I am trusting that one day we will listen to Samuel's story as he tells it in his words.

As for me, I still believe in miracles. Why, one called my name just the other morning.

...and all that is in the world...

The godly are concerned for the welfare of their animals, but even the kindness of the wicked is cruel.   Proverbs 12:10, NLT

Remember, it is sin to know what you ought to do and then not do it.   James 4:17, NLT

I watched nightly as the very life of Barbaro hung in the balance. Articles concerning the once-mighty racehorse dominated the sports headlines from the breaking of his leg during the start of the Preakness, to his demise some time later. The outpouring from horse lovers, both nationally and worldwide, rained down upon the Pennsylvania campus where he clung to life for months. I remember the news updates: "His attitude is good," they told us. "He is mentally tough and holding up well under the stress of his ordeal." His indomitable spirit may have tried to pull him through, and the cards, banners, fruit baskets, flowers and other expressions of love and support that concerned humanity heaped upon him didn't hurt either. But, like others before him, he had to be "put down." The comfort in Barbaro's passing came from knowing that the medical catalogue had been exhausted on his behalf. Even superhuman effort could not guarantee that the horse would live. I can hardly wait for the Hallmark movie—Barbaro! Gentle Giant: Portrait of a Warrior.

Yes, I tired of "news" over an ailing horse. It's another of those odd contradictions of life that I see here from the land of plenty-for-some. I recount so many people who are suffering, and yet it's horses that grab headlines and hearts. Those struggling with access to quality medical care will benefit little from equestrian celebrity. Humans dying for lack of timely care are strangely eclipsed by animals, here in this world of reversed values.

Still, I want to insulate myself from mounds of hate mail, so I will immediately state a simple fact: I enjoy animals, in their place. The uses of animals within the world for labor, transportation, food, and a host of other arenas are as old as the biblical word that declares their usefulness for us. Please, don't forward lectures about "advances in medicine" and "the importance of research for the care of horses and it's applications to the human arena." I'm not a total lout. I know these arguments and frankly, I agree. The imbalance I see comes from an elevation of animals to the "person" stage where many "Lassies" and "Garfields" receive care well beyond what masses of the world's human population could ever hope to enjoy. I know. It's the land of privilege. It's my dollar to do with as I please. My life and my pets are my business. Horse races, dog shows and chicken fights are all on the table for consumers to enjoy. OK, maybe the chicken one is in the back room somewhere, but you get my drift. It's not a new situation, granted. As far back as I might search, animals have been domesticated not only for labor, but as a show of wealth and status. Sporting events involving animals also enjoy a rich history.

I'm not a pet hater. Remember, I enjoy animals in their place. For loyal companionship, there are dogs. To keep me from thinking too highly of myself, God sends me cats. Gerbils I'm not too sure about, but I believe many cultures enjoy them, especially medium-well. My own pets enjoy healthcare that rivals mine, and maybe even exceeds it, because they are protected from fleas and ticks unlike yours truly.

Perhaps it's just the logic of this world and its luxury of imbalance that prompts me to say, "Enough about horse care!"

All of the headlines concerning Barbaro cause me to think of other issues where the imbalances scream out. Why would someone have pets and then horribly mistreat them? Further then, how can the abuse of children even enter into the mind as remotely permissible? These depths are beyond understanding from any person with half a heart.

It's the same for me as that mystifying logic that allows a protester to march in a demonstration to champion abortion rights, and then hurry across town to participate in another rally, this time to demand protection for earth's helpless baby seals.

It's the same baffling inconsistency that drives a bible quoting man or woman to picket an abortion clinic, perhaps verbally challenging young women entering there, yet before their pregnancy, not give a tinker's damn to the same young women even as they live next door or brush past one another in the community day after day for years.

It's the discordant mindset that opposes health benefits for some members of society, but can walk openly to church and sing "Make Me a Blessing" at full voice.

The book I want to live by tells me that animals deserve humane treatment, but they are not human. My opening verses to this short plea reveals God's heart for animals. The book also tells me that God values people more than any other created thing. His heart for humanity is in much fuller commentary. In fact, it's pretty much cover-to-cover in the Book. In one often quoted verse, the "world" of John 3:16 is the human population, not the trees and flowers and horses and puppies and kitties. Man is made in the image of God, it is man who has the eternal spirit, and it is man for whom Jesus, the God-man, laid down his life so that we could be restored in our relationship to God and one another.

And what a restoration we need.

In a race, a loss of physical balance can lead to a break, as Barbaro has experienced.

In the race of life, a loss of spiritual balance can also lead to a break. A break from reality concerning our true priorities, purposes and mission. Given the headlines, I conclude that we are at present, running this race badly.

Maybe Barbaro's survivors could send over a fruit basket to help assuage our loss.

"...*everyone who hears these words of mine and acts on them, may be compared to a wise man who built his house on the rock. And the rain fell, and the floods came, and the winds blew and slammed against that house; and yet it did not fall, for it had been founded on the rock. Everyone who hears these words of mine and does not act on them, will be like a foolish man who built his house on the sand. The rain fell, and the floods came, and the winds blew and slammed against that house; and it fell—and great was its fall.*"

Matthew 7:24-27; NASU

Like others before it, I read the updates and watched various news clips detailing the Cyclone—Nargis was this one's name—and its toll of devastation across Myanmar. And in keeping with the figures that fall from most of these steadily grim repetitions of hurricanes, tsunamis, earthquakes and other cataclysms, these newest casualty numbers are too staggering for me to really comprehend. Multiplied tens of thousands stuns my mind and my soul. For the average person in many of these regions, there is little that can be done to brace for a killer storm. Living conditions are often meager, some regions are susceptible to vicious cycles of storms, and even if there is the "help" of advance warning, there are logistical limits to how and how far a large scattered population could immediately travel to avoid loss of life. Often, by the time the storm hits, there is still nowhere one can go; nothing one can do.

Our nation's own fumbling in Katrina's wake tells me that many of these same factors exist even here in my "developed" world. Those that seem fully prepared on paper can be found wanting and hapless in second-by-second reality when the wind picks up or the earth sways.

One key to storm survival is having preparations in place. Earthquake-resilient structures can be engineered. Hurricane-tough building codes are proven to pay life-saving dividends. Hole-in-the-ground storm cellars still afford a great refuge when tornadoes spin. Even for cyclones, the existence of elevated and sturdy homes could offer some hope.

In a perfect world, all would survive the storm. Finances, priorities and planning would be challenges to overcome, not obstacles to end the conversation.

But even with the key of preparation, there still remains in every storm the element of the unknown. Some storms defy the models, break the records, and go beyond the foreseeable. In this life, you live with the tension: all you've planned for may never be enough when the actual storm hits.

In the scripture passage above, Jesus seems to major on this theme of preparation. For a spiritual application, he delivers an illustration straight out of our world. His language is very plain; uncloaked. And Jesus exudes a confidence. Being prepared spiritually by heeding his counsel will secure anyone, even when life's storms bring in those unknown elements.

How can that be?

Jesus will win no award from today's wave of "communicators" for the concluding remarks to his sermon recorded in this gospel. There is no feel-good, "You're OK" cheerleading, ending with a high-five run through the crowd.

Instead, he gives warnings.

It seems that Jesus runs contrary to a lot that we value about public speaking, feeding our motivational machines, scratching our significance itch, and appeal through the power of positive thinking. He shows us our condition, and plainly tells us we can do nothing to fix it. He tells (and ultimately demonstrates) how he alone will restore us. Then he calls us to change direction, or perish. To put our spiritual house on his footings, or watch all we independently build implode in the end-storm that brings us to judgment. His call is exclusionary. Security is found only with him. Disciples will abandon all competing "reasonable" or "moderate" spiritual approaches. It is a warning to build on him, or nothing.

I am led to believe that Jesus would probably have trouble packing the arenas today. Word would travel quickly that he hadn't changed his approach. His hearers would still be leaving more humbled, exposed, challenged and dependent on him, rather than inspired and affirmed in their present distractions. For those rejecting his word, their thirst for comfort and confirmation will lead them to other messages from other messengers; continual competition among popular "teachers," to both fill and fleece that clamoring crowd.

For the disciple who takes Jesus at his word, living life on the foundation of Christ will include present day storms. Derision, mocking and worse still blow through these days. False professors trash the landscape of Christendom. "Casual" believers obscure Jesus with the detritus of the world. Majority votes erode what Jesus actually said, or rip away what His meaning was if the jury determines He may have said at least something like it.

Little wonder the world cannot embrace Him, for He has been portrayed as nothing more than wispy "love," devoid of demands and incapable of any weighty judgment of man. There's little appeal to surrender all to an effeminate idealist that spoke in platitudes and left us with little more direction than "be good children and find your way home—any road you like will do."

Mention such of Jesus' teachings of commands, obedience, sin, or final accounting, and the world sneers, eye-rolling in their evaluation of you as quaint or queer: Jesus' words? They are "suggestions" for us to apply as we feel led. There are "exceptions" because god is my buddy, and we have an understanding. Practical necessity has led to our "new thinking," for no one in their right mind would ever take what he says as plain, literal truth. It is odd that you have not heard—god has learned to "lighten up" or risk losing even our token nods here in Vanity Fair.

We have built our houses. We have weathered much on our own platforms. We expect those storms ahead will not blow much worse. And we have time, lots of time. Play on the beach, don't monitor the sky.

I still take heartfelt instruction in this final sermon's word from Jesus. It is not a smug satisfaction that one day "they'll get theirs." The Lord has plenty of warning for those reveling in their own "righteousness" while condemnatory of everyone else. Splinters and planks have both had turns at residency in my eye. I am reminded that it's by grace that we don't all get what we deserve; that which we have truly earned.

The instruction I receive, from the position of one safe from the final storm, is to be steadfast now as a weatherman, a builder, a first responder, and a disciple. The Jesus who offered his storm plan still extends the offer today. His body the church is here to present his word, and eliminate obstacles to its reception. We are to both encourage and warn the world that, as storms go, we haven't seen anything yet.

And there remains one Way, offering both a future, and a hope.

Give your complete attention to these matters. Throw yourself into your tasks so that everyone will see your progress. Keep a

As I Was Saying . . .

close watch on how you live and on your teaching. Stay true to what is right for the sake of your own salvation and the salvation of those who hear you.   1 Timothy 4:15-16; NLT

Well, the tree has been planted. It's a sturdy maple with a complete root ball and good structure. With it receiving a long winter's nap, and with a few extra trips with my water bucket next year, it should be off to a good start in its new and permanent home. I can envision the shade that it will produce over our back yard in just a few summers. I would be enjoying the shade a year or more sooner, but the first maple I planted had its life cut short. Literally.

OK, it's a guy thing. I fall into a trance-like state whenever I run the line trimmer, and this was certainly the case last month when I was engrossed in cleaning off our lot line behind the house. In one deft move (although my wife substitutes another quite contradictory and unflattering word for deft) the business end of my testosterone-pumping trimmer encountered the young maple, taking bark, branches and leaves off faster than I could say, "uh, what was that?" I stood there dumbly, taking a full breath and finally realizing what I had done. One lousy distracted act, and there was no undoing, no going back. The tree was dead.

It occurs to me that much of my life is spent trying to sort out and avoid "the distractions."

When the lead off story on the evening news concerns a boy and his newly discovered two-headed frog, I know there's nothing but a half hour of distraction ahead. Click.

Even my American League team got their eyes on the seats and suddenly forgot to pay attention to the game they were in, resulting in sandlot errors and forfeited dreams. It was tough to watch distraction strip away what should have been a glorious finale. Click.

So, the economy of my state is basically in the toilet, my schools are struggling, and families in these communities I call home are on the ropes. I'm asked to go to the poll and finally weigh in on the extremely important ballot proposal (I know it's been plaguing my mind) that will set my great state back on its feet, and perhaps secure liberty for the entire universe at last. I can't wait until

Tuesday so the Mourning Dove hunting debate can finally be settled. Distraction? It certainly qualifies on my list of things that are an annoying diversion in my world.

As an aside, if I wanted to eat a dove, even a dead eye shot such as myself needn't tamp a charge and ball down my thunder stick. The Mourning Doves I encounter could be walked over to, picked up and throttled bare handed. Who knows? Maybe next year, with everything finally right in Michigan, we'll finally get to vote on my proposal, asking to legalize cluster-bombing missions on the Tufted Titmouse, evil menace of the Midwest States. Or perhaps, if things head any further into the cellar, next year we may all be out in the woods scrambling to eat Mourning Doves or anything else we can fill full of shot.

I was explaining my rage/frustration/incredulity over these and other distractions to a friend over coffee, but gave up when he gestured at me to hold my thought. He appeared to be experiencing an attack of the chiggers, but in actuality was simply trying to extract his cell phone from his pants pocket. The ringer tone, set at a painful but survivable 110 dB, was my giveaway clue. So there I was, put on hold while he took his call.

You know, there's just too much distraction in the air.

Sometimes it's easy to think that good Christian folk don't suffer from such worldly distraction. The truth is, it's probably even more pronounced in my species. One of the myths of coming to faith is that suddenly the problems are over, the air is cleaner, and struggles over priorities, profitless pursuits and yes, distractions will cease.

Last Fall, I sat on the deck and looked over the faded flower garden. Had I even taken the time to enjoy it in full bloom? Now it had the frost kill, subdued hues that would eventually matt down under winter's snow. What had been the steady stream of priorities that I had traded for lingering here for just a few more hours?

How many times I've talked to folks filled with an endless stream of regrets over children that are grown and gone too soon. People vexed by realizing that love was lost because of their neglect. Lives irretrievably scarred because life was frittered away. People leading trivial pursuit existences, too distracted even to notice the cost. Largely, these are people of faith, people who are supposed to "get it" when it comes to heeding the word of God and making the changes. I try to learn from the positive and the negative examples, always under the weight that somewhere, someone is watching to see how it turns out for me. It is no light thing to carry the name "Christian" attached to you. The world that does not know Him has every right to judge my life, for I have allied myself with His Name, and even the unbelieving world knows that this Jesus calls for life that is radically different to how it normally is on the streets. And I think for many, they secretly hope it's true…

We have a practice in the Masters household that concerns instruction for our kids. When we are talking, it's always "eyes up" for the people engaged in the conversation. Eye contact means, "I'm shutting out distractions and focusing on you and your words." It's also common courtesy. We've done extensive remedial training with the kid's friends, many whom aren't used to even speaking to adults except in monosyllabic grunts. Lately, I find myself envisioning my conversing with my Lord face to face. Not that I need to create a mind's eye notion of his appearance, but simply to help me continually realize that I am before him at all times and in every situation. He is not "looking away," distracted, or off in a neighboring state while I'm left to go it on my own for a spell. It has been refreshing to me to "maintain eye contact" with my heavenly father, as an obedient child should. He wants me to keep my eyes fixed on Him. I truly believe in some way this helps me to filter out distractions to my most important relationship.

I realize how easily I get distracted. And I see more and more the tremendous challenge to stay on task not only for my soul's sake, but also for that ever-present cloud of witnesses that wants to know if life in Christ really adds up in the end. Paying attention not only saves my life, but also could save others.

May all who name Him dig down deep, settle in, take root, and labor to avoid distractions to the real issues of life. May we not be distracted from the care and nurture of that which has been planted in us. And like the maple I planted today, may future generations benefit from what we have taken pains to leave behind.

. . . and all that is in the world . . . .

And, oh yeah, Mr. Tufted Titmouse: your days of insensate wickedness are numbered…

"… that they would seek God, if perhaps they might grope for Him and find Him, though He is not far from each one of us; for in Him we live and move and exist…"   Acts 17:27-28a; NASU

Recently, we had met for a walk. It was long overdue, this tradition of portable conversation that we enjoy far too infrequently. There was much catching up on all that had transpired in our worlds. Old friendships are often like that, and the topics that day were as you might expect, "all over the board." In one arena, which I would categorize as "the future," we shared ideas about what areas in the country would be likely spots to settle in to enjoy our last years. Not envisioning much of a change in my world, I spoke of perhaps a slight move, being fairly well rooted in southern Michigan unless the Lord clearly directed otherwise. My friend's situation will be more fluid, so the pros and cons of various regions were tossed back and forth between us.

I discovered that there was one region that would never pass muster for his relocation. This was the Pacific Northwest. Set out against the great positives of sheer beauty, variety, and quality of life was one hurdle that could not be overcome. It is an area ripe for the "big one" in seismic activity, and he wanted no part of "going down," either historically or literally or both.

The next morning—and I do indeed find this somewhat remarkable and noteworthy, for how rare it is for me to ever speak about earthquakes save when one is current news—I had just returned to my chair from putting our resident cat outside. It was early; I had not slept well and was enjoying a profitable time of reading there in the quiet. The furnace had just started again in its cycle, when quite subtly, I noticed that a very distinct east-west rocking of the house had begun. I have experienced minor temblors before in Michigan, and much more pronounced shaking on a couple of Central American journeys, so I had no doubt as to what was happening. It was slight. So slight in fact that all the household save me slept on, peacefully ignorant of what was in those moments occurring down deep, miles below their pillowed heads.

Megan came downstairs an hour later, wondering if I had been listening to the news. I told her no, but gave her the quake's start time and duration to test against her radio-facts. She was astonished. She had slept through an earthquake. How could it be? I assured her there would be many who had not noticed, given its occurrence at an early hour and the faintness of it in our region. Others closer to the origin would tell far different stories; you can't help but notice as you get nearer to the source.

In the book of Acts, Paul's dialogue with the Athenians touches upon this proximity factor, but in the spiritual realm. Their lofty ignorance, bred through minds focused on the rumble and sway of their own vain imaginings, blinded and deafened them against any discerning of His presence. Though evidence of God's authorship was displayed all about them, they were too far removed from Him to draw the sensible conclusion the facts presented: The unity of the creation points to a single creator. A single creator, Paul instructed them, who still, even in their age, was not silent.

In my times, what we call this more "advanced" age, it is notable that the God who is present and not silent still receives largely an identical reception. Man has in many ways refined further the Athenian mindset, swelling considerably the pantheon of his gods along the way. It seems man will embrace just about anything, so long as it doesn't involve the revealed Creator with whom he must one day give account.

Yet, as Paul explains, far from God's noisy rumblings in creation and sustainment of the world, He is often much like the distant earthquake in making His presence known to His created mankind. His subtlety is at times astonishing.

And, as Paul states, God is "not far" from us. He has formed us with the capacity to know Him, if we will but come to Him through the Way He has established.

The toughest distance His message has to travel is the span from the human head to the human heart. Sometimes God goes that distance through amazing, thunderous events, drawing one to

Himself in ways no one could ignore or misinterpret. At other times, His is a subtle call, a quiet shifting, a sensing of Greatness so delicate that one must focus in the stillness to discern its presence; its origin.

Have you heard? Have you seen? God still moves.

"Has anyone ever heard of anything as strange as this? Has any nation ever traded its gods for new ones, even though they are not gods at all? Yet my people have exchanged their glorious God for worthless idols! The heavens are shocked at such a thing and shrink back in horror and dismay," says the Lord. "For my people have done two evil things: They have abandoned me—the fountain of living water. And they have dug for themselves cracked cisterns that can hold no water at all!"

Jer. 2:10b-13; NLT

Exchanges and leaky things: two topics that I am familiar with in my world.

The verses above tell of the Lord's frustration with His people as they willingly replaced Him with the gods of their world. He compared it to digging away their lives on pits that would be profitless. His Word still speaks the same warning to me today.

I am well aware that in my world, the season for exchanging politicians is fast approaching. With the primary season having just passed, I am resting from the first wave of political advertising and getting ready for the second, this one to end mercifully with the November elections. I think I'll keep my barn boots ready, for if the primaries are any indication, the election ads are going to muck up the place quite a bit.

Soon I'll have the opportunity to vote for the candidates, and as the results are tabulated, wonder what good will come from the chosen field. I know many take the approach that these men and women are gods indeed; they alone can turn around the course of the state, the nation or the local dog pound, depending on their particular sphere. I am reminded at this juncture that Hope, at age nine, is eager to answer the phone, though the finer points of message taking and relaying such information are still a little ways off. I was informed that I had a call last week, rather casually by this youngest daughter of her mother. When I inquired as to whom had called, she matter-of-factly stated, "It was the president. I told him you weren't here, and then I hung up."

Well, maybe this time he'll get the point. I don't know how many times I've told the commander in chief not to call me at home.

As I stated, my world is a world full of exchanges. Besides politicians, there are gas cylinders, which not surprisingly come to mind directly after politicians. Cars and stocks are exchanged, books are exchanged, and life-mates are exchanged. Our nation has an obsession for "idols" that likewise are exchanged for new ones, once the voting is done and the ad campaigns and debut albums are released. My vote is for a new reality show—"Castaway Island: American Idol Has-Been Edition." Washed up "idols," having been exchanged for new ones, compete to stay alive in grueling tropical conditions while reinventing themselves for the ultimate comeback. Snide members of the general public, fed up with idolism, get to take potshots at them from a satellite-based laser cannon. Should be riveting viewing, in my estimation.

Leaks, to which the scripture above also refers, are commonplace for me as well. I have experienced firsthand the result of slow undetected leaks around the house. One drop at a time, the resultant damage required repairs all the way down to new floor joists and extensive mold removal in the walls. Oh, for the days of Saturday night bucket baths on the back porch. The sound you may be hearing is the mass rolling of eyes by the other inhabitants of my castle who are playful, water-loving otters. Just make sure the plumbing is operational and the bills are paid, and everybody's very happy in otter-world. I have another idea for a reality based show, but I've shared it in private with these people and their mother, and I guess it would never fly given their looks of utter distain, cries of "disgusting", and threats of calling in the officials if "Rough-it Island: North American Family Edition" ever made it even to pilot.

I've encountered leaks while on the road as well. My keen need for state-of-the-art transportation blended with real life economics has led me to drive anything midpoint between the scrap yard and Slick's Car Emporium. My Plymouth Horizon, a sturdy mid-eighties model, was no match for the pheasant who decided to end it all. There, northbound on the Waldron Road, I saw him from a hundred yards out. Rather than continuing across the road, he instead turned toward my snappy little car, lowering his altitude while picking up speed. Upon impact, an immediate fine mist began to coat my windshield... antifreeze. I pulled over and pried the bird out, his beak having made quite an entry into the radiator core, and limped my way home with the dead bird in tow. The family had pheasant for dinner, which I named "under hood" as opposed to "under glass." After repairs were totaled up, the cost of our entrée came out to roughly $87.50 a pound.

Of major, costly leaks, I know of another good anecdote. My father caught a leak at the property he managed in the south. The swimming pool had a defective drain which had gone undetected for who-knows how long before his tenure there began. The resultant repair saved thousands in water and chemical bills that were literally leaking away in plain view.

Exchanges and leaks. In my life, it's important to guard against "leaks" spiritually, for it can result in my exchanging the fullness of Christ for the eventual emptiness of this world's gods:
Jesus shouted to the crowds, "Anyone who is thirsty may come to me! Anyone who believes in me may come and drink! For the Scriptures declare, 'Rivers of living water will flow from his heart.'" (Jn. 7:37b-38; NLT)

Any time I exchange trust in my Lord for the gods of this world, I deplete and dehydrate my spirit by rejecting His Spirit living within me. Any moment I look to the idols of this life for my worship, focus, security or deliverance, I reject the living water for a trip to a waterless pit that will never produce. The caution in my life is to quit digging at the broken cisterns, and stay with the overflowing One who has provided life for me.

As to the woman at the well, Jesus still makes the offer today: *"If you only knew the gift God has for you and who you are speaking to, you would ask me, and I would give you living water."* (Jn. 4:10; NLT)

As I Was Saying . . .

Some things by God's design are exchangeable in this life. Others are best left as He intends. Leaks in this life are inevitable, but dying of thirst when water is freely offered is a senseless act. May God keep me from profitless exchanges, and self-inflicted leaks. And may November, our month for the exchange of the gods, come and go quickly.

Well then, if you teach others, why don't you teach yourself? No wonder the Scriptures say, "The world blasphemes the name of God because of you." Romans 2:21a, 24; NLT

More common than a congressional resignation or a celebrity's check-in to rehab, I am faced with reading of yet another prominent evangelical's fall from grace. This one's resignation from national leadership, dismissal as lead pastor of his mega church, and demise as all around champion of family values has left me wondering once again what has gone wrong with the church and especially the pastorate here in this nation under God. It occurs to me that more and more frequently, the "success" of a church leader by the world's standards: numbers, money, position, spotlight—is more a harbinger of a sensational plunge into ruin, than an assurance and sign that God is building His kingdom through a charismatic disciple.

I do not make a hobby out of recklessly shooting the wounded. There are certainly Christ followers who find themselves dealing with consequences of sin that are life shattering and unalterable. My heart goes out to them and the command of Scripture is clear: *"if another Christian is overcome by some sin, you who are godly should gently and humbly help that person back onto the right path. And be careful not to fall into the same temptation yourself."* (Galatians 6:1; NLT)

Although I was not acquainted with this man nor his ministry, the first difficulty I have with him and similar fallen "stars" of the church is not in the sordidness of their disclosed sins. Sin is sin; it's all a variation of the same theme. The primary issue for me is in the

reckless violation of their sacred position and trust. The compo-
nents of that violation are by now an all-too-familiar litany shared
by these who publicly tumble from their pulpit: living an amazingly
hypocritical life, walking secretly and irresponsibly, shunning
accountability, bashing the "sinners" of the world, and continuing
boldly on in their "ministries" until finally exposed and cornered in
such an irrefutable way that the awful truth is revealed.

The real sin issues were thriving in the heart long before they
manifested themselves through the outer man. It is troubling that
because of pride, they are unable to abandon the ministry and do
something—anything else—for a vocation while reveling in their
"secret" sins. The fallout sure would be a lot less troubling if they
weren't in their spotlight ministries when the meltdown occurred.
How do you function day after day with such duplicity in the heart?
I can't grasp it.

The second difficulty I struggle with is in the exit speeches or letters the "stars" bestow upon their congregations and the listening
world. The popular pattern is to insinuate that their particular beset-
ting sin is far beyond what even the presence of the Lord in their
life is able to overcome. In effect, the gospel they have preached,
taught and exhorted, and by which millions throughout the ages
have come to know as the power of God to totally, radically, and
victoriously transform lives, is strangely negated in its ability to
change one life—the life of its chief proponent amid a congregation.

Their parting charge? "Flock, you stay under the Word and continue to let God transform your lives. I am a special case where
even God could not deliver me. Lucky you; poor me. I am forced
to resign, disappointed that the power of God was ineffectual to
work in me. But for you, be faithful, keep giving, do what is right. I
know you'll forgive me, because the word says you need to. Did I
mention keep giving? Now I must go away, and try to heal from my
wounds."

Strange stuff, indeed. If I were on the outside looking in on the
world of faith, I'd have a hard time subscribing to the potency and
effectiveness of the gospel. Who honestly would commit to faith in
the random effectiveness of Christ? Yet through the swan song

comments given, that is exactly what is being offered up as the "reason" pastors fail so spectacularly and regularly.

I suppose on this overcast rainy day, I've reached a personal saturation point; a deeper cynicism (even for me!) where "I'm sorry" has been thrown out so much in my days that it really has lost its potency in convincing me sorrow is present. I wonder if the real "sorry" is just over the peripheral issue of being caught and having the ride end.

Dear brothers and sisters, not many of you should become teachers in the church, for we who teach will be judged by God with greater strictness (James 3:1; NLT).

Comparatively speaking, God's judgment must be a dreadful thing. The verdict by the world is God-awful in its mockery, condemnation and told-you-so jubilance. And once again, the world has been given ample fodder for their derision. One online news source charted a whopping 973 pages of public comment surrounding the man's demise by the first evening the story broke. I read three pages and pretty much got the public's drift. I don't get angered or bemoan their unbelief. The failed pulpit has gone overboard to confirm that the message is not truly to be taken personally or seriously. The script may be eloquently read, but it is dismissed as fiction due to the poor and halting performance delivered by the lead player.

I understand more fully with each publicized scandal why good pastors with godly lives and sincere ministry intentions choose to step out of ministry and content themselves with any quiet work where they can simply punch in, punch out, and go home. The shadow cast by the failures can eclipse the joy and resolve of even the most dedicated of God's servants. While smaller men destruct in smaller ponds with tinier ripples, the big implosions of the evangelical world cause tsunamis that sweep with chilling devastation across the land and around the globe. It is comparable to Dante's vision of the destroyers whose eternal task is to build up and tear down simultaneously. We in the church expect attacks and opposition to come; it is just beyond reason to grasp why the most deadly assaults seem to come most frequently from within. To the world we hope to reach, it makes the faithful minister look like a simpleton at best or corrupt-but-not-yet-caught at worst.

And those who know my heart know how much we tire of the Name of Christ being derided again due to our own men self destructing.

If you think you are standing strong, be careful, for you, too, may fall into the same sin.   1 Corinthians 10:12; NLT.

To those churches who have the gift of a pastor with integrity: guard him in prayer, surround him with faithful men committed to mutual accountability, and follow their example.

May we all take to heart the words of Thomas á Kempis, my 15th century friend:

It is a hard thing to leave evil customs and it is harder to break our own will, but it is most hard forever to lie in pain and forever to lose the joys of heaven. If you do not overcome small and light things, how shall you then overcome the greater? Resist quickly at the beginning your evil inclinations and leave off wholly all your evil customs, lest, perhaps, by little and little they afterwards bring you greater difficulty. Oh, if you would consider how great inward peace you would have yourself, and how great gladness you would cause in others by behaving yourself well, I truly believe you would be much more diligent to profit in virtue than you have been before this (The Imitation of Christ, Doubleday & Co., 1955, p. 43).

And for the pastor who still has his integrity in the Lord: may you never crave a taste of the success that the "stars" of the world have reveled in. The cost of that banquet is tallied not in dollars, but in the expense of souls; the first being your own.

As I Was Saying . . .

...let the peace that comes from Christ rule in your hearts. For as members of one body you are called to live in peace. And always be thankful.
                                                              Colossians 3:15, NLT

I was reminded of my status as a middle-aged chunky guy again this morning. Getting out of bed is no longer a sprightly act, it having now evolved to an orderly series of slow and deliberate moves. Let it ring if you call early. The otters are sleeping, but I'm coming. My back would be in better shape if it weren't for all of these thankless jobs.

Last evening after dinner, I labored on sanding drywall. It's a good reminder to me of how some of the necessary jobs in life go unnoticed and often without thanks. I had no audience or applause or sideline encouragement of any type for sanding, let alone the hanging of the blasted stuff last month. The process of applying "mud" and then sanding is a tedious job that demands care and precision, but there were no accolades from the living room. The only time I really get even a passing level of acknowledgment is when I show up with a pizza box. Or use a sentence with the word "mall" in it.

I've invested even more evenings out lately, attending various commencement ceremonies around our area. They have been for the most part very crowded, very warm, and appropriate except for length, which upon a bleacher for me is anything under nine minutes. At that point, I tune out the actual event and lose myself in deep thought over what type of expensive surgery I will be requiring to restore feeling to my southern regions.

Notably, the content of the speeches made during the graduation exercises changes very little from year to year. There are numerous "inside" jokes and obscure references to the class that makes me feel like I'm eavesdropping on someone's cell call. (That actually did occur, five times at the last ceremony, but hey, who's counting?) The one unifying theme that connects the speeches is the giving of thanks, usually broad enough to include all in attendance and special teachers that gave their all for the graduates. All appropriate, all expected.

I wonder if those with the "drywall" jobs ever heard a "thanks." You know, the janitors, cooks, aides, drivers, and the host of staff and volunteers that also labor, albeit in the shadow of the machine. Try running a zoo without a zookeeper. Things would pile up quickly.

I wonder how many times the police, fire, or civic officials actually get a positive comment in the course of their work. I wonder what would happen to the attitude of community and nation if thanks instead of jeers were the standard. I can well imagine what it would do to the morale across the various fields of work and service. Soldiers. The lady at the drive thru window. Your postal worker. The independent business owner. The bagger. The maintenance laborer.

It is striking to me that the Christian community should well be expected to set a high standard for thanks-giving. We of all people should be first to realize the tremendous blessing we hold in respect to this faith, our place in this world, and our responsibility. This is certainly expected "in house", but if it is strained, rare or artificial in its practice there, what trickle-down into the community can we expect? In order to give thanks, we might well rehearse some of the blessings that envelope us.

So today, I nurse aching muscles and recount many things. I had a meal today. Many in this world have not, and will not. I was able to assemble for worship this week because people have laid down their lives and continue to do so, that I may have freedom. I had no checkpoints to pass through on my drive to the office today, and no roadside IED's to contend with. I have little currency in my pocket, but I have some, and am more blessed than most occupying this planet. Should my back fail me, and history repeat, I have access to the finest medical care, period. Many have no options for even the simplest of medical needs. I have enjoyed a splendid education, access to information and a free press to keep abreast of events around the globe. Many will never read or write, meeting only closed doors to even the most basic education. They will live and die in isolation, ignorance and fear. In my mind, I could expand this list into chapters...

In all these things, God shows me that even sincere "thanks" is not enough. His call is for me to go beyond my voicing thanksgiving, and live it in service for the physical, emotional, and spiritual needs of others. This is not just selective laboring within my Christian community. There are those around this world that also have needs I am able, because of my blessings, to help meet. After all, as a Christian, the greatest need of my life has already been met in the person of Christ. It may be the same for you, as well.

I could grumble about drywall, and you're right, I have. But at least I have a wall to sand, and in this, I will choose to be thankful. How about you?

First, voice it. Then, live it.

I'll be the first to say it.

Thank you.

But many who are the greatest now will be least important then, and those who seem least important now will be the greatest then.
Mark 10:31; NLT

There's a proud legacy in our land of honoring those who have gone before. It is fitting to have our Memorial Days, Veteran's Days and Independence Days, even Thanksgivings and President's Days to remember those who have paved the way. From the majestic tranquility of Arlington to the out-of-the-way battlefield cemeteries that span the globe, we have places to go and remember, to honor, to pray, to respect those that gave us this day. We also use our parades, concerts, fireworks and solemn assemblies to help create our sacred spaces and traditions of remembrance.

Our Christian celebrations of Christmas and Easter are marked by the truly devout as a time of remembrance, much as we regularly observe the ordinance of communion and ponder afresh what God has done through His Christ. It is good that we pause to remember. We are a forgetful people, indeed.

We are not alone in our tribute to the generations that have been. While I have read in recent articles of a Civil War soldier reunited with his grave marker, I too have read of the city of Kokura, Japan.

It participates regularly in remembering Nagasaki, the city that providentially took the bomb sixty-one years ago instead of Kokura, due to weather issues.

In the midst of this, there is also much troubling news I read of cemeteries receiving vandalism. I would prefer to think that there is an especially appropriate level of hell for such individuals who commit these acts. Dishonoring the dead seems to me among the basest of crimes—destroying sacred space and opening wounds afresh for normal human beings who respect the resting places of their dead. These crimes of brutish minds are part of the natural spiral downward of self-centered life without regard to God, adding another entry in my notebook to refute upward evolution of the human species.

Honor is a fleeting thing in our world. Even the most recognizable names to us will slowly slip from memory and tongue in the generations to come. Lost records of kings, pharaohs and whole civilizations cause me to take stock of the wispy nature of honor.

Thankfully, as a believer in a God who has fashioned me and has eternity in mind, I do not have to spend my years here struggling to receive this passing honor of men. The issue at hand for every Christ-follower is to have His honor at the center of one's life and motives. The result of prayerful, wise living will be, *"the way you live will always honor and please the Lord, and your lives will produce every kind of good fruit. All the while, you will grow as you learn to know God better and better"* (Col. 1:10; NLT).

I was in the cemetery lately. Pastors get there more than others do. Some people, busy with the affairs of the living, only make one trip there, to stay. This day was not "business" however, but simply to walk and reflect. I've known so many that have gone before me. I was observing the names and dates when I came across an old friend. I knew the spot; I had been there before. The grave was well kept and a large granite stone was adorned with a newer wreath. In my mind, I flashed back to the memorial service. It had been well attended and full of testimonies and praise for this one, and rightly so. There had been many who knew, remembered, and honored. The honor evidently was still there as evidenced by this maintained spot.

I stepped back a bit, and my foot caught in a depression. As I turned to look, I saw that there indeed was another grave, with the marker just beyond my step. This was a very plain flat stone, nearly obscured by a matting of cut grass. It was obvious that no one had been here to tend this grave since the long-past committal service. I remembered that day as well. Another faithful believer. A much quieter, less public life. Not so much flash or vocal crowd for the final service. Not much honor, in the here and now.

I wonder, which one of these two was the Lord more pleased to welcome into His heaven? Which one received of the Lord greater things for their earthly life? Which one truly was greatest in the Lord's presence?

How I answer those questions has everything to do with how I live my life, how I approach the subject of honor, what motivates my service for Him, and whether my understanding of grace is accurate.

Honor from man is much like smoke. As much as you may grasp for it, it slips away. In the final analysis, the only opinion that matters comes from the One who has created me, and the only honor that matters is His. His alone.

...I am quite content with my weaknesses and with insults, hardships, persecutions, and calamities. For when I am weak, then I am strong.   2 Cor. 12:10b, NLT.

Scarring is the fad I'll never understand. Come to think of it, I'm not overly knowledgeable about the frame of mind that drives multiple piercings or billboard-sized tattoos, either. It seems to me an odd paradox: the quest to express individuality through body art, and yet the lemming-line to get it done just like thousands of other "individuals." When I was a kid, we carved wood, and unintentionally ourselves on occasion. Yet scarring, that ancient tribal ritual-turned-trendy, has continued its sweep of the land as the latest way to say something about you, this time by deliberately carving on you. Scars are a part of normal life here, usually accidental and unavoidable in this body that wounds so easily. My first scar of memory occurred when I, perhaps at age eight, hurdled a fence and came down with one leg into a coil of barbed wire still being strung for our horse pasture. Stop by some time and I'll show it to you. I think it expresses my individuality and whimsical artsy side. As a bonus, it was free.

There are many scarred around the world simply for living for their Lord they know as Jesus Christ. The Islamic backlash that sprang from depictions of their prophet Mohammed in Danish cartoons left many Christian communities scarred, but not destroyed. In Nigeria alone, 52 church buildings burned while 51 Christians were brutally murdered. The "elephant in the room" is that these Christians, like others around the globe, had no complicity to what the Danes had printed an ocean away. The bull's-eye was on them during the riots purely because of their faith in Christ. The second "elephant" concerns murder and mayhem as a viable response to cartoons, but that beast is too large to try to dissect in this book.

Here in America, many news agencies buckled, speaking of sensitivity toward the Muslim psyche and restraint for media to reprint the hateful comics. It is offensive, we don't want to upset them, and besides, isn't there a new stage revival of "The Last Temptation of Christ," a South Park episode ridiculing Him, or some DaVinci coverage to highlight for the newscast? Welcome to America, where it's a continual open season on Christ and His followers. He and they can be lampooned with impunity, because our system protects free speech, no matter how repulsive. Just be sure to stump for kindliness and understanding for any other world religion, or you'll be labeled intolerant.

The scars of our near-Christian neighbors are also multiplying. Venezuela has given most Christian missions the boot, and as of today Morales is following Chavez' nationalizing lead further south in Bolivia. The Christians, churches and missions there may now face the same trying path, but this, like terror in Nigeria, will work to strengthen the church. Scars always push the church into a truer faith and a deeper walk with Christ. After all, it was His path as well.

I am disquieted by the conflicting message the church triumphant brings to the world in our little bubble of North America. While many congregations have willingly embarked on the downward

path to greatness by emphasizing a body life of service and sacrifice, others seem bent on their quest for popularity, acceptance
and avoidance of scars. It seems for many the markers of "success" are numbers, books in the black, smooth services and warm
fuzzy holidays. Others draw a line in the sand, opting for in-your-
face activism and political maneuvering to trump their worldly foes
in media, capitol, or court. Forget spreading the gospel; let's just
legislate it.

I think of the Lord on His journey to Jerusalem. He was on mission, resisting and facing off even His own disciples who tried to
push Him on a fast path to power, kingdom, and domain. He had a
single downward focus, to be lifted on a cross. The last time I
checked, His Word still read, "Follow me."

A pastor friend recently reminded me that the risen Christ still
displays His scars. Forever He will carry the evidence that demonstrates His love for us; scars He willingly opened His hands to
receive. Perhaps the church triumphant will have to readjust her
thinking here in wonderland, and come to grips with the fact that
Jesus taught servanthood, not success. Indeed, the first is the only
gateway to the second. But it's His way, His standard, His timing. I
pray that the church—the body of Christ—will once again be willing to open her hands to receive the scars. A body of wounded
healers known not for its flash or fight, but for bringing Christ's
healing to those they encounter on the path. This is scarring I think
even I am beginning to understand.

No, it's not faddish, but it is the only viable markings for those following the Master.

Have you no scar?
A jagged scar on foot, at side, in hand?
Yes, I know you're praised as mighty in this land—
I hear you're hailed a bright and rising star.
Have you no scar?

Or, where's your wound?
See, I was wounded by assassins sent.
Spiked to a tree to suffer, my side was rent by

mocking souls surrounding me.
In death I swooned—
Where is your wound?

No wound? No scar?
See, as the master must the servant be.
Pierced are the dusty feet that follow me—
but yours are clean and smooth.
Could you have stayed so close and followed far,
yet bear no wound? No scar?

--my rewriting of an original verse by Amy Carmichael, as contained in J. O. Sanders, Spiritual Leadership (Moody Press, 1994, p. 117).

———————————————

Work hard and cheerfully at whatever you do, as though you were working for the Lord rather than for people. Col. 3:23; NLT

I have the makings for a great, crotchety old man if I live that long. My wife says that I already have the driving habits down cold. Admittedly, I occasionally wander into rooms with no idea of what I am after, and lately I slip into comment about how things used to be when I was young. Like now.

Recently I was again bemoaning the sorry state of our union as I drove home from shopping. The manager who needed to figure my sale had instructed me to wait at the counter until he was freed up. Not freed up from pressing business, or providing quality customer service to another, but by reaching a convenient point to pause his solitaire game on the business computer and tend to my interruptive transaction.

[There has been a pause mid-typing as I stepped outside to vent by hollering "Aaargh!" at the backyard woods and (unintentionally) my neighbor who now thinks I am psychotic and/or displeased with her late-winter yard work.]

Work and work ethic are nothing new to my world, and hopefully yours. Dad ran a small business, turning wrenches to turn a profit. And we, by virtue of being family, assisted in the endeavor. Hard work never killed me, though I am pretty crippled up at this juncture of life. We were taught a way of life that still motivates me: the old adage of a job worth doing is a job worth doing right. The reality that how you performed the work you did—however menial—said a great deal about you. How much greater this truth expands for those who claim to have the Lord at the core of their lives.

I'm reminded of all the different jobs I've held on the way to my career. Each had good and bad points, but they paid the bills. I would suppose it's the same across all fields. You take the good with the bad, but always give it your best. This simple lesson is often where we seem to fall down, to our individual and societal shame.

I've been a supporter of job shadowing for our kids, and recent news featuring Junior Achievement confirms the usefulness of this tool. Rather than landing on "forensic pathologist" because it looks so chic on the tube, students can get behind the driver's seat in areas of their interest to see if it is truly—realistically—what they would pour themselves into for a career. I hope that every school, business, student and parent can cooperate to expand these exploratory opportunities.

Sharing the truth and giving guidance are needed, but modeling is perhaps the critical key. Each of us model life and career, whether we realize someone is looking or not. With a focus on serving something or someone bigger than ourselves—even at the core of our work—our future could once again reflect the values that we all were created to uphold.

Careers are more than looking slick, or what the job pays. And in work, like life, we never truly play solitaire.

Then Jesus said to His disciples, "If anyone wishes to come after Me, he must deny himself, and take up his cross and follow Me. For whoever wishes to save his life will lose it; but whoever loses

. . . and all that is in the world . . . .

*his life for My sake will find it. For what will it profit a man if he gains
the whole world and forfeits his soul? Or what will a man give in
exchange for his soul?"*　　　　　　　　Matthew 16:24-26; NASU

By all accounts they had it made. Lucrative, upwardly-mobile job.
Good marriage. Bright kids. The retirement account grew steadily.
Vacations were fun and frequent. Life was as it should be under
the bright sun of the American Dream. Success, by the numbers.
The feeling came gradually, but then in fullness would not permit
them to overlook it. There was something missing. Something
being left off, that needed to be done. It would not let them go. So
they chose, trembling, to obey. Or perhaps they at first chose just
to consider to obey. Tiny faith steps, of exploration and conversation and fact-finding and setting out fleeces, so to speak. One by
one their defenses came down. There was nothing more that could
be objected to, definitely answered, absolutely guaranteed, or confidently assured. They had, in effect, reached the end of themselves. The only thing remaining was the step. The following.
Resignations were tendered. Belongings were sold. Goodbyes
were said, many to bewildered family and friends who could not
understand such a radical step.
"Serve the Lord by raising your kids here."
"Think of your future."
"Let someone else do that. Just stop and look at all you'll be losing."
Today, they serve where He has led. It hasn't been easy. The
obstacles have been, and are, great. "Success" by the world's
measures is light-years removed from them. They wouldn't have it
any other way. They do possess a joy that comes from the One
who has ensured their true ultimate success. In that, they are
indeed rich. Success, as His numbered.

*　　*　　*

She sits alone for a good part of her days. They are gone now;
the ones once so close. Life has moved on, and the changes it has
brought were not always the pleasant variety. But her days are
presently filled in other ways, a different vitality and communication

with those to whom she is now utterly given.

Her room is full of treasures, but you would not see it so. To the uninitiated soul, it holds contents well-suited for an incinerator; nothing of note for Sotheby's auction block. Pictures, some rather poorly taken. Letters, jumbled and worn. Books showing great use; broken-spined, dog-eared and copiously annotated. The table by her chair holds numerous objects; knick knacks of foreign lands to which she has never traveled, yet she has been there, to every corner of this earth they represent. Most prominent amid the sacred clutter is a Bible, turned loose-leaf by its frequent consultations. The room is dark; the lone exception being the lamp at chairside. It spills out a magnificent wattage, allowing dim eyes and tiny print to at least try and coexist peaceably.

There are also fresher holdings here in this archive. Another stand reveals an orderly supply of paper, stationery, cards, envelopes and postage stamps; purchased at great sacrifice. An adorning tray holds contents better suited for a writing desk drawer: pencils, pens, scissors. A magnifying glass rides sentry atop a well-thumbed address book.

Then there are the lists. One cannot help but also notice them. They occupy table space and counter space and even an arm of the worn chair which has become her command center for the duration of her current mission. These lists are marked with dates, cryptic notes—"perfect peace," "strengthen faith," "needed workers!" She has evidently developed a shorthand method for recording bits of scripture for each of these entries, and quite frequently you see the word, "answered!" followed by what seems to be a comment of praise or thanks.

And so she daily takes her place, and goes to battle. The correspondences are read, the names and requests are poured over. The words of her God she also reads from, or quotes from a memory still sharp and attuned to its gleaming guidance and promises. She writes to each saint with a hand quavered by age but grasped by the Lord. And when the mail has gone, she still returns to her work, for more has arrived. She lifts them up, silently now, sharing her heart and their need with the First One to whom she is given; the One who always occupies this war room with her, heedless of the hour or its lean appearance.

*   *   *

They never have had a lot to spare. If you saw the way they prioritized their world, you'd know why. Of course, it was easier before the kids came along. It usually is. In those days, it didn't seem like such a sacrifice. One less meal out, a few less new clothes, keep the car another year. Time was freer too, and the volunteering, like the giving, was never as much of a challenge before diapers, recitals, minivans and mortgages.

It never made sense, all this giving. Their friends told them so. Coworkers laughed them off. Her folks were particularly unimpressed.

"What are you going to do about the future?"

"The more you give, the more they'll want from you."

"Don't you think your family is ministry enough?"

"If you don't wise up, you'll be the ones needing help."

But still, they have stuck to their priorities, their convictions, their beliefs. They have never gotten away from the reality that there are others here that they are called to serve. That there are food issues and housing issues and care issues that require more than a token nod when the mood suits you. That the church is a body, and each part must function or the whole being suffers.

He likes to say that it's no sacrifice. The really big sacrifice was made by the One who served them. She likes to tell others that they have really given up nothing. That their needs are always met, and they turn their wants into wants for someone else. They both stress that they do what they do to draw attention to their Lord, and not themselves.

And their worship is more than filling a seat for the attendance record. And their service is often in being the answer to the very need they have prayed about. And their lives through open hands have really grasped what this life is all about. And they acknowledge that every value has a corresponding price tag.

Now, even their children are of age where they too are making this value of following the Lord their very own. This is no little thing; for it ensures that this influence to find life by losing it may shine in a dark world for at least one more generation.

121

As I Was Saying . . .

Come. Take up. Deny. Follow. Save. Lose. Find. Profit. Forfeit. The words of the one who alone is worthy to be my Lord. Three brief tales, of which there are thousands more to tell.

What will your story be? Our accounts, even now, are being written.

We all make many mistakes, but those who control their tongues can also control themselves in every other way. James 3:2, NLT

Cell phones are all the rage, and are fueling mine. Or maybe it's just too much talk, with phones simply being the current frontrunner in the yak race. Talk TV and radio are growth industries with no ceiling in sight, and obviously no basement for crudity. New musical "artists" are launched into the spotlight by their prowess in rapid-speak. Kids pore over chat rooms, copying the parent's obsession for casually shot-off e-mail over in the next room.

I know—a pastor bemoaning "talk" is delightfully absurd—but let me press my point. Much that passes for speech today is not on the weighing of words, or the appropriateness of words, but simply the quantity of words. Somehow, a sheer abundance of words has come to equate itself with actually having something to say. It seems that "free speech" can be often better characterized as thought-free speech. This plague of profitless speech is certainly not a new arrival in my world; every generation seems to give me a warning about the danger of idle words.

This caution against cheap talk is amplified for me in my Christian walk. The Word I would live by reminds me that the world has every right to judge my life as a Christ-follower, and <u>that</u> based on the fruit of my life, which includes my speech. So what can I do to safeguard myself and keep my speech profitable? One help is to practice a delightful early Christian discipline: pursuing silence and solitude. This discipline, embraced habitually, acts as a buffer on my lust for the noise and flash of the world. Without it, a moment of silence even in my worship can seem to be an awkward intrusion. If my life is a world of constant chatter, I might respond to quiet worship with, "Can't we skip this and get on to something meaningful?"

As I close, I propose an anthem for us all. To stress the fact that I am not wound too tight and do have a playful, lighthearted side, I chose musical lyric. David used Psalms, but my libretto may have more of a nod to Weird Al than Hebrew prose. Try this, to the tune of "On the Road Again."

On the phone again,
Just can't wait to get on the phone again.
Spreadin' gossip, Lord I know that it's a sin,
But I can't wait to get on the phone again.
On the phone again,
Let's see now, where do I begin?
Sow some discord or invent a little dirt—
What can it hurt to be on the phone again...

On the phone again,
Ramblin' on and on about some things best left unsaid.
On the phone again,
Reachin' out to touch someone with scandal in my head—
The Spirit's fled.
On the phone again,
Just can't wait to get on the phone again.
Spreadin' gossip, Lord I know that it's a sin,
But I can't wait to get on the phone again.
On the phone again,
Grievin', quenchin' with the tales I spin.
Every idle word is written, I'll allow,
But for now, I'm gettin' on the phone again.

While I do express my apologies to Willie for besmirching his hit, I hope you can take this word constructively. If not, why don't you give me a quick call and...

I Will Build My Church...

Then all the disciples left him and fled. Matthew 26:56b; NASU

In this high holy week where the church recounts the agony and victory of the Christ, I pause to consider the state of the flock that would claim Shepherd Jesus as their very own. It is of little use to revisit the first century cross and tomb if there is a refusal to bridge the ages and soberly allow the Spirit of Christ to judge the effect of that message of death and resurrection upon our twenty-first century lives as his purported followers.

To be sure, keeping the observance without having life in Him is simply practicing religion. In every congregation, there are doubtless those dabblers who keep this yearly remembrance by little more than sentimentality and a display of new wardrobe. It seems their message-through-life would be, "Queue up for the big pageant events and flower-littered rituals, but don't get hung up about any personal connection to this One we're making all the fuss over today." I wonder, does Jesus know them by name? The naysayer will immediately fly to Scripture and quote to me ample warnings about judging, but I'll hold my ground on this very hill: where is the disciple found, when the good times are gone? That location, more telling than any other of their behaviors or collection of their eloquent words, may well be the dividing line between the false and the true.

It is an inescapable fact that even in the walk of the true, failure will be a companion, constant and unrelenting. The fleeing disciples are evidence enough. But I wonder, did the false one, steeled by his newfound celebrity and jingle in his pocket, accompany the arresting party in their escort of Jesus back to the murderous leadership?

The true ones, flooded with anguish and shame, responded in the following hours and days with tears, introspection, prayer and quiet camaraderie. The false one took leave of life at the end of a rope. The true were greeted by the resurrected Lord, receiving from Him that commission which restored and refocused their lives. Not all was lost. They were not without remedy. This time, God's forgiveness and the unshakable truth about eternity would grip them. His Spirit would fill them. Jesus had broken the power of sin and death, granting new power to those who were true. Nothing for the disciples would ever be the same again.

It would be pleasant to report for twenty-first century drive-by disciples, that the true ones enjoyed relative ease and public acclaim as they lived their unencumbered lives from that point forward. Nothing could be farther from the truth. While Scripture is relatively silent concerning life's end for most of them, extant church history bears out the truth that Jesus meant exactly what He said concerning their call.

"He who loves his life loses it, and he who hates his life in this world will keep it to life eternal. If anyone serves Me, he must follow Me; and where I am, there My servant will be also; if anyone serves Me, the Father will honor him." John 12:25-26; NASU

Is there a different call upon His church today? Can the church continue to be the church, if in the swell of popular culture the voice of Jesus continues to be relegated farther and farther from the pulpit and closer and closer toward the exit? If the "disciple" of today thinks no differently than, acts with no distinction from, and speaks with the same voice as the world, who will be the last one left in the church to even discern in the Spirit when Jesus has indeed left the building?

In an honest exercise to examine the heart and confess the sin of self and the church, perhaps what we need for this high and holy week is a little less festivity and a little more contemplation. More reflection concerning our walk the other weeks of our year, and less concern about how much religious commotion we can cram into one week each spring. More care for Jesus and His Word, and less tolerance for tickled ears and culturally acceptable acquiescence. More resolve to walk as a near servant of Christ, and less allegiance to the world and its languid, insipid portrayal of discipleship as random and trifling.

125

As I Was Saying . . .

Then Jesus told him, "Follow me."   John 21:19b; NLT

In this coming spring Sunday, I pray we each not neglect our remembrance of the Friday that grants us the opportunities to both ponder and celebrate. May your Easter be filled with joy as fragrant as the lily, meaning as deep as God's reach to Earth, and resolve as weighty as the stone that was, nigh unto twenty centuries ago, rolled away.

Then the eleven disciples left for Galilee, going to the mountain where Jesus had told them to go. When they saw him, they worshiped him—but some of them doubted!

Matthew 28:16-17; NLT

As Resurrection Sundays go, this one now just past was pretty good. Numbers were up, attention was fixed, and there were a lot of compliments after the services by regulars and visitors alike. On the man-scale, by all appearances and exit-polls, we seem to have had a winner in the conducting of the Easter services this year.

It is a common feature of our gathering, last week notwithstanding, to thank the Lord in prayer for simply blessing us, as His worshippers, with His presence. We remind ourselves that He is the audience and we are the instruments tuning ourselves to be pleasing bearers of his praise and adoration through song, word, sacrament and fellowship. We need frequent reminders of this heart-check in attitude, lest we twist the creator/created relationship and supplant ourselves as the focus and recipients of our own worship. If "I, me, my" are frequently invoked in the design or evaluation of worship, evidence indicates that we will both be planning and attending "self-services," with our own preferences, tastes and biases as the trumping criterion. The inviolate standard becomes, "I like it, so He (and everyone else who wants to worship with me) had better be OK with it too." Is this really what worship in His presence is to center on? "Lord, please receive this that makes me feel good, for I am so very comfortable with it."

The eleven, fresh off of several encounters with their risen Lord in the past handful of days, made their way to a Galilean mountain Jesus had used as a teaching spot in his previous ministry within that region. There, when they encountered him, there was the wholesale prostrating of themselves in absolute worship. He was indeed the living Son of God. He was undeniably come from the dead, fulfilling all he had foretold them concerning his death, burial and resurrection. They were given to him there; heart, soul, mind, strength—a focused veneration that literally had them undone; lost in wonder at his feet.

And Jesus came up and spoke to them, saying, "All authority has been given to Me in heaven and on earth. Go therefore and make disciples of all the nations, baptizing them in the name of the Father and the Son and the Holy Spirit, teaching them to observe all that I commanded you; and lo, I am with you always, even to the end of the age" (Matthew 28:18-20; NASU).

He would commission them, and they in worshipful response would go. The living and telling of the good news would be expensive worship; it would cost them all things earthly. For most of the eleven, it would in time cost them the last thing earthly: their very lives. They would not be known for personal quests for power, or notoriety, or slick campaigns for the biggest crowds. They would be content to tell of Him, and fearless of what man could do (and would do) to them. The very men who had hidden, allowing the faithful women to be the first at the day of discovery, would soon be emboldened by the resident Holy Spirit, having a zeal in Christ's bodily absence they had never unwaveringly demonstrated even while in his presence. The whole of the Roman Empire could not obliterate the truth or the messengers of it. The proof it seems, was not secured only by the visible affirmation of His resurrection. The proof more clearly was demonstrated by the lives that were completely transformed by receiving this gospel. It started with the women, then the eleven. It continues to this day, still impelling its messengers to "go" and present good news.

Into this scene of rapt worship, Matthew interjects a brief comment that both adds authenticity to his report and breeds discussion spanning the centuries: "…some of them doubted!"

So who were these "doubters" that he has referred to? I would assume that there must be others present on the mountain. I would appeal that there has to be. Paul may be alluding to these "others" in one of his letters: "After that He appeared to more than five hundred brethren at one time…" (1 Corinthians 15:6a; NASU). What did they doubt? Why was this included in the closing lines of a document carefully written to affirm that Jesus is the Messiah, Son of God, Lord and Christ? I can hazard a response to these things, but mind you, I am but a man.

It seems implausible to me for these eleven to be simultaneously worshipping and doubting. I would hazard to say that the terms should be considered mutually exclusive. For those walking by faith, there will always be that given element of the unknown; that is why it is called "faith," and not "sight." But to enter into true worship while shadowed by doubt seems for me to be a spiritual impossibility. These had met the resurrected Lord in previous days. They had been invited to examine hand and side. Meals had been shared. Now, on the mountain, all of their confirmations converge. In previous years, they had followed, and learned, and loved him. Now, they do what is reserved solely for God alone; God present beyond any doubting and questioning. They worship Him.

Yes, others mixed with doubt must be present. Others, perhaps in addition to these five hundred "brothers" of which Paul records; an assortment from Jesus' "followers" in all their various walks and spiritual attitudes. See, look. Here is another fallen prostrate before Him. And yet another, who stands trembling, trying to comprehend, praying for answers, daring to step a bit closer. And yet another, skeptical and hard, knowing the facts of Jesus' death and resolute to uncover who could be perpetrating such a thing as to portray a resurrected healer. Or bread and fish provider. Or good teacher. Or prophet. Yes, this is the group seasoned both by worshipper and doubter. This is the mixed multitude upon the mountain. This is the varied crowd drawn to Jesus, as were the crowds in earlier days, and in the days to come…the centuries to come.

And here, in my days, the crowd once more departed at the conclusion of Easter services. Unsurprisingly, perhaps, a mixed band of worshippers and doubters. Possibly there was that one that this day has seen doubts destroyed, faith come to life, and entrance into the joy of belief. Then there were the worshippers, both humbled yet emboldened to "go" with the news that has given them life. And, to not be naïve, the doubters in some number, quietly walking away, thinking perhaps, "Wishful...but it can't be."

Does doubt change the truth? It cannot, any more than closing my eyes at sunrise could obliterate the notion that the sun still rules the day. My boy Samuel still plays the "I'll close my eyes so you can't see me" game. When he is mature, he will put away such childish notions. Likewise, the God of the universe still occupies the room whether He is rightly acknowledged or not.

But there is another tough question remaining. For the worshippers—and by this I mean not the person performing in form or posture or words or participation, but the one poured out in heart, spirit, mind, soul, strength— does their worship flow out naturally into obedience? To fall prostrate, recognizing His authority, listening to His word, confessing allegiance while shoulder to shoulder with others—this is truly an aspect of worship, one that we recognize as a corporate reality and delight. The real test begins when the worshipper arises, and is faced with the command of commission, and expectation and obedience and accountability.

It is good news. Others can meet Him as they experience His presence in our true worship. They should also be encountering Him, as we, His worshippers, carry the message beyond the walls and into our waiting world.

How is your worship? Is it God-centered? Whole hearted and genuine? Unmixed? Passionate? Guided by Spirit and Truth? And oh yes, is it portable?

Genuine worship of Him demands these things, without a doubt.

"Ask, and it will be given to you; seek, and you will find; knock, and it will be opened to you. For everyone who asks receives, and he who seeks finds, and to him who knocks it will be opened."
Matthew 7:7-8; NASU

"Ask, and it will be given you..." I used to think it was all in the asking. Having been "grounded" in the Word, it was all made so simple; so clear. So...one sided. All you have to do is ask, because, well, that's what Jesus said. I've heard it all before:

He will not deny that which you ask of Him. Name his will for you, and it is done.

He is ready to give you what you desire in your heart of hearts. You know your need; tell him so he knows too.

He is poised to bestow upon you any and all things you want. The receiving is delayed only because you are slow to request... to petition... to ask. Remember, he must honor his word, and finish his obligation to supply your demand, for he has stated it so.

If the demand isn't met, ask longer, harder, with more faith, in his name, with more reminders to him of what he said. That should do it.

Pretty passive it seems, this supplier-of-the-miraculous called Jesus, and this pipeline called prayer. But then, I've also observed that the words of the Christ continue. What will I do with these?

"Seek, and you will find..." Following on the heels of his command to simply ask, the Lord launches into yet more emphatic language, this time to send me on a hunt. I've sought for many things over the years, from lost keys to lost rings, and once a child at an amusement park (but that's a tale for another day).

What strange topical leaps the Lord takes in his mountainside address! Has Matthew slipped out for a bit and failed to notify us that he's missing some notes from a few minutes of the sermon? Here, I thought we were having a lesson hammered home about prayer, and now suddenly I'm to be up and active and looking for something he hasn't even bothered to specifically name?

What could it be? Maybe Jesus wants me to find a personal sense of well-being. Easy search; there's shelves full of such published "resources" to help me fill that ticket. Or maybe it's self-help: uncover some trendy spiritual psychology guides to boost my esteem. I could find a boatload of "3 easy steps" or "7 keys" instruction in a mere heartbeat. Is that what I need to be seeking? Is Jesus here on a mission to be my wish-genie and my private therapist too? Hallelujah. How could it get any better than that?

"Knock, and it will be opened to you." Just when I was settling in on creating my list of "wants" to present, and scheduling sessions to work through my inner issues, Jesus again takes off on another tangent. This time, it seems he would send me to an unnamed door where I am to make my presence known. That is an uncomfortable command, especially intrusive within my private world amid my closed, independent society. You know, there are reasons doors are shut and bolted. People who go around banging on closed doors can expect often to be ignored, yelled at, chased away, or even worse. My own residence has a plain "No Soliciting" sign placed right at the bell. You don't want me answering the door to meet you perched on my stoop offering free water analysis, discounted meats, or sweeper demonstrations. There's a reason I posted the sign there. Why would the Lord command me to go knocking on a cold call? Can't He give me a little more information? What with getting all I ask for and having my therapies for personal fulfillment, I really do need some more information to help me with my decision on whether or not I want to do this knocking.

The isolation of this passage into three separate, unlinked "thoughts" from Jesus can lead me to such faulty conclusions as those I have penned. Only if I retain the unity of Jesus' words, will a far different (and coherently sound) theology of prayer make its presence known.

Prayer, it seems, is more than offering up my requests to Him. As wonderful a promise as "Ask and it shall be given" is, I cannot trap it in isolation and lever from it the conclusion that my naming and claiming has God's stamp of approval upon it. His word amply reinforces that my quest is to be focused upon holiness, not my mere happiness. He also states that asking in offhand ways is "amiss," usually concerned with earthly cares and frequently more about my comfort than his kingdom.

And so comes the seeking. Through intake of His word, reflection, counsel and corporate confession, we take in holy guidance to inform our prayer. His desire is that our asking would be in perfect accord with His will, for He can answer for our good in no other way. It is still, "Thy will be done." He has given us ample resources within and around to guide us in our seeking. Heeded, they will keep us from the evil of promoting our self-will as His perfect will.

The proximity of knocking brings with it an image of persistence, boldness, and expectation. Unlike our modern aversion, the Father is neither annoyed nor reluctant to hear our "knocking" of faith, and dependence, and desire for simply being in His presence. The sum total prayer-life then also requires motion; action. To ask and seek without traveling the ways of God and to God in the day-to-day leaves off a core element of the disciple's life: consistently doing what He reveals. To knock means that I have approached His abode and that I seek entrance by the prescribed way, according to His clear path. I anticipate his warm reception, because it is my pleasant habit to travel purposefully and resolutely for fellowship with Him. I have walked His paths, performing His will. I have joys to share and orders to receive. He will swing wide that door.

Whole prayer.

A complementary weave of spirit-guided thought, and word, and action. A discipline focused on the intents of the heart, not necessarily the ring of the words that spill from often halting lips. It is living, moving, adapting, transforming. It is in its very essence described by the Word as "without ceasing" (1 Thes. 5:17).

Ask. Seek. Knock.

Do it.

But do it all.

———————————

Now after Jesus was born in Bethlehem of Judea in the days of Herod the king, magi from the east arrived in Jerusalem, saying, "Where is He who has been born King of the Jews? For we saw His star in the east and have come to worship Him." When Herod the king heard this, he was troubled, and all Jerusalem with him. Gathering together all the chief priests and scribes of the people, he inquired of them where the Messiah was to be born. They said to him, "In Bethlehem of Judea; for this is what has been written by the prophet: 'AND YOU, BETHLEHEM, LAND OF JUDAH, ARE BY NO MEANS LEAST AMONG THE LEADERS OF JUDAH; FOR OUT OF YOU SHALL COME FORTH A RULER WHO WILL SHEPHERD MY PEOPLE ISRAEL.'" Then Herod secretly called the magi and determined from them the exact time the star appeared. And he sent them to Bethlehem and said, "Go and search carefully for the Child; and when you have found Him, report to me, so that I too may come and worship Him."

Matthew 2:1-8; NASU

It is fitting for me this evening to recall this story from Jesus' early years, here on the cusp of this high and holy season that commemorates his coming to that obscure village named Bethlehem. We in Christendom like to remark about His lowly birth, and the significance of the savior coming for the insignificant. This is certainly truth and bears up well in scripture's account. In our celebration and pageant, we even rush to merge the events given in Matthew and Luke by imposing the visit of the magi at Jesus' birth, rather than some later point when He is a child but definitely not an infant; when He is found in a house and not a stable. I'm not one to quibble—yet there are some striking points to ponder that are easily overlooked by slipping into another sentimental treading of the tale, and not seeing it for what it is and when it transpired.

I talk to my bible, and ask questions I may never fully understand this side of eternity. What was the reason for Joseph and Mary, compelled as Luke tells it to enter Bethlehem for a census, to be there long after the numbering and Jesus' birth, seemingly putting down roots and calling it home? Was it a respite, having a new start in a quiet village where obscurity was a blessing? Was there sacredness in anonymity for this couple who had perhaps known Nazareth's disapproval and the barb of relentless tongues that saw more scandal than miracle in this betrothed couple being found with child? Scripture does little to aid my inquiry, but a reference found in John's gospel may shed more light than a casual read would notice. As the open hostility for Jesus escalates, the retort is thrown at him, "We were not born of fornication; we have one Father: God." (John 8:41b; NASU) Jesus had probably heard the taunts before, and I suspect His earthly parents knew more of the same. It doesn't take a biblical scholar to observe the common traits of human nature.

I am struck too by the presence of the star, appearing to the magi coming from the east to discover this new ruler heralded by signs in the heavens. The duration of the star's appearing, along with its frequency, intensity, and path, is unknown. What is known from Matthew's account leads me to other points to ponder. Here at the core for God's people, the city of Jerusalem, the star was shining with little if any notice. It took gentile seekers to draw attention to what should have been the focal point of every God worshipper in the region. Herod's inquiry to his religious scholars bears a stunning witness. They knew the word of God, and it foretold that the rural village of Bethlehem would usher in the king "born"—not appointed—to rule the Jews as Messiah. Citing their scriptures of Micah and Samuel, Herod's counselors were plain in their conclusion: it is as the Holy Word says.

The magi are sent to complete their quest, naïve to Herod's true intents for when the child is located. Of course, as we read and learn, God intervenes so that day will not result in the young Messiah's demise. Many others will perish, but not the Chosen One.

It would seem to me that given the star and the involvement of the religious elite in affirming the Christ's location, every able bodied God fearer would be scouring Bethlehem to find The One. The magi have no difficulty, as the star is on the move reminiscent of the pillar of fire in Exodus, coming at last to rest directly over the house where the holy family now resides. The remainder of the population seemingly has no interest or desire to come behold their King. I wonder if it is fear of Herod, fear of God's coming, plain disinterest, or other priorities that prevented their running to meet their Deliverer. And I will have to content myself with that wonderment for now.

There is one additional point in the story I ponder now, a bit later into this crisp end-of-November evening. It is the problem of distance. The distance, that is, from Jerusalem to Bethlehem. According to common knowledge, rooted in the fact that both settlements still exist today, that distance spans the paltry sum of somewhere around six miles.

Six miles.

The Savior of the world was abiding, six miles away. And a population that existed through God's sovereign plan could not bridge that distance to go and welcome Him to their world. A caravan composed of members from the pagan world traveled a far greater distance, being given a God-directed, rudimentary understanding that someone amazing had arrived, and they couldn't miss out on greeting, and gifting, and worshiping him.

I wonder, in this merriment-fixated world, what distance mankind today refuses to go—in ignorance, indifference, or fear—to avoid encountering the Christ of Christmas. I wonder more fully if those who would readily number themselves among the God fearers also labor at keeping, rather than spanning the distance to welcome the Savior into our personal worlds. Is the Savior distant? What span might I traverse to behold His presence? Consider these "six mile" separations:

• The family that will know no Christmas, while across the street all is merry and bright.

• The myriad of congregations that will offer open hearts and doors to share the real meaning of this King's coming, yet will see very little interest from the masses going to great lengths to keep the holidays, but avoid the Holy One.

• The pantry that faces the pain of yet more empty shelves and yet more empty stomachs—a willing toolbox with limited tools.

• The young woman struggling in her plight, receiving as Mary, soulless stares from those intent on keeping their righteous distance. And finishing their shopping.

• The man, woman or child, isolated from family by states or oceans, contemplating the prospect of the loneliest day of the year approaching.

• The patient, the resident, the overlooked, the marginalized—those who are beginning to see that perhaps Christmas is only for the strong, the mobile, the pleasant, the acceptable, and the connected.

When we come near to others, we discover that the Lord Jesus is also present. How very often He beckons to us, and often from much closer than even a six mile journey. When we span those distances, laying down whatever time, treasure and energy they require, we find, in following his star, the privilege of entering in and ministering to the Christ who inhabits that place. That place where

As I Was Saying . . .

He abides, significantly still coming for the insignificant.

Insignificant, that is, to every eye but His own.

Where is His star shining this season, bidding you to come? To find the Savior, it is there you must journey.

But when the fullness of the time came, God sent forth His Son, born of a woman...

Galatians 4:4a; NASU

Christmas doesn't just happen—ask my wife.

Plans are being drawn up for the festive holiday decorating to begin at the ol' Masters Estate. Mind you, there have been plenty of reminders all this fall to keep me cognizant of the fact that Christmas is coming. The carols have been pouring forth from the CD player during breakfast and dinner times for just over a month now, and I have been under strict orders to not touch the mail or any advertisement until she has gone through them all to glean out the pertinent information every Christmas shopper wants and needs. It's not just a holiday—it's an endurance sport. If I mess with her plans, I have been assured it will turn into a contact sport. She can be so menacing with that rolled up newspaper...

Soon I will come home from a day in my ministerial routine to discover that once again, the jolly Christmas gnomes have descended on my residence and turned it into Winter Wonderland Festive Village: Southern Encampment. The real fun this time around will be watching Samuel at age five, and how he responds to all the décor. He's already picked out a couple of favorite carols, and tries his best to warble out the words and melody with his own distinct stylings. It too will be interesting to see how our new tomcat Bob takes to all the frenzy and buzz in and around the house. Bob, so named because he showed up this summer sporting half a tail, has adopted us as his new family. He has steadily grown more receptive and affectionate, although I truly believe that a full food dish and a warm place to take a nap have a lot to do with displays of affection from a cat. As his first residence seemingly was the woods behind our place, I'm sure it won't take him long to launch a full scale frontal assault and ascent of the family Christmas tree. Given Samuel's penchant for following the cat, I will also go out on a limb and assume that there will be collaboration from the two of them that will result in said tree coming down. I have resolved to speak with Samuel privately this week, encouraging him to plan that event for when I am away for the day. I don't do well being around my wife when her tree comes down. Neither does the rest of our county.

Unfortunately, due to tiny printed clauses in my marriage license that I failed to inspect before signing, I am bound to contribute both time and muscle to the display. My arena for deployment is the exterior of the household. I lug up and illuminate a simple front yard nativity set, along with an accompanying pine tree trimmed with deep blue bulbs. The lights barely made it through last season, and figuring they finally were irreparable, I took the liberty to (stealthily) scrap them when the decorations came down. I figured joyfully, albeit quietly, that at last I was free. Not so. The reminder came this morning, with her firm but not-yet-threatening commentary, "I see the outdoor tree is bare. Have you picked up the new lights yet? That needs to be ready for next week." Sheesh.

Other ways I contribute to the festivity and my peace of mind are through hiding all my power tools and the shop key, which of course just sets me up to do more of the display work. Since I don't want a long list of repair projects generated by, let's say, her encouraging son Ben to put up the icicle lights on the eaves with my power stapler, I had best commandeer those jobs and trudge around doing them. I will give a resigned smile later, in a couple of months when it's all put away and I've avoided property damage one more time. I still have nightmares about that stapler thing…

Soon it will all be over for another year. Christmas will be a memory. The power company's congratulatory letter on another record month for a single family dwelling will arrive, and I will contemplate lucrative careers as the bills accrued for our "preparation" roll in.

And she gave birth to her firstborn son; and she wrapped Him in cloths, and laid Him in a manger, because there was no room for

As I Was Saying . . .

them in the inn. Luke 2:7; NASU

There comes a strange contrast at Christmas. In all the preparations God made to bring His Son into the world, even the most primitive of rooms was not arranged for the King of Kings. His residence would be in the heart of man, and His coming would be for the ones not drawn to pomp and splendor, but drawn by their sin and need to One who would indeed identify with them in their barrenness. Their bankruptcy. Their exposure.

With all of the preparations swirling about me, it behooves me to not overlook the preparations of my heart. In all my keeping of Christmas, the last thing I want is to miss it by not having that room prepared within. I have a few good reads for the season; devotionals somewhat worn that have become like old friends as I meditate through them in this month to come. The opening matters of Matthew and Luke bear their mark on my morning quiet, and I find a solace in pondering the carols, some familiar and some quite new to me even in their antiquity. It is illuminating and cleansing, as I consider how pens of another era voiced their praises to the Word that became flesh and dwelt among us.

For He was foreknown before the foundation of the world, but has appeared in these last times for the sake of you... 1 Peter 1:20; NASU

Begin your preparations. The season is upon us once again. Let there be lights, for it is a season of lights. Let your traditions start or remain, all those good things which bring the focus to the One for whom we sing, and share, and celebrate, and fall silent.

But do not overlook the preparations of the heart. It is there that the wonder is birthed, and it is there that the wonder must reside.

"But as for you, Bethlehem Ephrathah, too little to be among the clans of Judah, from you One will go forth for Me to be ruler in Israel. His goings forth are from long ago, from the days of eternity." Micah 5:2; NASU

PBS has been good to me this week. Nursing my annual

cold/sinus infection/throat malady, (which thankfully as a hearty Michigander never continues on much past the arrival of spring) I took pity on myself and deliberately grabbed a little down time Saturday afternoon to hibernate in front of the tube. No meetings. No events. No desk work. No home repairs. It was a rare "off" moment; a welcome respite from the normal pace.

The program that I stumbled upon went on for some time, albeit broken up regularly by appeals to viewers like me for funding pledges. These contributions, I was told, would ensure that such educational and inspiring fare would continue on without commercial interruption, and that other high-brow programming would survive on this and other public stations, safe from profiteers' influence and lowest-common-denominator fare that—ugh—regular television spewed forth. The great implication was that PBS stands alone, virtuous in their agenda-free programming, head and shoulders above the teeming mass of mediocrity that occupies the airwaves and satellite feeds.

Yeah, right.

Now don't misunderstand. They offer some good stuff, but I chafe at their insinuation that agendas are checked at the PBS door. Slogans and intents aside, bias is unavoidable in any institution. Some market widgets. Others, ideologies. Most combine the two. Be mindful that the church triumphant can also be accused of these joint charges, and often found glaringly guilty.

Still, I don't want PBS to lose heart and write me off entirely. My pledge may come in the future, when I actually have the time to become a regular viewer. For now, a deep thanks to all viewers like you who support my occasional leeching will have to suffice. So, anonymous, ill, and with only traces of a guilty conscience, I watched the show. And it was a show I truly did enjoy.

Through the miraculous gift that television can be, I was transported for a few hours to various points all across Europe, being invited to peer in at how Christmas is kept and celebrated among the differing nations, regions and peoples. I saw some that was familiar, much that was a distant cousin of my Christmas-keeping, and an awful lot that was wholly foreign.

Not surprisingly, many of the larger cities have elaborate productions that accompany their Christmases, drawing the masses to ogle over spectacular displays, circus-like attractions, and lavish gatherings. These crowds conveniently help to boost the gate receipts as well. Reference was occasionally made to pockets of the devout scattered within these populations; those content to observe the sacred and bypass the hype and flash. It was apparent that this is not the majority European view, and obviously a Christ-focus in the keeping of Christmas is not a huge draw for the bulk of the festive crowds. It would also make for a much duller travelogue, which by its very nature is biased to draw in the world traveler and not the common Christian.

The lesser venues, those small towns included in the film's itinerary, seemed to more naturally retain the elements of a purer Christian celebration of Christmas: sacred concerts, Bible readings, candlelit worship, nativity scenes and processionals. I found myself drawn to these more intimate snapshots, feeling at times uncomfortably intrusive. Through the camera I entered into hallowed spaces, observing publically a very private worship.

While these unmixed observances were an encouragement to me in this season of His appearing, many of the other foreign customs had a common root with the celebrations I am familiar with here in the west. Even an oceans' distance and depth does not detour or drown the competing holiday of Xmas. And Xmas is indeed about big business. Nothing more, but definitely nothing less. In the wash of Xmas here, it seems oddly incongruent to me that there is such a fierce resistance to grant even a passing recognition to the one who stands at the center of the event. It's as if the honored guest was not invited to the party given to honor him. After years of dropping the invitation, even the reason for the party—he himself—has been forgotten. Today, if queried as to why we have Christmas, the best some might honestly muster is simply, "Well, we do it because it's just what we do." At least those who champion "Xmas" or "Happy Holidays" are honest in their declarations. In their world, it's not about Him at all. After all, that whole Christ thing is so backwater...so small town.

I find this year and in this season, a great comfort in the celebration of Christmas in a small town. There is very little gloss and very little use for it in a place where real people face real life, all the while still working at making a difference by stepping out of their homes, pursuing meaningful connections with their neighbors and community; wanting more than a bedroom and a drive-through utilitarian hub. In a small town Christmas, there is a value for family and tradition, demonstrated from tree lightings to nativity scenes, volunteerism and pantry donations, caroling, giving, and worshipping—all as one's spirit, not fashion, leads. Christmas helps the small town to retain and reaffirm its identity and its values, guarding it from sliding into the faceless Main Street that has claimed so many victims; the "used to be" villages, skeletal and ghostly all about us.

There is a certain vulnerability and honesty that is demanded of those who celebrate Christmas in a small town. You know and are known; there is precious little room to hide. The proof of one's heart for God will not suddenly be discovered by the town at Christmas. Dickens can get away with it; we cannot. One's keeping of Christmas will be either further evidence or glaring contradiction. The face-and-name reality of these streets contrasts strongly to the nameless and faceless locales where anonymity is king, detachment is queen, and eye contact is strictly avoided, save for confrontation.

Remember with me another time, and another small town. It has failed to make it onto the "cool cities" list year after year. To add to its struggle, it lies in the shadow of the big sister city, bustling and smug with its temple, its king, and its brand-name recognition. Big sister city is running the table, and by all indicators of success, it is holding the winning hand. But then, the small town hears from God, quietly calling. The news is stunning.

Small town Bethlehem holds His Son.

Behold the bias of God.

Those that receive the call come to see. What a band of small-towners they turn out to be. Not a mover or shaker among them— just shepherds. Ordinary working class folk, definitely not top-shelf material. This one has on a worn-out robe, and that one over there could stand a morning at the spa. And what about that young one, who dares to come up so close? What business has he with the

As I Was Saying . . .

king of the universe? Is there no dress code? No guest list? No decorum whatsoever?

What of these surroundings? We know that kings may humor themselves by mingling with their vassals on occasion. But it is unthinkable for a king to lodge in a stable ripe with the smell of animals. Only commoners would find a pleasing fragrance in the stink of sheep. This mean place will not bode well with the wealthy land owners, or the cultured who reside in big sister city. What does He hope to bring about by holding court in this offensive cave? Surely He doesn't expect decent, respectable folk to meet Him in such an undignified location, does He?

But yet it does happen, as the prophet had told that it would. Then, as today, the giants by the world's standard become insignificant as they come against Him. The mighty stumble and fall as they encounter this rock that is both foundation and cornerstone of the new kingdom God is building. His teaching will turn man's wisdom on its collective head. His miracles will confirm his every word and His very identity. His mission will defeat hell, and death, and the grave, and the enemy of our souls. Forever.

And the humble, and the meek, and the lowly, and the insignificant, and the helpless, and the frail, and the sinner, and the undone, and the hopeless, and the lost, still come. Pressing in, we rub common shoulders to better view Him in our amazement and wonder. He hasn't passed us by.

Once, He chose a stable to be the sacred birthing room for His advent. Now, He elects to bring his new birth to all who by faith receive Him as Savior, King, Christ.

Rejoice. He has chosen to come to us, this Christ of the Christmas.

And He delights to come, even to a small town.

...but Mary quietly treasured these things in her heart and thought about them often.   Luke 2:19; NLT

Sentimentality is not my strong suit. Ask anyone I live with, especially her. Maybe it's the genetic thing; my certain doom to primitive thought patterns and behaviors, all because of the undeniable

142

presence of my resident male factor. Then again, perhaps it's the culmination of all my years conducting maintenance and exercising practical make-do in keeping the homestead in quasi-working order. I'd rather think that like a Pavlovian mutt, I've been gradually conditioned to my present mindset. Rather than drooling in a rage as I encounter more busted stuff, or even allowing myself to entertain vain thoughts that perhaps something I possess will actually remain unscathed, I have instead experienced an extinction of that response. Now, in my recent years, all that energy has been replaced by a dry-mouthed resignation, stoically facing the truth that becoming attached to any possession will simply set me up for certain and often swift disappointment. As sure as the sun sets, all things are destined to burn out, rust out, wear out, or fall into the hands of a nine year old. I have shed my last tear for hair dryers, heavy duty washing machines, "commercial grade" vacuum cleaners, bicycles, double hung windows, or anything in general that in another life I could really like.

This cathartic mindset also extends to the smaller items of the household, what I have been known to lovingly refer to as bric-a-brac, kitsch or knickknack. These sophisticated terms sound much better to the feminine ear than "junk", "stuff" or "clutter." The good news is that I never had an attachment with these myriad items to begin with. This has made letting go extremely easy for me. The wife's sense of import to this collection is of course, a far different story.

Celebrating Christmas at our place includes the unloading and placement of objects from several boxes, all of which would fit into my category qualifying them as knickknacks. For her, however, each piece has its own history, family tie, and value. She can recall with razor precision the story of each piece, and stares dumbly at me when I simply can't bring to mind, say, that special trip we made shopping on December 12, 1987, and that Countdown-To-Christmas Calendar that we discovered at that certain store on the bottom of the third shelf six aisles from where it was supposed to be stocked when they had told us it was sold out and we were sure we'd never find another like it, ever. And how we've enjoyed it every year since and how much it means when we hang it up and the delight of the children as we keep our great tradition year after year and they take turns moving the mouse closer to Christmas Day and retrieving their chocolate from the tiny compartments and… I am now squirming as I desperately need to duck this blinding spotlight of once again being discovered as a common Neanderthal, devoid of even the basest of sentimental recollections. I don't remember where we got it. I didn't know the kids were so enamored with taking their turns. And besides, I was never asked to take a turn moving the stupid mouse, for cryin' out loud. Maybe if I got chocolate, I'd reserve some space in my noggin to recall it fondly as well. Two can play at this game, so cleverly I counter by asking her what type of spark plug the chainsaw requires and what the gap should be set at. In retrospect this was not a sensible tactic, and I wouldn't recommend it at home, guys. On a positive note, the swelling has gone down this week…

Tonight, all the décor is finally up. All the boxes have been emptied, and the mouse was moved this morning for the first of twenty-five mornings. The family is watching a Christmas movie, and I am recalling the story of that first coming of the Christ, and what constituted Mary's celebration as she extolled the Lord God for His plan and her inclusion. *For he, the Mighty One, is holy, and he has done great things for me* (Luke 1:48; NLT).

Of all the events mundane, miraculous and tragic that composed Mary's life, I discover in the Word only the most skeletal of details. Still, it would seem to me a very reasonable assumption that Mary often took time to recount Jesus the Savior—her Savior—and his advent. I would dare to believe that she probably retained precious little of the artifacts from his life to aid in her recollection and worship. She would instead hide the imperishable things in her heart, and from this collection of guided thought, worship the One that she could not hold on to, constantly protect and ultimately preserve from death, much as her mother heart would die in his place if she only could. But you cannot die in your Savior's place. You can only die to self, and live for Him.

For now, in my family, we have many traditions that add to our celebration of this great and wondrous season of Christmas. I know that over time, things will change and some traditions will be set aside. That is the nature of things, the very definition of the temporal side of life. It is a good reminder for me of Mary's discipline—the discipline of the heart—to keep the Christ as the true keepsake. For the meaning of His Advent will never change, though the celebrations and accouterments will vary often, and widely.

I could say more, but there now is apparently a string of lights that needs my attention for repair. And when no one's looking, I'm digging into one of those calendar pockets for a chocolate. I can always blame it on the kids. Or plead ignorance to the whole concept of the calendar thing.

After all, it worked for me last year.

He came into the very world he created, but the world didn't recognize him. He came to his own people, and even they rejected him. But to all who believed in him and accepted him, he gave the right to become children of God. John 1:10-12; NLT

Christmas is found in Jesus

Not in trees and snowflakes
Not in candles and lights.
Not in bells, and choirs, and carols
Or quiet starlit nights.
Not in sleighs or reindeer
Not in partridges and pears.
Not in ribboned boxes
Or stockings hung with care.

Christmas is found in Jesus
It's all wrapped up in him.
Many things may speak of the Savior
But some, his light, they dim.
Where do you look for Christmas?
What makes your Christmas so dear?
With all Christmas brings, will it bring you to Jesus,
When Christmas comes this year?

As I Was Saying . . .

Not in a rich stately palace
Not to the regally named.
Not for the crowd who rested in plenty
Not for the fortuned and famed.
He came for the lost and the dying
For a world where trouble won't cease.
He offers a gift to all who receive him
True love, true life, true peace.

Christmas is found in Jesus
It's all wrapped up in him.
Many things may speak of the Savior
But some, his light, they dim.
Where do you look for Christmas?
What makes your Christmas so dear?
With all Christmas brings, will it bring you to Jesus,
When Christmas comes this year?

Keep the light on the child in the manger
He is the hope of the nations.
How can we share the gift with our world,
If we focus on cheap imitations?

Christmas is found in Jesus
It's all wrapped up in him.
Many things may speak of the Savior
But some, his light, they dim.
Where do you look for Christmas?
What makes your Christmas so dear?
With all Christmas brings, will it bring you to Jesus,
When Christmas comes this year?

Bread, by the sweat of your face...

The Lord placed the man in the Garden of Eden to tend and care
for it.   Gen. 2:15, NLT

It's garden time again. I'm sure I come by it naturally, as I am just one generation removed from the farm. I know the language of the planters; how they describe "the east forty" or, "the front section." I have "the back twenty," a garden spot approximately twenty feet square. I use the hugely popular French-intensive method, which is a fancy way of saying, "Cram the garden full." Obviously, I'm not into mega-farming. My total harvest will supply the family for a handful of meals, tops. Still, I need to do it. Far more satisfying than any entertainment, sport or other diversion, it is in the garden that I find my vacation spot, therapy couch and prayer room.

Why is it that the garden is so important for my life? Maybe it's the simple reward of standing back and actually seeing accomplishment—something not always possible in my profession. Or, it could be the process of breaking soil, planting, nurturing, and harvesting; observing and participating in a full cycle of life on a micro-scale. Why, developing an asparagus bed alone closely mirrors parenting: tend and care, wait patiently for years, don't rush by confusing growth with maturity; find reward when it's finally established! The love of gardening could also come from the rigor of the process. Along with sweat of the brow, I find discipline, disappointment, wonder, and reward. I need the garden just as much as the garden needs me. After all, man was created to be a gardener.

The garden, near and dear to God's heart as well, is also a ready illustration of the work He does in me here in His field. The master gardener provides what is needful for me to be fruitful and beneficial. He grants me life by the sowing of His Word, the seed. The rooting of that Word is established, as He breaks up the tough clods in my life that resist it. Through the needful pain of weeding and pruning, He spurs my growth so that I can reach my greatest potential in service to Him for His purposes. The master gardener is not interested in showy foliage; it is all about fruit. In due time, there is the harvest of a life lived for Him. The acceptable yield for the gardener is first the fruit of His Spirit (Gal. 5:22-23), evidence that the plant has drawn its strength from Him. Second, the yield should produce a legacy of heirloom, not hybrid seed. A plant reproducing under the gardener's touch will provide an increase of similar, fruitful plants for Him (Luke 8:15).

This week I will labor on planting the garden. It is a ritual steeped in tradition and meaning for me. As my toil continues through the summer and fall, I know I cannot guarantee the yield. Yet I will work hard, doing my part and watching as God supplies what I cannot. Above all, whether this year's harvest is great or small, I am acutely aware that as I labor under the sun, the master gardener is active in my life, preparing me for the day of great harvest. One future spring, I will stand in awe as I see a new garden birthed where the labor will be sweet, and the weeds will be no more.

Don't be misled. Remember that you can't ignore God and get away with it. You will always reap what you sow! Those who live only to satisfy their own sinful desires will harvest the consequences of decay and death. But those who live to please the Spirit will harvest everlasting life from the Spirit. So don't get tired of doing what is good. Don't get discouraged and give up, for we will reap a harvest of blessing at the appropriate time. Gal. 6:7-9, NLT

In His Kingdom, I will find contentment to be just His gardener... again.

"Do not let your heart be troubled; believe in God, believe also in Me. In My Father's house are many dwelling places; if it were not so, I would have told you; for I go to prepare a place for you. If I go and prepare a place for you, I will come again and receive you to Myself, that where I am, there you may be also. And you know the way where I am going." John 14:1-4; NASU

It almost went in the wastebasket, that's for sure. Usually the fun mail goes to the youngest kids; stickers, books, and animal fact cards from the zoo. The teens get college or trade school invites, cell phone offers and coupons from every store in every mall in

America. Me? I get the bills, and it's a rare day indeed that one of those doesn't grace the pile. This letter was innocuous enough; one of those with the appearance halfway between "used car sale by invitation" and "you may be a winner already." Still, with this sad influx of junk mail almost overtaking my mailbox daily, I paused in mid-pitch, and added it to the stack bearing my name.

Hours later at my desk, I opened the mail. The nearly tossed letter caused me to take a sharp inward breath when I read its contents. After forty-six years in the same home, we were being reassigned a new street number. The neighboring blocks of our street had been a jumble of addresses, with no rational sequence in the house numbering from one end to the other. Now government had swiftly acted, and we had just less than two weeks before the change would be in effect.

On one hand, it is now comforting to know that we have a logical progression of street numbers, as other people enjoy on virtually every other street in the county. It will help deliveries and emergency responses, and it all makes very good sense. But there is now an end to driving the pizza delivery guy nuts. The "Thirty Minutes or it's On Us" campaign was pulled largely in part of the vast number of freebies we collected on that easy winner.

The notifications for an address change are somewhat standard, but certain entities are not equipped to handle a reassignment of street address. I have explained our situation so often now that I have a crib sheet of useful phrases to make sure the party on the other end of the phone has truly grasped what is happening. The best phrase to date has been, "it's a change of address, but not a change of location."

I find in this little gem of living a spiritual application for my life as well. When I came to Christ, my state changed spiritually, though I am still in the same location here on earth. Many things of life do not change at all. There are still the same struggles, hardships, and trials. But through Christ, I have a completely new set of tools with which to face the day to day on the street where I live. He addresses me now as "child" and I address Him as Lord and Savior. I may still tread the streets of Brooklyn and tend the same plot of land at home, but positionally life has changed dramatically. Paul says that God "raised us from the dead along with Christ, and we are seated with Him in the heavenly realms—all because we are one with Jesus Christ" (Eph. 2:6; NLT).

I spend my time reading His word; His letter He has sent to earth. As noted in the passage that begins this story, He gives his promise that I have awaiting me a great and glorious "moving day" one day. Until that time, I will walk where He has planted me, fully aware that I am presently a citizen of his kingdom. Though not "at home," I still bear His name and strive to live for Him in the ever-changing world I occupy, for now.

Check your mail. You too could be a winner.

Then Jesus said, "Come to me, all of you who are weary and carry heavy burdens, and I will give you rest. Take my yoke upon you. Let me teach you, because I am humble and gentle at heart, and you will find rest for your souls. For my yoke is easy to bear, and the burden I give you is light." Matthew 11:28-30; NLT

Click. Pop.

It was frustrating enough to be rushing from one item to another on my "to do" list. The projects were steadily being checked off, one by one, while a stealthy hand seemed to be penciling new projects onto the end of the list. Like some Sisyphean task, my home maintenance will never be "caught up." One project done; two more added, forever. Then a casual pull of the light cord in the pantry. A brief flash, small noise, and darkness. A new task that won't even make the list: change the bulb, now.

Burned out lights are normally not that big of a challenge for me. In a home that gets congratulatory cards from the power company—"to our dear highest residential billing friend"—we go through bulbs at just slightly less a rate than bathroom tissue. In one of my rare insightful moments, I switched over to fluorescent bulbs for conservation purposes. Now granted, these are much more costly up front, but the promised energy savings was too much to resist. That, and the free travel mug with every purchase. But alas, they too are no match for the challenge of kids that need 400 watts worth of night-lights alone. No chance in a house where a toddler flicks on and off light switches a few hundred times a day for pure toddler entertainment. Not a prayer with a wife who thinks Kincade gets his painterly inspiration by driving past our house, nightly resembling a four-alarm blaze minus the smoke. Hopeless with a house full of otters-at-play who think bulbs and electricity grow on trees. Or some other colloquialism that is even more appropriate and to the point, but I can't think of it right now because I have to change the bulb. Stupid bulb. Stupid travel mug. It drips, too. But now I digress...

At the end of our summer season, I know of many who are feeling, like that bulb, completely burned out. You might think I'm a little short and testy myself after these days of work and working vacations, but rest assured, I'm normally this way. Actually, I'm a lot more level than usual. No, it's not from endless good times, or even a change in my meds—my God has been revealing to me some truths about burn out, work, leisure and rest.

I know what you're probably thinking. What could be more idyllic than the life of a pastor? Like a night watchman or the lighthouse keeper of old, isn't a ministry position simply guaranteed work in a quiet post? I mean, show up on Sunday for a couple of hours, then disappear into the wilderness for a week of contemplation, leisure, and of course, golf. Put something together from a resource book on Saturday night, and voilà!, you're good to go. Too many years ago, I received advice from a veteran minister who learned of my desire to enter the pastorate: "Young man, if you are able to do anything else that the Lord blesses, do that." So began my sobering welcome to the world of the clergy.

It could be the same in your world. People may consider your work simple, or they may not consider your work at all. But you find yourself staggering under the load, wondering when the break will come, or sitting disillusioned at the end of break time, feeling more tired than before the vacation started.

That, I believe is the grand illusion of the world. The illusion that somehow by getting away from it all and switching scenery, placid thoughts and true rest can finally come our way. I read of the ministry of Jesus and His disciples. There is quite a differing take on

151

work and rest and travel if I want to believe the Word and its account of their experience. Pressing crowds. Stolen quick, quiet moments before and after busy days. But always—always—a priority to be with men and women who needed God's touch. Jesus, finding His rest simply in being with the Father and doing His will. The disciples, finding their rest in simply being with Jesus, and going about their lives, their ministries.

Here's what I've come to know. In the passage that begins this story, Jesus tells me that I need to come to Him, and I need to stay with Him. There's no season of "with Him," followed by a season where I set Him aside for "me" time. We are joined, and only by staying joined do I have the rest in Him that I so crave, the true rest only He can provide. In plain language, I can find rest within my life, freeing me from the world's lie that I must pursue rest from my life.

The busyness is always with me. The list continues to ebb and flow. The demands of life and ministry are always before me. The bulbs are always burning out, but I don't have to. Every day can become a "day of rest," as I stay focused on my Lord and allow Him to bear my burdens. This understanding compares to having an inner light turned on in my world. What could be more restful than to start with Jesus, stay with Jesus, and simply share the light?

Keep your light on. A connection with Him guarantees it'll never burn out.

"Do not store up for yourselves treasures on earth, where moth and rust destroy, and where thieves break in and steal. But store up for yourselves treasures in heaven, where neither moth nor rust destroys, and where thieves do not break in or steal; for where your treasure is, there your heart will be also."

Matthew 6:19-21; NASU

It would have been a wonderful gift. The timing was what ruined it.

Being a 20th century guy stuck in the 21st, you can probably well imagine the struggles I face with all the emerging technologies and my lack of savvy for them. Yes, it is indeed a marvel at what can be accomplished with the microchip. Communication tools are absolutely amazing. My new computer stares at me, waiting for input from this molasses-slow dolt that has purchased it, and will forever not use it to its capacity. When it is by industry standards functionally obsolete (best guess, about six months) the dolt will continue to use it like it was some irreplaceable collectable. Why couldn't there be a weekly gathering for us retro-techno types to showcase our fossil technology? They do it with cars and nobody laughs. As I slip farther from the cutting edge and slide into the dulled, no-longer-supported abyss, my computer tech eldest son will be unable to refrain from unkind tech-remarks, and will finally shame and so hound me that I will have to give in and…here comes the fateful word…upgrade. Good grief. I still have socks from college days, and they're not in that bad a shape. Why spring for more?

Anyway, the recent gift was a result of technological upgrade. Not on my behalf, but on that of the gifter. Seems that with the bite of the digital bug, his days with the standard camera had ended—some time ago. Knowing of my occasional travel, and often punishing conditions for cameras, he located and brought his dusty old stuff over, declaring it mine. Naturally, I was thrilled for, remember, I prefer the non-techno technology. Forget full auto—I like the old manual 35mm cameras. I know all the snooty arguments against them. I endure the techno-geek scoffs. Their rolling eyes as I occasionally pause to change film. I have endured their 400-digital-shot presentations of baby's first tooth like the best of them. Why not just video, and record every waking second of junior's day? Sheeesh. Surely they can tolerate my quirks, kind of like an eccentric uncle or that guy that lives across the street who talks to himself. It's just who I am, and I am unabashedly old school.

I had barely glanced at the bag of free camera and goodies during the day, but when I got home and dinner was finished, I anxiously headed for the shop with my treasure in tow. My joy was extremely short-lived. The great nemesis of classic cameras, besides water, dirt, children, or drops onto concrete slabs, is leaving the batteries in for extended periods. Old batteries rupture, leak, and create havoc, ranging from the need for a delicate cleaning, to irreparable-at-any-price damage. You can probably connect the dots and guess what the old battery havoc had led to on this particular night. I was a bit crestfallen, as this had been a peach of a camera in its day. But my friend, holding on to it so long in disuse, had unwittingly caused it to be worthless in the end. That of great value had been reduced to that of no value. It had been treasure; now it was trash.

When he asked, I had to be truthful, and tell him about the demise of the 35. He was mortified, but I told him about it being the thought that counts. And that I've been guilty of the same oversight with the things of my world.

I was reminded of a passage of scripture (as often I am) from this life-as-it-happens observation. That scripture begins this story. How could this truth from Christ about my life and "stuff" be any clearer? Treasure on earth is flat-out fleeting. I see the sense of His words, but do I dare to get beyond mental assent to it and actually trust Him at His Word?

This theme about the right treasure should sound familiar to me, because every age has had its idols, its pursuits, its golden rings. Many of the desirable things for people a century ago are simply curiosities for museum displays today. I wouldn't remotely even want the bulk of what they clamored for—the things that consumed their days, hopes, dreams... The Word, which is denigrated but has not degraded, still points to investing my resources for God's purposes, hanging on to the stuff of this life loosely at best. Cameras are only a slight illustration.

Any "treasure" time, or talent which is hoarded will naturally degrade if left in isolation. It seems a law is at work to demonstrate to mankind that security cannot be drawn from that which is continually wearing out, flying away, or silently eroding into dust. How good to recognize the law, but better to have the giver of that law residing within, directing one's life investment.

Am I holding on to any treasure that needs to be released for the good of God's kingdom? Is that the portfolio that I am laboring to grow? Is my drive for investing in that which cannot devalue? Only

I can answer that question. Oh yes, and One Other, who indeed owns all that has been entrusted to my brief season of steward-ship, here in this snapshot we call life on earth.

Jesus, knowing that the Father had given all things into His hands, and that He had come forth from God and was going back to God, got up from supper, and laid aside His garments; and tak-ing a towel, He girded Himself. Then He poured water into the basin, and began to wash the disciples' feet and to wipe them with the towel with which He was girded. So He came to Simon Peter. He said to Him, "Lord, do You wash my feet?" Jesus answered and said to him, "What I do you do not realize now, but you will under-stand hereafter." Peter said to Him, "Never shall You wash my feet!" Jesus answered him, "If I do not wash you, you have no part with Me." Simon Peter said to Him, "Lord, then wash not only my feet, but also my hands and my head."   John 13:3-9; NASU

It's only right that I think about cleansing at this time of year. Having been raised in an upper Midwest family that knew how to keep the seasons straight, the term spring-cleaning has deep, pro-found meaning to me even after all these years. I am not too young to remember hanging huge oval rugs over the clothesline and beating the tar out of them with a wooden tennis racket (what a joy for a kid that wants to help and can have fun at the same time)! The steady progress over several days, from scrubbing walls, floors and windows to "ridding out" the amassed clutter of dark wintry months is still a routine I can recall on this fine spring day.

Once the interior work was done, we were turned loose to attack the yard, creating from the downfall branches and winter-drop oak leaves a huge burn pile, a sure source of entertainment and enter-prise for this rural boy growing up way back there in the late six-ties. Looking back, there was only one time I felt the fire depart-ment might have to be summoned, but the wind dropped as my brother and I raked feverishly, and all ended well. Though the hors-es were on edge for a few days, the pasture returned greener than ever, and we spun the story to say it turned out just like we had planned it.

I recall the cleaning routine being stepped up to an über-pitch when visiting the grandparents during this season. Truly, there never was any dirt that called grandma's house "home." It seemed strange to me that spring-cleaning was ever performed at that residence. You see, cleaning was an ongoing exercise that was never out of season to grandma. Why, the garage floor was kept in a pristine state—I could've taken my meals off it and never balked for a second. Even the basement, block walls and all, was scrubbed down in this annual ritual—such is the drive of good Germanic stock. With the grandparents now gone, I have had opportunity to study the tiny handful of tattered photos that showed the original farm and primitive house that they "started" in. Now it strikes me as less odd to recount the compulsion for cleanliness at their latter address. There had been a lot of toil to get where they were at, and it was obvious grandma was not going to relive the old, lean days when there truly was nothing to clean.

I am reminded that my drive for spring-cleaning is tempered by the fact that today our house always resembles a structure under either construction or demolition. Vacuum sweepers throw themselves from the upstairs landing in a desperate attempt to end it all before having to tackle another bedroom. Mini blinds resemble some horrid footage from hurricane-ravaged territories. The front room has taken on a murky smell and is best left dimly lit, now that long-sodden winter boots mingle with sweaty tennis shoes under the benches that grace its walls.

While the actual house may sway back and forth between "clean" and "toxic site," there is good news in knowing that the occupants are virtually germ-free, due to the increased shower use that springtime awakens in them. I have reminded them that in some cultures, bathing is rare and quick. I have asked these children of my wife to consider that perhaps too much showering could be detrimental, causing them to have weakened immune systems and a lower tolerance to common germs, simply because they are not allowing any resident bacteria to live on them, whereby they could develop "resistance." This theory, as nearly as I can surmise, has been completely dismissed by them, given the open-mouthed stares, choruses of "ew, gross" and the obligatory eye rolling that accompanied the aforementioned theatrics. They indeed have developed resistance—to me, the voice of cleansing reason.

My gracious wife rides herd over the occupants and the system, to bring cleansing order to this home. I am blessed for her efforts. Personally, my attack would involve a dumpster, a power washer and a leaf blower, so it's better for all that she manage the plant. She would concur.

As a gesture to this spring cleaning frame of mind, at least I can still venture out and build a burn pile, but even that has to be done with care and permits so as not to disrupt the neighborhood. The horses and pasture are long gone, but the woods and all the tangle of winter deadfall give me sobering pause to striking a match. I don't rake as fast as when I was young.

Yes, cleansing has gotten more complicated, as has so much of my life in the spring of this year. Oh, to be clean, again.

The cleansing of Jesus, referenced in the opening scripture of this story, reminds me of how much I need what he provides for my life. It is only because of his cleansing sacrifice for me, that I can even dare to address God as "Father." It is only through His continsual cleansing that I can find grace, forgiveness and peace as I plod along with these grimy feet of clay. His cleansing even covers the areas of my life that are yet to be revealed as needing change according to his master plan. Like Peter, I would be quick to desire the wash from head to toe, but I am often forgetful of my need.

When I look at my life and imagine I've made it upright all by myself, how much I need his cleansing.

When I find the focus is about me: my feet, my world, my concerns, my ease—how much I need his cleansing.

When I look to the sins of others and figure I'm alright, how much I need his cleansing.

When I secretly believe Jesus got a pretty good deal when he got me, how much I need his cleansing.

When I rail about insults against Christ, yet live aloof from his body while claiming to know him, how much I need his cleansing.

When my allegiance to him is as changing as these passing seasons, how much I need his cleansing.

In this season of spring-cleaning, may Jesus have access to wash every area of my life. When springtime is done, may I still find myself surrendered to his basin and towel, experiencing his continual cleansing that renders me acceptable for his service. And may I wash the feet of those I meet, encouraging them that no matter the stain, there is a cleansing that is effective to the very soul. That is why, in the spring of the year, a spotless lamb was offered on a hill outside Jerusalem.

When God performed his spring-cleaning, he did it once.

And He did it right.

Your adornment must not be merely external -- braiding the hair, and wearing gold jewelry, or putting on dresses; but let it be the hidden person of the heart, with the imperishable quality of a gentle and quiet spirit, which is precious in the sight of God.

1 Peter 3:3-4; NASU

The cycle never fails, and they are banking on it. I cave in, watch a little television, and the unease creeps into my mind. Soon I'm walking around with newly realized frustrations that I am incomplete and unfulfilled as a person. I thought I was doing OK, but corporate sponsors have knowledge that deep down, all is not well with John D. They have honed their craft at placing the evidence before me, making the pitch, and clinching the sale. After all, it is their mission to create need. This most recent ad demonstrated eyeglasses with new, stylin' designs. According to Eyeglass World, I'm missing out. I'm flat-out less than I should be. Worse, I'm less than I deserve to be. They of course have the solution for my emptiness, and it's available today at a store near me. I can be momentarily fulfilled once again and — good news — they take plastic.

That which has been is that which will be, and that which has been done is that which will be done. So there is nothing new under the sun. Is there anything of which one might say, "See this, it is new"? Already it has existed for ages which were before us. There is no remembrance of earlier things; and also of the later things which will occur, there will be for them no remembrance among those who will come later still.

Ecclesiastes 1:9-11; NASU

I would imagine that ever since the first sale of an extra apple or a spare lamb, man has been hooked with the thrill of making the deal. Centuries come and go, and the only things that change are the legal tender and the product selections. In this age of onslaught advertisement, I reflect back to a day when picking out your glasses was an easy, quick task. You had black horn rimmed, brown horn rimmed, and...you were back to black. Today, choosing the "right" frame from among hundreds takes nearly as long as wandering aisles nine, ten and eleven trying to select a box of breakfast cereal. I'm almost set to pursue this next purchase, however. The advertisement has me swayed that when I don those designer beauties, they will transform my life, improve my outlook, and make me as hip as their models parading about to the beat of a snappy jingle. Then, there was also the pull of that phrase that heaped urgency on my decision: "Come in now, and get your new look for fall!"

And you know that I'm all about a new look for fall.

I wonder where this "seasonal look" for glasses came from, but I know it's not hard to figure out in a world where demand has to be created. When I was a kid, glass frames were indestructible. I had a pair once so sturdy you could've pried rocks out of the creek with them. It's just a descriptive phrase, in case you're wondering if I ever did that. It was also common to pick out a pair that you could "grow into." Here's how that worked: Over the years, while your prescription changed, your frame stayed ruggedly in service, receiving lens after lens which in short order would be riddled with chips and scratches. For the first years, the oversized frames were akin to wearing prescription picture windows, but that would change as one ate their spinach and enjoyed recess. Finally, when your bows were visible from frame to ear when looked at straight on, it was time to go for a slightly larger frame. Some day they'll dig up my skull and think a missing link has been discovered due to the presence of pronounced bone creases incurred from said frames.

With all the fuss about the new look for fall, it's probably best for me to skip the television and focus instead on what I am "wearing" that will have some eternal value. Peter's admonition that begins this story may have been written with the fairer sex in view, but there is certainly application in his thoughts for all believers. Being people of spiritual substance in a world of skin deep values is certainly a constant theme throughout the Scriptures.

The apostle Paul also speaks of a "spiritual wardrobe" in this way: *Therefore consider the members of your earthly body as dead to immorality, impurity, passion, evil desire, and greed, which amounts to idolatry. For it is because of these things that the wrath of God will come upon the sons of disobedience, and in them you also once walked, when you were living in them. But now you also, put them all aside: anger, wrath, malice, slander, and abusive speech from your mouth. Do not lie to one another, since you laid aside the old self with its evil practices, and have put on the new self who is being renewed to a true knowledge according to the image of the One who created him—a renewal in which there is no distinction between Greek and Jew, circumcised and uncircumcised, barbarian, Scythian, slave and freeman, but Christ is all, and in all. So, as those who have been chosen of God, holy and beloved, put on a heart of compassion, kindness, humility, gentleness and patience; bearing with one another, and forgiving each other, whoever has a complaint against anyone; just as the Lord forgave you, so also should you. Beyond all these things put on love, which is the perfect bond of unity* (Colossians 3:5-14, NASU; emphases mine).

As Paul plainly states, the wardrobe of a "season" without Christ needs to be put out—disposed of—not "hung up" in my heart's closet, reserved for slipping into if I feel like going back to the old, dark days. And why would one reborn by the Spirit of God go back to the worn, rotten garment when the new has arrived? *Therefore if anyone is in Christ, he is a new creature; the old things passed away; behold, new things have come* (2 Corinthians 5:17; NASU). Along with the need for this internal attire, Paul also gives me plenty to dwell upon in his description of another spiritual outfit, this for guarding one's heart and fending off the attacks that come to all who would live for the Lord. This outfit, like all other "garments" of Christ, has no optional accessories. It is to be worn in its entirety, every day. Without it, the battle cannot be won. *Put on the full armor of God, so that you will be able to stand firm against the schemes of the devil. For our struggle is not against flesh and blood, but against the rulers, against the powers, against the world forces of this darkness, against the spiritual forces of wickedness in the heavenly places. Therefore, take up the full armor of God, so that you will be able to resist in the evil day, and having done everything, to stand firm. Stand firm therefore, HAVING GIRDED YOUR LOINS WITH TRUTH, and HAVING PUT ON THE BREASTPLATE OF RIGHTEOUSNESS, and having shod YOUR FEET WITH THE PREPARATION OF THE GOSPEL OF PEACE; in addition to all, taking up the shield of faith with which you will be able to extinguish all the flaming arrows of the evil one. And take THE HELMET OF SALVATION, and the sword of the Spirit, which is the word of God* (Ephesians 6:11-17; NASU).

Yes, fall is approaching. The kids are distraught that the back-to-school ads have again appeared, earlier than ever. Some movers and shakers that I will never meet have determined what the new styles will be. I guarantee that much of it will be a rehash of another era that has come around once again. So choose wisely when making your fashion decisions, for it all will be passé in short order. Instead, why not pour your energy into not only reading these Scriptures, but purposefully "putting them on" in each day He grants you? These will never go out of fashion.

Maybe together, we can leave off some of the hype, and not

worry quite so much about putting on the new look. I'm not going back to black horned rims, but you get the picture. Follow the styles of the world, and that will get you noticed. But resolve to put on a new outlook, and that will draw attention to the Lord, the Changeless One. I think that is a far more preferable reveal for your life, and mine. All else is simply the seasonal, passing fashion of an ad-mad world.

But hurry. This limited time offer ends soon.

"For this reason I say to you, do not be worried about your life, as to what you will eat or what you will drink; nor for your body, as to what you will put on. Is not life more than food, and the body more than clothing? Look at the birds of the air, that they do not sow, nor reap nor gather into barns, and yet your heavenly Father feeds them. Are you not worth much more than they? And who of you by being worried can add a single hour to his life? And why are you worried about clothing? Observe how the lilies of the field grow; they do not toil nor do they spin, yet I say to you that not even Solomon in all his glory clothed himself like one of these. But if God so clothes the grass of the field, which is alive today and tomorrow is thrown into the furnace, will He not much more clothe you? You of little faith! Do not worry then, saying, "What will we eat?' or "What will we drink?' or "What will we wear for clothing?' For the Gentiles eagerly seek all these things; for your heavenly Father knows that you need all these things. But seek first His kingdom and His righteousness, and all these things will be added to you. So do not worry about tomorrow; for tomorrow will care for itself. Each day has enough trouble of its own.

Matthew 6:25-34, NASU

Life is great once the cares are dealt with. Having talked about this recently in a Sunday message, I have in sad reality noted that this is not always so in my world. Worry over the little things can quickly distract me. Case in point: my residence.

Things are shaping up nicely at the Masters ranch this year. The garden is in, and a woodchuck that leaves Jurassic Park-sized footprints is edging closer to it each evening. He (she, it, whatever) is now on the bounty hunter list for quick-draw Slim (that's me).

Outside of the bounds of the rototiller, I have abandoned all hope of ever having a lawn. A lawn is a place where men in white jackets and women with parasols stroll, sipping iced tea and laughing over a stately game of croquet. I have no lawn. I have a yard. A yard is a place where the dandelions can thrive. Their chief competition, grass, has been dispatched by an army of soil-dwelling insects that has earned me accolades as home business of the year under the category, "Grub Farms of the Midwest." The dandelions do suffer somewhat from the moles, which have done a job rivaling the rototiller in their pursuit of grubus delectibulis. The moles are gaining in number and size, given that the cats won't go out alone anymore and the kids are reenacting scenes from the movie "Tremors" amid the tunnels.

The coup de grâce comes as I mount my nineteen-year-old steed, "Simplicity" and buck it out over the moonscape terrain. At one time, I referred to it as a riding mower, but given the absence of grass and the abundance of mounds of dirt, it has in effect become more of a surface planer for the yard. The deck never clogs, but it's murder on the blades. The occasional pulverizing of a toy or other abandoned article is followed by a shower of "lawn glitter" in various shades of plastic, tin or paper. This adds a festive aire to the residence, and it was even more fun before the returnable bottle bill became law.

In the front of the house, we are now being commandeered by Bucky, the new mom squirrel. Actually, Bucky is a creation of my own foolishness, as this is the third year of her feeding at our pine tree. She has determined in her own squirrel-logic that we are simple, harmless creatures that are loaded with squirrel-delighting food. Her approach now is to walk up boldly whenever a family member is present. The children often encounter her as they disembark the school bus. It is delightful for me to hear their little shrieks of joy when happening upon their aggressive wild kingdom pet. No... sorry... I guess those are just plain old shrieks of terror. Anyway, the kids aren't talking to me much and I suppose it is unnerving to have a squirrel squatting on your shoe all uninvited and everything.

We are also celebrating national potty training month by getting Sammy into that pull-up state of mind. I say "we" speaking of my wife's efforts and my encouragement of her. This is usually by phone, or an occasional visit with them inside the house. She sees it as a break from diapers and one less thing to clean a thousand times a day around the house. I see it as yet more maintenance for that last piece of the yard compendium, the drain field. I am vigilant in drain field management, as when it stops working, everything stops working. Given the fact that residing in our house is a bit like living on a major river during flood stage—you always hear running water—I am consumed by worry over these oft-neglected yard vaults—the septic tanks. Even with plans in place for lid risers and more frequent pumping, it still weighs heavy on my mind. Things are quiet and seemingly up to snuff mechanically inside and out, so I know something major is about to blow, somewhere. And then, the nagging night questions creep in, starting with, "What if...?"

The words of Jesus beginning my story remind me not to worry over the issues of life. Food. Clothing. Yards. Septic fields. This is no license to "Let go and let God" as some would advocate. I realize I am responsible to work, plan, maintain, and otherwise live up to my responsibilities. Yet the command is simple: do not worry about life as I go about my life. Instead, I am to focus on my living before Him, as a child of His Kingdom. To live rightly before Him is the weightier issue; as I keep that perspective, the other lesser things of life will find their order in my world.

I arose early this morning and had opportunity to head out hours ahead of what the normal school year allows. As I walked to the truck, I noticed a small object on the edge of the road directly across from my drive. I approached to discover it was a fledgling cardinal, a few tufts of down still clinging amid the new, ruby feathers. There was no injury; it was simply sitting on the road's edge perhaps resting from experimental flight. I carefully placed him on the lowest branch of the squirrel-diner pine and waited. A few seconds later, he responded to a parental call from the oaks across the road, and took to flight as though he'd been at it for years.

The cardinals of the air. The dandelions of the field. The Creator knows them, supplies their need, and instills within them a beautiful proverb for my life. Don't sweat the small things. Observe them, learn from them, but leave off worrying over them. God's care never ceases, and He delights to direct me to care for His priorities. Sometimes it's hard lessons about my walk with Him. In other moments, He even lets me feed His squirrels, or have a showdown with the occasional, marauding woodchuck.

———————————

Every good thing given and every perfect gift is from above, coming down from the Father of lights, with whom there is no variation or shifting shadow. In the exercise of His will He brought us forth by the word of truth, so that we would be a kind of first fruits among His creatures.   James 1:17-18; NASU

I have contended for many years now that one of the joys of home ownership is that of having a hobby that will last me well into my retirement years, if I indeed hold on that long. I admit bewilderment with those men that have time for other hobbies, such as golf or fishing or inhabiting a lawn chair. I just never seem to get it all caught up. I'm not particularly slow, and it's not like it was a hovel when we moved in, either. I believe my malady is mainly due to my wife and all of her children exceeding the warranty limitations and violating the normal operating procedures for nearly every item in and around our residence.

Some of my maintenance and repair jobs push the envelope of "homeowner sanctioned" activities, crossing that fine line into "Dangerous" or "Really Dumb" for the handy guy to attempt. For example, while unclogging a drain would rate relatively low on the "D-RD" scale, other tasks such as a total replumb of the house or rebuilding the electric dryer would rate quite highly; tasks usually reserved for the trained professional. Armed with a manual or two,

As I Was Saying . . .

I usually plow into the riskier tasks not for any sense of accomplishment or delighting in the challenge of learning a new skill. I wish it were that glorious and self-actualizing. The truth is, I'm cheap. Really cheap.

I have developed for my wife a codeword when embarking on one of my frequent tasks of that riskier "D-RD" nature. The origin of this codeword is as follows: I keep a file cabinet of important papers, as do most folks of the beaver-mentality such as myself. This attractive blue file is tab organized and complete in all of our household information, so that there will be minimal confusion if, for instance, during the trial run of the dryer rebuild, I end up inadvertently "buying the farm" so to speak. For the last several years, as I set out on a dicier task, I am prone to shout out to her, "Blue file job!" whereby she is given notice that today could end up not being so bad after all. Now, to be sure, she protests and tries to convince me that there is no humor at all in the prospect of leaving her an attractive, rich widow. Still, while tending to business at my desk, I occasionally notice that the life insurance folder has been rifled through, and there is a slight drift of her perfume lingering around the blue file zone...

To be sure, there are occasions when I come alongside a neighbor to help them out with a maintenance job or repair, but the usual stance is that of everyone taking care of their own place. After all, it is their place.

I am reminded of how the act of caring for one's home mirrors the art of caring for one's spiritual house as well. In the scripture I began this story with, James is quick to remind me that God gives generously, deliberately and perfectly that which I need to bring "success" to my life by His standard. The Word of God is indeed like that homeowner's manual; it tells me what I need to know, and guides me through the care and maintenance of that which I possess. It keeps me from destroying that which is precious to me, and is written by One who knows, not one who has an uneducated or fallible opinion about the topic at hand. Wisdom Himself delights to give me wisdom.

Life's manuals are often ignored in my home. They are misplaced easily, thrown out inadvertently, or admittedly go ignored, because after all, I can figure this out by myself. That often leads to one "D-RD" scenario after another. Similarly, I can fumble pretty badly when I leave off His manual. When that guidance is abandoned, light is left off for darkness, and it can get real dark, real fast when I go it alone.

I am struck too that as a people we Christians can get awfully vocal about calling a nation to get its collective house in order, when the real lack still seems to be in focusing on our own. If there's scanty proof of the "new life" in my life, why would anyone want what I say I have? It is also helpful for me to remember that while I often despair over my nation adrift, I cannot legislate Christ upon my world. God's Manual is for those who know him, and it should be obvious to us that Joe Nonchristian can't live for Him until Joe comes to Him. Veneer on plywood is still veneer on plywood.

I fumble pretty badly at upkeep of the family home, and often in the spiritual house as well. Nothing is perfect, but that is no excuse. God calls me not to earthly perfection, but to steady progress. True life in him has no other direction. When that sense of direction is lacking, I had best see who is heading up maintenance and prioritizing repairs. If it's not of Him, the collapse is inevitable; a "Blue file job" that could have eternal consequences, not only for me, but also for those observing my life.

"You are the light of the world. A city set on a hill cannot be hidden; nor does anyone light a lamp and put it under a basket, but on the lampstand, and it gives light to all who are in the house. Let your light shine before men in such a way that they may see your good works, and glorify your Father who is in heaven." Matthew 5:14-16; NASU

So Christian, my goal is to maintain, spiritually speaking, my own house. I'm not there yet—and truly won't perfect it in this life. But, the task is important. It's the only "house" I'll ever have. And rest assured, all my neighbors are watching…"Wonder what that Masters is up to now?"

And it's probably much the same for you.

As I Was Saying . . .

Then King Rehoboam consulted with the elders who had served his father Solomon while he was still alive, saying, "How do you counsel me to answer this people?" They spoke to him, saying, "If you will be kind to this people and please them and speak good words to them, then they will be your servants forever." But he forsook the counsel of the elders which they had given him, and consulted with the young men who grew up with him and served him.

2 Chronicles 10:6-8; NASU

The confession you all are waiting for finally surfaces in this book. Run for the scissors and frame this admission: I too am a man who does stupid things. On occasion.

I feel somewhat singled out that even this great nation has stooped to recognize and official Stupid Guy Thing Day. This festive event is an annual day to recount with levity some of the things that men do to make the world a little more unstable. I am fairly safe in my assumption to say that this day has most likely been organized by a woman. That hypothesis should in no way be misconstrued as chauvinistic or politically incorrect in any fashion on my part. It just sounds like something a woman would say. A hurtful, sexist, crude and thoughtless woman. But I will mask my pain, refrain from counterattacking, and continue my poised and dignified writing of this chapter. She probably wears a man-suit, too.

Now truly, we as males cannot shy away from the long running historically documented connection we have for engaging in brainless activity. Scripture is replete with brainless guy antics. Rehoboam, in the passage above, couldn't bear the thought of exhibiting judicious and gracious behavior in his kingship. The advice of his imbecile friends cost him the kingdom and plunged the nation into civil war. It's good to realize that cronyism still has its place in the world of politics today, with equally devastating results. This Stupid Guy Thing, shared across all generations, is the evidence that we are very slow to learn, if we learn at all.

Others noteworthy of the award for ready-shoot-aim conduct include Samson and his demise, King Saul and his demise, Solomon and his demise, the blunders of David, Noah, Moses, Abraham, Isaac, Jacob, Esau, Jonah...You get the drift, and I'm nowhere near exhausting even the Old Testament examples for that list.

The New Testament is somewhat uglier in its portrayal of Stupid Guy Things, due mainly to a steady parade of men who rejected both the Lord Jesus and those who followed Him. Many are simply unnamed amid the masses, but there are others readily listed, such as Judas, the Herods, Pilate, Alexander, Felix, Festus and Demas.

Some Stupid Guy Things are maddening, such as rejection of their God.

Other actions you just have to live and learn from, or at least fudge a little while recounting, just for the sake of the insurance adjuster. Things I am aware of a man doing, though identification of said male will forever remain obscured, include:

• Removal of yellow jackets from clothesline pole by the M-80 firecracker method. Messy but efficient, with an interesting spray pattern.

• Discovering the presence of a 220v circuit with an 110v hammer drill.

• Operation of all tools without guards or safety shields. The bigger and more dangerous the instrument, the quicker the salvation-for-the-idiot protection features disappear.

• Substituting gas for lighter fluid to jumpstart the bonfire. Theory: more gas equals quicker time to s'more production.

• Studying angles, calculating distance, and skillfully notching a looming box elder tree, to drop it with heat-seeking missile accuracy 180 degrees off course. The fall obliterated the kid's play set and a good chunk of the neighbor's pricey fence—so I am told. Stupid wind shift.

• Discerning that a lingering crawl space gas smell was indeed due to a faulty shut off valve. This revelation came hours after gas pipe replacement and some accompanying work of soldering in new water pipes. Oh, the looks on the quick-response utility team's faces—and all men, too.

• Engineering hornet nest removal employing only a five gallon bucket, a high-reach pruning hook, a blazing burning barrel, and a pair of good running shoes.

As I Was Saying . . .

• Days before hosting a major public gathering, embarking on a frenzied "surprise for the wife" landscape project with a borrowed Bobcat® articulated-steering bucket loader. This inaugural run in his operation of "heavy" equipment would result in the complete destruction of a side and rear yard, the machine itself rendered inoperable until extricated from waist-deep mud, placing the land-scaper/husband/offender in a precarious marital state for most of the remaining summer.

These unfortunate Stupid Guy Things, of which I have enumer-ated but few, all carry within them a hidden underlying current. I have thought about this in deep, reflective meditation for nearly a full minute now. It's not about us guys at all. It is because of the women in our lives that we men do such inane things. Face it. Without our women, there would be no need for indoor plumbing or kid's play equipment or flower beds or endless home improve-ments. The world would exist peaceably with the advent of one enormous pizza delivery grid. There would by necessity be the times of routine maintenance for our Stratolounger® reclining mechanisms, but that would be it.

This insight leads me to recall the original Stupid Actions Day, back in Eden, which incidentally I do believe was orchestrated by the woman, not the man.

And the man, abdicating his accountability and responsibility before God, fully chose to fill his mouth. Adam then chose to blame Eve, and the downward spin of Stupid Guy Things had begun. Thankfully, at the right time God provided the release for our stu-pidity, by placing our guilt upon his Son, who took our punishment willingly.

This life we now live may still find us engaging in various Stupid Guy Things, but at least through Him we have the present day opportunity to escape the eternity of Stupid Guy Consequences. Some Stupid Guy Things are maddening, such as rejection of their God. This rejection has been mediated and corrected. The reme-dy exists. But we need to choose the Savior for ourselves.

The Lord won't always rescue you from the day to day Stupid Guy Things, but he can begin some serious change if you'll let him lead. And He will absolutely rescue you from the wrath that is to come.

And as a Guy, and a believer, I am beginning to better understand these things.

After all, I'm not completely stoopid.

"Come, let us return to the Lord. He has torn us to pieces; now he will heal us. He has injured us; now he will bandage our wounds. In just a short time he will restore us, so that we may live in his presence. Oh, that we might know the Lord! Let us press on to know him. He will respond to us as surely as the arrival of dawn or the coming of the rains in early spring."   Hosea 6:1-3; NLT.

The rain gauge filled early on the first weekend of June. It then overflowed as a matter of course through the evening of the first Sunday of the month; that first day of the first week.

I had expected it to come.

With all of the remarkable extremes in weather happening around the nation, lately I have been prone to again offer my remark that for all our other struggles, there's still much to be thankful for about living in this drained swamp commonly referred to as South Central Michigan. Sure, I can recollect a few whopper storms and so can you, but overall the weather here is neatly predictable, and like it or not there are other seasons than "golf" to try and enjoy. Of a most predictable nature is the coming of the rains. Whether early or late in the spring, they are known for their appearances, and the life-giving refreshment they bring.

Granted, this was indeed the mother of all rains in my recent memories. My measure—the kiddie swimming pool on the deck—was a great visual tool for tallying up the inches that fell. I think I may take up phoning the area weathermen with my Little Tykes® Accu-gauge regional report. Maybe they'll even want to shoot some live remote broadcasts from my deck, and I could be in the running for something snazzy like a free mug or hat or t-shirt from the station. You have to love the weathermen—job security no matter how far off they may have been. "Whoa! Didn't see that flood coming! Now, over to Tim for sports!"

Other useful indicators that these were no slight showers included several deluged streets, two ill-timed power outages (like there's a good time for one?), and the birth of "Lake Masters." This scenic backyard floodwater, resplendent from the downed box elder trees all the way past the compost pile, is now spawning a mosquito population of biblical proportions, synchronized perfectly for Emily's upcoming graduation open house. (Note to self: be sure invites include the wording, "Bring lawn chairs, DDT, tennis racket, and your own plasma supply.")

I had made my preparations as best I knew, so that I would be ready to receive the rains. The garden and flowers were in, with the soil being worked deep so as to accept the moisture and not lose it to run off. The roof was in good shape, the eaves were clean, and the children were schooled once again about the importance of quick showers in days when the drain field borders on inundation.

Without too much poetic license, I can refer to the Word of God and also offer the knowledge that other rains are held in reserve, to be sent in a fit season. As much as God graciously sends the water the earth needs, designing and orchestrating its cycle to and from the heavens, he also delights to send the spiritual rains upon his people. God is no miser with his water; the meter is not read.

These other God-rains also require preparation. God's sown word—the good seed—cannot root and thrive in a heart's soil that is uncultivated, hardened, and weeded over. The Lord has ways of laying bare one's soul, in times of introspection, confession, repentance, and restoration to his ways alone. Pride is dug out only by great violence to self, and ambitions cloaked even in spiritual leaves must be pulled up roots and all if one is to make ready for the rains to be received. Then, and only then, the growth in his ways becomes as a flourishing branch upon a deep-rooted vine.

I tire quickly about talk of revival when there is often no desire for the painful heart preparation that must come before God's outpouring. With no anticipatory action, there can be no reception of God if and when he would visit the spiritual rains upon us. The blessing would instead like a cloud pass by, guided by an invisible breath toward more receptive soil. Or the rain could indeed fall, but simply to run off, unappropriated and unappreciated, like much of the ample rain that just fell upon the unplowed earth of field after field in this land.

I know the storehouse of blessing is there. God has it prepared, though there may be evidence of only the tiniest cloud on this present day's horizon. Open your heart. Allow the breaking to begin. The painful preparation of heart cultivation can be borne with patience as you truly anticipate and desire His coming rains.

And they will come.

They must come.

Let them fear You while the sun endures, and as long as the moon, throughout all generations. May he come down like rain upon the mown grass, like showers that water the earth.

Psalm 72:5-6; NASU

The LORD is my rock and my fortress and my deliverer, my God, my rock, in whom I take refuge; my shield and the horn of my salvation, my stronghold. God is our refuge and strength, a very present help in trouble. Therefore we will not fear, though the earth should change and though the mountains slip into the heart of the sea; Though its waters roar and foam, though the mountains quake at its swelling pride.

Psalms 18:2 and 46:1-3; NASU

On my list of unpleasant things, ranked somewhere in the near vicinity of "personal surgery" and "diaper duty," I would place the experience of encountering cobwebs across the face. As you know, manly men do not shrink from spiders; they need to keep them in sight until their helpmeet rushes in to dispatch the nasty things. When encountering the dinner-plate-sized tarantulas of Bolivia unexpectedly, even the manliest of men may tend to lose composure, but that's another story and would not lend itself to today's topic, or to preserving any shred of personal dignity I may yet possess.

As I Was Saying . . .

The cobwebs I despise are a constant companion in my walk-down crawlspace. I seem to now be the one responsible to take care of any and all business in that netherworld region of the Masters' Estate; it is my usual lonely chore to deal with the cobwebs, conduct the business that brings me there, and scream for backup that never arrives when sizeable things are seen scurrying in the shadows.

There was at one time a rule on the books, where the joyous task of sweeping the crawlspace was delegated to my wife's kids. The vision of the recruits heading off to grim underground duty was indeed a remarkable sight. They were field combat ready, decked out with safety goggles, rubber gloves, scarf, two anti-cobweb baseball hats (perched with bills opposed front and back for maximum protection), long sleeved shirts, and pant cuffs tucked strategically into long athletic socks. They shouldered the business end of the shop vac like a trusty M16 in those days.

Unfortunately, I also had the vision of a chance passerby glimpsing them, and cell phoning an overzealous agency to report that some children looked like they were being exploited into working a clandestine nuclear waste operation run by their deranged male parental unit. So I flinched, and now the cleaning is left up to me. This is why I tackle cobwebs. A lot of cobwebs.

The crawlspace is a useful space to store our garden canning bounty, file boxes of old paperwork awaiting the seven-year rule, and miscellaneous items my wife considers necessary for her world. I was sorely tempted to pass along a few of these wifely items during a recent youth group's arrival on their "trading up" road rally treasure hunt, but I thought the better of it. That, and she was home, watching me like a hawk. Drat the timing.

Anyway, my point is, the only time I ever seem to get any voluntary movement toward the crawlspace by anyone, is when the spring storms roll in. This is the season of the storm in our region, and we have by necessity adapted to the routine of occasionally needing to head to the "cellar" when a bad one is blowing through. The survival rate for nasty storms is exponentially better if you can get to a basement, and our crawlspace fits the bill close enough to merit beelining for it when needed.

Our typical routine is to catch the local TV weather, or hear the area siren, and make for the stairs. There are of course a few other rituals, as calling for cats that never show up, grabbing the extra flashlight that the youngest has made sure the batteries are stone dead in, and toting down the cell phone and weather radio so I personally have something to fiddle with. The younger kids spend their time in fervent prayer for the safety of their prodigal felines, the older kids sit on the benches and scan the dim floor and walls for signs of arachnids, and Mom obsesses about the actual storm, getting panicky-vocal about how long the power is going to be out this time. Me, I'm trying to tune in weather from seven feet underground on a radio that can't get reception of the closest station from the peak of our roof on a clear day. I also enjoy reassuring the kids that in a worst-case scenario, we can live down here for weeks, what with the sump pump pit, the mild temperature, and all the pickles and tomatoes we have preserved on the shelves. As I drift into a lighthearted commentary about the protein value of certain cellar creatures, I am abruptly cut off by my first wife, so I go back to frustrated radio fiddling. Nobody appreciates humor in the crawlspace. With this audience, it's tough enough up on the main floor.

Dear brothers and sisters, when troubles come your way, consider it an opportunity for great joy. For you know that when your faith is tested, your endurance has a chance to grow. So let it grow, for when your endurance is fully developed, you will be perfect and complete, needing nothing. James 1:2-4; NLT

It's obvious that the storms of our state usually come with warning, and are typically seasonal in nature. The trouble-storms that James writes about in the verses above come out of nowhere, and remain constant throughout life. A Christ follower doesn't walk around picking fights and persecutions; James affirms that these are little more than the normal feature of a world not enamored with Jesus or those who love him. It is a truth only experienced firsthand. As faith and trust are exercised in the "little" storms of life, the "cellar" within the heart is prepared and stocked; provision for the inevitable "big blows" that are sure to come out of a seeming blue sky. When I am tested, God is true to show himself as my refuge, fortress and rock, as his word amplifies and familiarity proves.

We have learned a lot about weathering the storms of the seasons here in this Midwest place we call home. Our preparations are a little more refined, our routines a little less chaotic, and our rolling with the inconvenience a little more relaxed. There is always a tension, and occasionally we suffer damage or a loss from the blow. Still, we Midwesterners are a resilient lot, and we will always bounce back.

I pray the resilience is also to be found in the spiritual storms that rake my days. After all, the shelter is provided, the safety is ensured, and the companionship is guaranteed. I will never be abandoned in the storm, or herded into a doomed shelter. *But the salvation of the righteous is from the LORD; he is their strength in time of trouble* (Psalm 37:39; NASU).

Fittingly, this heart-cellar in the Lord has no hint of cobwebs, due to its increased use. His shelter feels more comfortable with each passing season, and has begun, finally, to take on the unmistakable familiarity of home. Real, safe, secure home.

But as for me, I shall sing of Your strength; yes, I shall joyfully sing of Your lovingkindness in the morning, for You have been my stronghold and a refuge in the day of my distress. O my strength, I will sing praises to You; for God is my stronghold, the God who shows me lovingkindness. Psalm 59:16-17; NASU

Who may worship in your sanctuary, LORD? Who may enter your presence on your holy hill? Those who lead blameless lives and do what is right, speaking the truth from sincere hearts. Psalm 15:1-2, NLT

I have a compartment for everything. From the smallest nuts and bolts to the larger items necessary to maintain the Masters' estate, every object has a place. Now granted, it may take me a day or two to actually find the item I need, but it is tucked away in neat fashion…somewhere. I have perfected the art of tracking down a needed item from my shop. I go out and buy what I need, use it as needed, and then walk into the shop. The first shelf, drawer or cupboard I then search will reveal the exact item I just purchased and used. Works like a charm, every time.

One can never have too many compartments for life's collections. I get a bit flustered to see how many compartments are disappearing from my world. In my youth, my '69 Bonneville was actually a compartment system on wheels. The trunk alone could hold three sets of golf clubs, a full sized spare, tools enough for a roadside rebuild, groceries for a week, and a rigid plastic blue kiddy swimming pool. The glove box—remember those?—was large enough for an atlas, three changes of clothes and Chilton's repair manual, hard cover. With today's models, you might get sixteen cup holders and a doughnut spare mounted somewhere underneath. I don't get it.

Isaac, at ten years old, is following nicely in his balding parental figures' lumbering footsteps. That's me. The other parental figure has thick, beautiful hair and tiny poised footsteps. And reads. Isaac has been collecting items for his camping/fishing/backpacking/outdoorsy woodsmanship/he-man/chop something down/build a fire/aarrgh we're-all-men-here interests for some time now. And, as he has learned, this involves lots of compartments.

His tackle box, when opened on the shore of a favorite fishing hole, has a look reminiscent of beachfront condos I've seen on the Florida coast. It has several levels that tower over the waterfront, each floor a home to numerous lures, bobbers and sure-fire gadgets for the serious bass man. I have become intimately acquainted with the contents of each compartment, as I had the sad misfortune of picking up the box without the lids being latched. Needless to say, I didn't get much fishing done that day as I had a hands and knees assignment that pretty much consumed my morning. There were the occasional pauses to bait his hook, unhook a fish, undo snags and replace lures every two minutes, but outside of that, it was pretty much arranging compartments the rest of the time. Of course trying to concentrate and get everything in the right spot is a little harder when you have a lure the size of a hummingbird

As I Was Saying . . .

whipping past your ear at approximately 45 miles per hour. That's on both the windup and the release, virtually a split second apart but on totally different trajectories with your head as the common passing point.

I'm reminded of how easy it is for me to slip into thinking about my life as I do my shop or my vehicle or a tackle box: full of compartments. How natural it is to try and divide out my days and my roles into compartmented units. There's the Sunday "pastor" compartment, the home "parent" compartment, the relational "spouse" compartment, the community "citizen" compartment... Certainly, I have various duties, responsibilities and expectations upon me, as does everyone. Yet the caution I find in the word of scripture opening this story is a good check for my soul. The psalm writer uses a great term to describe one who can walk in God's presence. The word he uses is blameless. The word speaks of one who is living in fullness, completeness, soundness, openness, or transparency. Another suitable word in our language for this Hebrew gem is integrity. That's the root of our word integer: a whole number, not a fraction.

God desires me to be whole before Him, in all things, at all times. I cannot partition off a section of my life where I go it on my own. I cannot enjoy His fullest blessing if I have a compartment-a fraction- that is filled with my living apart from Him. Anywhere that God does not figure in the course of my day and the path of my heart, I have created a compartment. And these compartments must be removed.

I appreciate organization, and I know I have a way to go in my life. Just getting my world organized is a constant project. Compartments are wonderful tools for shops, cars, and tackle boxes. New surprises await me every time I explore a compartment long forgotten. The inspection of my heart likewise is ongoing and probing. Compartments I regularly find there are harder to empty, but I must be compartment-free, whole and open if I desire to be wholly filled by Him.

Bread by the sweat of your face

O Lord my God, you have performed many wonders for us. Your plans for us are too numerous to list. You have no equal. If I tried to recite all your wonderful deeds, I would never come to the end of them.

Psalm 40:5, NLT

Somewhere on earth, a forest has been planted to replace the one felled and processed for the tiny Post-it® notes that now flag my world. I admit openly that my addiction to the 3M brand 1.5" x 2" sticky note is (notably) out of control. I am, in the final retrospection, a list junkie.

It started innocently enough, the product of my work experiences and the need to be answerable for tiny, trivial-yet-essential details of production. Making lists soon grew from a work-based activity to overshadow even my home life and downtime planning. Soon I seemed to have a list for everything. Everything.

I had never thought of myself as a type-A, wired and ready-to-go-off kind of guy. I'm more comfortable in jeans than suits. I actually like PBS and don't normally talk to the television during shows. I enjoy my beaver den studies and like to think of myself as easy-going, flexible and relaxed in a Red Green-meets-Fabio sort of way. My wife uses similar descriptors of me, but also works in other words like "delusional" and "warped." But back to my story. This list thing really has me spooked.

Oh, there were warning signs. The craving to write out menus and shopping lists weeks in advance. The urge to plan a year's worth of worship services on paper. The drive to write out page after page of detail over trips, training, packing, instruction, and things to do. Even home improvement projects would fill a notebook before any actual work started. There were even the periphery issues of an addiction to French roast with double shots, and frequent dark chocolate indulgences. Then came the day I started trying out larger sizes of sticky notes, lingering in the office store to purchase color-keyed journals for task-specific lists. Still, I was in denial. I never really let it sink in, until this morning.

On this sunrise in early summer, the air smelt clean and cool. I sat and read with the back door open, enjoying the calm after the rain. I had a notebook and pen in hand along with my Bible, as is my normal custom. This quiet time is only available at these hours in this busy house; a time for devotional reading and writing, a delicate reflective moment that will immediately vaporize upon the sound of myriad feet in the hall looking for breakfast, open bathrooms, and most importantly, Mom. Still today, I was faced with a steady interruption of my own thoughts over what to do with my upcoming vacation. I found my writing suddenly drifting from thoughts of God to lists of to-do's.

This vacation carries a work-at-home theme with it. I take home improvement and maintenance projects very seriously, as the homeowner is a good friend of mine and I have a vested interest in her well being and cheerful state of mind. It wasn't always this way. My youthful failures in this area of nest-maintenance have yielded for me two very valuable, evaluated lessons. First, her happiness has a great impact on my happiness. Secondly, the former garage (which is now my workshop) is at best a three-season room, and decidedly not the place for extended overnight stays. These two lessons are a great incentive for me.

And so I scribbled out yet another list of vacation chores, actually looking forward to getting finished up on some long-standing projects. As I paused, figuring I had gotten it all on paper, I nearly came out of my chair as there issued a mighty crash from our back yard. A box elder tree, the nemesis of my attempts for order at the woods' edge, had given way under the immense soaking of these past days' storms. Now the yard was buried under its carcass. Irony. Sheer irony. I hastily scribbled another line to the list at hand: clean up stupid tree.

I went back to distracted reading from God's Word, and there I encountered the text that begins my story. A psalm from King David, a man who knew the importance of lists. He probably had a whole department of scribes and list-keepers. After all, the man wasn't a preacher in a small town—he was a king, for crying out loud.

And David's Spirit-inspired word brought me back to the reality I need. How much time do I spend listing out the benefits of knowing my God and living in His ways? How much of today did I blunder through, failing to recognize His hand on my life? Is this a list I choose to write, or is there no time for it in a world that I need to manage through scraps of yellow paper and scribbled lines?

Most of the lists I scramble to create have limited use and life-times. They are usually project or time-sensitive, then tossed away. The listing of God's influence and blessing in my life, whether on paper or internalized, is a catalog that will never be outmoded or exhausted. Am I taking time daily to compose and rehearse that list? If not, perhaps I need to find a new priority for the list that matters.

I'm glad the Lord has pointed this out to me today. And I'm happy to have this opportunity to share my story with you. My hope is that it gives the encouragement you need to gain perspective for your day.

Then too, I'm glad I can cross off "write today" from this list I've been carrying…

He gives snow like wool; He scatters the frost like ashes. He casts forth His ice as fragments; who can stand before His cold?
Psalm 147:16-17; NASU

A Short Primer for Family Survival When the Lights Go Out
Or,
How to Step Up Mental Erosion in Manly Men

I often speak of dependence upon the Lord alone. A couple of days and nights off the power grid betrays my many words. It has been a revealing exposure of just how reliant I am on the things of this earth, especially those wired objects that grace the castle of King John. As we plunged into darkness early Monday morning, I began a careful journal of observations and actions to help others who may find themselves in similar "no power" days.

1. Have your generator "good to go." By this, I mean that it should take you a good long time to go and find where you stored it. Conducting a frenzied search for your generator in freezing, pitch-black darkness, using your toddler's "Blue's Clues" AAA bat-

tery flashlight with a beam the intensity of one lit match should at least keep you warm for a while. Mine was neatly tucked away out in the barn. I extracted it from behind the power mower, wheelbarrow, rototiller, summer toy collection, and several bags of quick mix concrete that aren't the same since they got damp last fall. The term "generator" is multi-faceted. Generate electricity later; generate a migraine now.

2. Keep a big supply of gasoline on hand. The older, larger, and more unwieldy the gas can, the more fun it is to try and top off a generator that features a fill spout with the diameter of a sparrow's throat. It is best to use really old gasoline. The incessant running from house to generator to pull start the stalled-again engine will keep you toasty warm, for sure. The family, strongly resembling Nordic indigents in their multilayer wardrobe of hats, coats, gloves, comforters and blankets, will stare vacantly out at you through darkened windows, envying your brow of sweat and swarthy limp as Sparky roars to life for the eighty-third time today. They may be mumbling other things, but they're really just jealous. And don't worry about what they may or may not be saying. Your hearing won't be recovering anytime soon. Good thing you never replaced Sparky's muffler when it blew off during the historic "big backfire" of '97.

3. For light entertainment, tell the kids there'll be school. Go ahead, they have it coming. Mess with their heads; you know they do it to you all the time. Tell them the new school Health and Wellness Guideline 807f.3 demands attendance in all conditions except winged-monkey attacks. If they scoff, use the phrase that'll get 'em studying and loading their packs: "You don't want a wimpy unexcused absence going on your permanent record, do you?"

4. Realize that the response of teen females to the electricity going out is an immediate need to shower. It should be of no surprise to you; the teen female response to happy, angry, sad, tired, bored, hungry, calm, anxious or any other emotion or situation is always, "must shower...now." Keep your jogging shoes on and don't forget

to stretch that pulling arm, because the generator will have to be reset and restarted like crazy as the showers will be followed by extended times of consolation with every girl's best friend: Max Watts, Blow Dryer. While manning the pull starter, dream about a cushy hotel room with heat, cable and room service. You could pack it in and go, but the nearest room now available is somewhere on the outskirts of New Delhi. Still, it won't sound so far away by tomorrow night. Too bad, you never got the furnace set up to run off the generator. Tell the girls you need to do some bathroom maintenance, and while you're enjoying a few minutes with Max thawing out your frozen toes, make a few notes with sketches about these needed electrical upgrades.

5. The thrill that children experience when their school name scrolls across a generator-powered television screen is short lived for certain types of power outages. The outage that is accompanied by perilous roads, downed wires, and warnings from the constable to stay in or be ticketed, is not well received by homebound schoolchildren. The thought of being in a dark, cold, entertainment-devoid house, incarcerated with each other and edgy parental figures while condemned to miss a free day of gadding about, will have everyone reaching for the bottle of Nervine. To reduce stress and reconnect the family, why not set up a game that everyone enjoys? We recommend the homespun version of a popular amusement, where everyone draws something and others try to guess what it is. Setting up for the game and getting everyone into the same room can take a while, but once we were settled in, our bonding over lighthearted competition and zany humor lasted almost a whopping three minutes. Not to be outdone, several family members invented another game, "irritate the five year old." Put away the egg timer, for this game can last indefinitely, morphing into "irritate the teen," "irritate the mom," and the granddaddy of them all, "send dad into orbit." As an unanticipated cold weather bonus, this pastime will raise your blood pressure to the point where your face is warm and tingly.

6. Take the opportunity God has given you to clean out your fridge.

My recommendation for speed cataloguing your items runs to only four simple categories: Safe, Pretty Safe, Let the Kids Try It, and Definitely Toss. As you sort and move items to a cold area for safe-keeping (a good cold area is at this point most anywhere outside the fridge) use your time to plan out the menu for today's hearty meals. Remember, contrary to the ranting of celebrity chefs, any food can be prepared in a fry pan over a single propane burner. Corn dogs. Chicken patties. Waffles. Leftover spaghetti. Sure, it will smoke a little. It may well be completely unrecognizable on the plate. Yes, it will have a bit of "off" flavor attached to it, but it can be done. It must be done.

7. Steel your resolve to endure the question, "When is the power coming back on?" This will be asked continuously from the moment the last bulb flickers until every light is once again blazing in incandescent glory. In its contribution to forehead vein popping and left-eye twitching, this question leaves the traditional child-whine, "Are we there yet?" in the dust. Especially unnerving is when you start asking it, too.

Take a deep breath. Go out and stand in your shop for a while. Tend your generator. Experiment with different coffee strengths. This too will pass, and you will be the better for the learning experience.

****

I sat and thought, there in the dark. Reading by candlelight and bundled against this strange crisp air at my desk, I thought of how little I have known of being powerless. Not just the abundance of heat, and food, and working light, but also the power I have enjoyed by living in a land where personal freedom has kept me from so many powerless situations. I've not faced the struggles that many others have.

Often I have been hungry and thirsty and have gone without food. Often I have shivered with cold, without enough clothing to keep me warm.   2 Corinthians 11:27; NLT

The latest trial I've experienced might be meaningful to me, but it pales when I reflect on what others have faced and will face. I have the freedom to worship, or not. The freedom to pursue God, or not. The freedom to follow the Lord of Light. Or not.

"While the earth remains, seedtime and harvest, and cold and heat, and summer and winter, and day and night shall not cease."
Genesis 8:22; NASU

The Lord brings the earth's seasons, as well as these seasons of my life. I see clearly on this frosty evening, that my foundation in him must endure no matter what the winds may bring my way. What does tomorrow hold, and how will I respond? I trust that I will be true to Him, and endure—better, triumph—in whatever befalls. But as always, I only have today, and it is enough to walk with him through the trials that have come.

I may be a poor and miserable creature without my electricity, but that doesn't hold a candle to how wretched and undone I'd be without my God.

Then, at his command, it all melts. He sends his winds, and the ice thaws.
Psalm 147:18; NLT

——————————————

Don't store up treasures here on earth, where they can be eaten by moths and get rusty, and where thieves break in and steal. Store your treasures in heaven, where they will never become moth-eaten or rusty and where they will be safe from thieves. Wherever your treasure is, there your heart and thoughts will be also.
Matt. 6:19-21, NLT

My retirement years are being funded, one genuine collectible at a time.

On the village square, Jerry over at our local antiques dealer is seeing to my secure future by the sale of certain treasures I've been uncovering in my garage and barn. Sales have peaked, I've run out of classy items, and at the rate the big checks are accruing, I anticipate retirement around the year 2120, give or take a decade. The core problem, as he subtly points out, is that the things I believe should be hot in the antique market are in sad reality not desirable to his savvy buyers: a broken hand plane, part of a brace and bit, most of a dresser, something rusty that looks old. I think the subtle term he uses is "junk." Frustrated that I can't raise the bar for the public's tastes in antiquities and objets d'art, I am grudgingly swallowing the bitter pill.

He may have the eye and experience to know antiques, but I have been taken a few times. Treasures abound, but so do fakes. From currency to King Louis, this world is awash in counterfeits unscrupulous people are hawking as the genuine article. I'm still smarting from the ashtray incident.

Years ago we bought the item from Al, one of the street "vendors" who wandered our city in need of cash. He often graced dad's shop, especially in colder weather. The ashtray was antique, he had told us. Pedestaled and refined, a fitting gem for our office decor. We didn't need an ashtray, but he needed a donation, so Al collected. Some hours later, we took a minute to examine our "treasure." I had no idea 19th century plastic was so crude and flimsy. I'd no previous knowledge that China had been capable of extrusion production way back then. The wing nut that crowned it was decidedly not refined, but Al was long gone. So was our 5 bucks.

The televised antique appraisal shows have also done their part to fuel my treasure quests, and summarily dash my hopes. Occasionally watching PBS, which my wife and her children say stands for "Pretty Boring Show," I'll see people stand moon-eyed as they learn the object they just bought at a garage sale (after haggling the price down from three bucks to a quarter) is worth more than my neighborhood's combined assets. If I were they, you could forget about provenance and the "estimated value for insurance purposes." Heck, show me a buyer, right now. In front of the tube, my mind races as I blurt out, "Hey hon, haven't we got one of them?"

Hon's retort is, "Well, we did, but you pitched it last week."

Her reference was to my newly found freedom to let some possessions go, period. I was struck with that urge a few days back, as I had finally reached the breaking point in the stuff/space continuum. To the roadside by the driveway I dragged load after load, and then in a moment of liberty and abandon I fashioned a sign from cardboard, marker, screw gun and stake: "Hi. We're FREE!" The resultant traffic jam was something to behold, and in all seriousness (for as a pastor I never joke), the pile was foisted off—err, taken away—in ten minutes, tops. People were incredulous. A few folks still offered crumpled bills to me, too amazed to think I'd just be giving away all those high quality items.

Sure, things are nice, and who doesn't enjoy some "stuff?" I've found several items to add to my collection by browsing at the shops, and I'm sure there'll be more acquisitions to come. Still, it's good for me to remember that there are very few valuable—priceless—things that are in my life. One day when I lay down stuff—and much or little, I'll lay it all down—the most valuable thing will remain. That's the thing I need to focus on in my life, now. This Word that I learn and teach and endeavor to practice confirms that value, shaping my life and preparing me for the life to come.

You too may desire to experience freedom by releasing your grip on things that will one day be laid down. The Word I believe in is a great place for you to start, because it relates that we, not stuff, are what our Creator values.

You may also need a "Hi. We're FREE!" sign if you want to do it right. I have one, sturdy and proven, and I can let it go for you my friend, at a good price of say, three bucks. Hey, don't walk away...make me an offer!

Besides, it's going toward my retirement.

Yes, I am the vine; you are the branches. Those who remain in me, and I in them, will produce much fruit. For apart from me you can do nothing.   John 15:5, NLT

As a full blooded, full-bodied male of the commonest variety, I have several traits that are beyond my understanding. I quickly add

As I Was Saying . . .

that my wife voices a hearty "Amen" at this opening line, but as I repeatedly tell her on a daily basis, "You really do love me, y'know."

Personal oddities I cannot explain make up a familiar male pattern list. I have a magnetic field that attracts stains to my clothing. My hair is never right. I get excited and slightly sweaty whenever 5W30 is on sale. I pause and salute when encountering green and yellow farm machinery. I languish in a world that refuses to make pants that actually fit. I am drawn in a strange moth-flame dynamic to tools, especially tools that require power.

My escapades with power tools are truly tales of the miraculous; odds defying and not for the fainthearted. The first memorable experiment involved my unwitting connection of a power drill to a 220-volt circuit in the crawlspace. And people say it's impossible to make a quality built tool explode. As an aside, I still maintain that eyebrows are highly overrated. I functioned fine without mine all through the grow-back stage.

Then, there also was the oops that I now refer to as "the table saw incident."

Now I know, a lot of guys have the good stuff in their home shop. You know, Craftsman, Porter Cable, Delta, Bosch, Makita...My budget didn't allow for too elaborate a nameplate for a table saw. The salesman steered me over to a more fiscally conservative model, the same type he himself proudly owned, he told me. I should've known something was up there on the showroom floor by the way Mr. Commission was keeping one hand hidden in his pocket. That and the limp... Soon I was at home, setting up my very own Plywood Launcher XP—XP standing for eXtreme Pain.

There were several pieces of the PLXP that seemed at the time to be elaborate packing materials, or a mysterious bonus item, like on the TV infomercials where you get a 400-piece knife set if you call "right now" to order the FlabMaster 2000. Later, I would come to realize that these "extras" were instead the safety shields and anti-kickback devices that enable guys like me to walk out of their shops and enjoy dinner with all their extremities intact.

The events surrounding the actual recoil and impact of the plywood sheet with my midsection are a bit blurry today. It's probably because I was deprived of oxygen for let's say 20 minutes as I groaned and rolled around on the shop floor. Looking back, I'm glad I had on a down vest, and it was useful to have an abdomen that was, to delicately phrase it, well padded. The resultant bruising was a palette of colors that Van Gogh would've loved to explore. Hues changed over the days that followed, and I did finish my woodworking project, albeit with several "extras" carefully installed on my powered marvel. The sudden twitch and wide-eyed stare that come over me whenever I now switch on the saw, I consider as my actual bonus items.

Last month, the neighbors had a bit of excitement when the power line overhead snapped and fell onto their front lawn. I wandered over, another male trait being "walk toward emergency lights and situations that look incredibly dangerous." The lawn was scorched in a perfect path traced by the arcing line. The bluish shower of sparks was spellbinding to watch: this was power, raw and temporarily untamed. I stood transfixed, watching as the line crew and responders did their job. Besides, there was nothing I could do at my place since our power had also been cut off through this severed line.

This whole quest for power and connectedness to it brings my opening scripture passage to life. I need power to function, and my life in Him is sustained only by staying in contact with the one who supplies this power. If I am disconnected, there is no power, no productivity, no light, nothing. Abiding in Christ is not a switch on, switch off option for my life. Severed lines, like severed branches, are not easily put back in service. Deadness occurs rapidly when the cut is made.

Many times in my world, I find myself craving more tools, more machinery. Perhaps my focus should be instead on seeking more power for my life, not more toys to plug in. It's the same in the world of my spirit. I don't need more diversions. I need to focus on keeping a good connection with my Lord, and using the outlets he gives me for the release of his power through my life. There is probably a good lesson for the church—the body of Christ—in that notion, but I'm meddling now.

I'm gaining a healthy respect for power. It has its uses and abuses to learn from. One thing I know for sure: when I'm not connected, the collection of tools, great or small, will sit useless in the dark. This has great spiritual application for my life. It may be the line that needs connecting in your life as well.

Look here, you who say, "Today or tomorrow we are going to a certain town and will stay there a year. We will do business there and make a profit." How do you know what your life will be like tomorrow? Your life is like the morning fog—it's here a little while, then it's gone. What you ought to say is, "If the Lord wants us to, we will live and do this or that." Otherwise you are boasting about your own plans, and all such boasting is evil. James 4:13-16; NLT

Labor Day is gone. Don't look now, but your calendar is out of sync. This has occurred because while you were enjoying the lazy days of August, eating sweet corn, lounging lakeside and ruining your arches shuffling around in those flip-flops, September stole up on you. And now, the march downward begins. We are at that great dividing line on our calendars that separates the fun of summer from reality's slap that we are returning to the world of school, fall and a long spell until another well-needed break. Children will now appear, catatonic-like at bus stops. Pool toys will be supplanted by leaf rakes and furnace repairmen. Air conditioners will receive their requisite blue poly tarp covers, and you may find yourself bringing out a few extra covers for yourself at night. The lights will be needed a bit earlier each evening, and later each morning. Like every other post-Labor Day season, our journey into the fall has begun. We may not like it. It would not be our first choice. But it is inevitable, and at least out here in Michigan, you have to roll with the calendar; roll with the seasons.

There is a familiar cycle in September. There is an expectancy that things will go as they have in seasons past. Still, the lasting pall of 9-11, now denoted by our observance of Patriot's Day, has a way of reminding us that change, and not always welcome change, is part of this life we are now calling the new normal. Since that day when the towers fell, we have been more acutely aware that our preparation is essential to stave off other coming aggressions. It was a strange advance into our secure bubble here in North America, but certainly not a foreign experience to this planet. History is a record of unexpected aggressions, and it is a natural move of self-preservation to do what has to be done to secure one's family, nation and world. The exchange of aggressions has taken many forms throughout the ages, from open wars to terrorist plots, secret assassinations to embargoes and sanctions. Read all about it in your news today, or in several texts including one called The Bible. Maybe the new normal isn't so new after all. People have had to flex with an insecure world since the invention of the pointy stick and hand-held rock. Towers coming down, and man trying to come up with meaning from such a catastrophe, are likewise nothing new. Jesus relates such an incident from His time in Luke's Gospel, Chapter thirteen, verses one through five.

The U.S. Department of Homeland Security has also taken the month of September and turning it into National Preparedness Month. This is the month for me to stockpile my goods and draw up my emergency plans for the "big one." My mind races as to what sort of depot I will be constructing to squirrel away the goods necessary to support my wife and the kids for even a few weeks. The cereal alone will occupy a buried semi trailer; perhaps there is a used Super Dome somewhere cheap that I could have hauled in for the paper goods area? I could use reverse psychology and simply get a pallet or two of MRE's; chipped beef or something in grey gravy as the main entrée. That way, "Hey, I offered 'em food, but they didn't want any." On second thought, if I had to be bunkered down with that grumbling brood, I would probably be on the surface with a white flag in a matter of hours. I know when I'm beat. You see, the heart of the problem is, I don't know where the "big one" will be, or what form it will take. Couple that with the dilemma of what to stock, where to put it, expiration dates on all my cache, and the need to occasionally leave my bunker for let's say work or the shower, and I'm in a real quandary.

Yet I realize that there is nothing wrong with preparedness. No one should be caught flat-footed if the power grid goes down, the snow piles up, or terrorists run out into the streets. The point becomes one of balance for me, especially in light of God's Word that I have begun this story with. "Being prepared" sells many things, but as a follower of the God who has created all, will judge all, and has my eternity in view, I must allow God to be God, even as I do my work to which He has called me. He has placed a brain in my head, and I must use it to plan for my days. He cautions me not to act as if I will live on earth forever, nor stockpile goods for my own selfish isolation, as if I lived apart from Him (Lk.12:13-21). He also shows me it is foolish to live in isolation. I am to care for those He entrusts to me; wife, children, parents, relatives, church family, community, world. There is no luxury for the believer to be consumed with ease, removed in self-preservation, and existing with a goal to live large and die with stockpiles. It just doesn't fit with the preparation for life to come.

How would I envision National Preparedness Month for the Christian? Here are some maxims I would choose to follow:

Live each day preparing for eternity. Dig into God's Word.

Admit my total dependency upon Him for the day He has given me.

Do anonymous, random acts of kindness every day.

Pray more. The more I have to do, the more I would pray.

Comprehend that prayer is not a substitute for action.

Get involved with my community. Volunteer to give a child a future.

Sacrifice for things bigger than my days.

Do the best of things in the toughest of times.

Have vision for the world beyond my days.

Remove "I," "Me," and "My" from all conversation for one day.

Learn about the other person's hopes, dreams, fears and needs. Act upon what I learn.

Walk knowing that every day is the Lord's Day.

Have confidence that my preparation for all things comes from knowing Him.

September. Patriot Day. National Preparedness Month. Labor Day. All now serve as reminders to prepare for what may lie ahead. For some, preparation means school supplies. For others, preparation entails stocking up on duct tape, drinking water and ammo. While physical preparedness has its merits, I am reminded that true preparation for life's challenges should be primarily an issue of the heart. Once the "big questions" of life, death, purpose and "what next" are answered, then a person is truly prepared to live as our Creator intended: walking with Him, serving others, championing truth, and doing battle against the evil that for a season is still loosed upon the world.

Unless the LORD builds a house, the work of the builders is wasted. Unless the LORD protects a city, guarding it with sentries will do no good. It is useless for you to work so hard from early morning until late at night, anxiously working for food to eat; for God gives rest to his loved ones.   Psalm 127:1-2; NLT

Labor Day is gone; get up from your rest, and change your calendar. It's time to get back to the work God has set before you. The time is short; there's still much that needs to be prepared.

Life's summer is once again gone.

And like September, eternity steals up ever so quickly.

Have you entered the storehouses of the snow…?
Job 38:22a; NASU

A Guy's Guide to Snow Days and Mental Wellness

Snow days will often occur when the children have already been home for several days on "winter break" from school. Plan accordingly and resolve that, no matter what, you must leave the house and go somewhere…anywhere. A beaver being trapped at home with the otter gang cannot be a scene that ends well. Remember Nicholson in The Shining, man, and get a move on for the door. I don't care if you need to dig out with your hands.

Older youth, on break from say, college, have totally forgotten the concept of voluntary manual labor and will be somewhat startled if you suggest they at least work at snow removal around their personal vehicle. Grin and bear it, and continue your work at night on drawing up plans for that one bedroom retirement bungalow. Actually, they won't be too startled because that would require being awake and alert enough to mentally process your request in the first place.

Be sure to have the snow blower ready to go. This includes such things as flat or severely underinflated tires, last years' gas still resident in the fuel system, misplacement of the electric start plug-in cord, oil the color and consistency of blackstrap molasses, and one auger shear pin that was never replaced the last time you used it maybe two or three snowstorms ago. By the time you get it running, hey, spring might be here!

Given the complexity of our winter weather, and the probability that the weatherman is making wild speculations with the forecast anyway, it's always a good idea to have your winter outerwear ready for donning at one contained spot, sort of like firemen and their profession except without all the skill and training and focus and expertise and all that stuff. It is also good to remember that if you want to put on dry items, it's best to have your stuff squirreled away in a locked indoor wardrobe, or the outdoor shop to which you alone hold the key. I have no such luxury as a private indoor wardrobe, though once I had a shoebox under the bed that was all mine for about three days. Over the years, my gear-at-the-ready has often been reduced to either a heap in a closet, or a pile by a door. But now, by laying claim to man-land, my old garage-now-shop, I have a place to keep my gear, reminiscent of that great superhero grotto, The Batcave. The downside is that my winter wear, stored in the unheated shop, tends to retain its numbing coldness due to its superb insulating qualities, for just about as long as it takes me to dig out from the latest snowfall. The upside is that I start out dry, knocking out a huge contributing factor to hypothermia; that is, until the sweat starts to pour off me like a fat boy.

Above all, boots are the one thing you don't want to leave laying around. It is a scientifically proven phenomenon that any child from walking age up will wear your boots outside after they have soaked their own, even if yours are so huge on them it means dragging them sideways through the drifts or half-submerging them in icy puddles. You will not discover this until slipping them on and promptly soaking your only good pair of insulated socks. Mom's old trick, plastic bread bags slipped over the socks, will at this point only help slightly. The resultant clammy-cold foot condition, besides being incredibly unpleasant to work with, usually requires several podiatric visits and a ten-week course of odd smelling cream to abate.

Get up early. Real early. Manly men have drunk their strong black coffee and wedged themselves in their Nordic wear by at least 4:30 am. This ensures a good start to snow removal duty, and having good position in the driveway for when the snow truck goes by. You want to have a good portion of the drive done, so you can nod, raise a hand (manly men don't actually wave, mind you) and thereby experience the man-bond with the plow's driver. You might also experience other man-emotions, triggered in part by the fact that once he's passed, his blade has added about forty-five minutes' worth of work to clearing out the head of the driveway. Again. Thanks a lot, buddy.

Along with the early rise, don't forget that your testosterone rush will also fuel a desire to go over and get the neighbors rescued as well. Nothing says manly-man quite as well as coming to the aid of others. Try to keep an eye out especially near their doorways, as I have personally noted that objects are sometimes chucked at me from these darkened portals as I blow past them. I figure it's just their way of trying to get my attention to thank me for digging them out first, at least two hours before sunrise. But thanks enough is in the knowing that you've been a great help, and boy, do they have a good jump on their day, thanks to your early bird service. That, and that rusted-out muffler on the blower you were going to fix last season.

Invest a couple of minutes in a refresher course on medical self-diagnosis. I recommend my upcoming text, When Large Men Fall Down, which will be available at your local bookseller in the very near future. In it, you will find advice and mental exercises to help you in experiencing your fall in seeming slow motion. There are tips on choosing the precise location for your plummet, as well as stylistic approaches to employ in your actual event that will virtually ensure maximum damage: brief black-out, seeing stars, rear-

As I Was Saying . . .

ranging disk/vertebrae spacings, and combination surface and deep muscle bruising. As a bonus, there is also a helpful phrase guide to assist you in garnering utmost sympathy from your wife, once she quits laughing her head off from her wimpy warm house where she's been watching your misery unfold from the stupid picture window.

Be careful out there. It's a true Michigan winter for sure. The treasuries of the snow have been opened, and we are receiving blast after blast of its rich dividends. Do your work. Help your neighbor. Keep your perspective. The days are getting longer. My first seed catalogue arrived just today. And soon, spring will embrace us once again.

By the way, is your mower serviced, and ready to go? Sure as the snow, the growing season will fast be upon us. And take it from me, start early. You don't want to be caught.

Unprepared.

Teach us to make the most of our time, so that we may grow in wisdom.   Psalm 90:12, NLT

There are several traditions at our house that surround the annual Thanksgiving gathering. We gather to feast at precisely noon. We pause before the meal, for each to share about some things for which they are truly grateful. We recite a psalm together. We sing a chorus. We have prayer. We then enjoy way too much food. We opt not to view football (or any show for that matter) until well into the afternoon pick-a-spot-to-relax dessert session. At this point in our day, several break into their own personal traditions. Some choose to pass out in a classic turkey-tryptophan stupor. A large coalition opts for watching one of several holiday movies that cumulatively they have viewed four thousand times, quoting en masse line after line in delirious unison. Others (such as yours truly) consume endless mugs of fresh coffee (origin of choice; Costa Rican or Guatemalan) and converse wildly with animated hand gestures while sampling chocolates and other delicacies.

After the day winds down, the company has headed out, and the last of the cleanup is done, I usually go outside to wander around a bit. This is a result of discomfort from my hedonism, coupled with the effects of a heady overdose of caffeine. On this past Blessed Thursday, I managed to meander around the yard for a few minutes, but soon found myself standing at the door to my shop. I headed in, turning on the overhead lights.

The shop is the former garage, known as "garage" in name only. "Garage" implies that a building is designed to have a car parked inside. In all of my years here, this "garage" had never enjoyed the opportunity to fulfill its function and actually house a vehicle. Instead, it had gradually become the repository of tools and "stuff" that there was not room for in the house. Finally, due to age and obsolescence, the overhead door was removed, entry doors were added, and the "shop" was born. Oh, that and we added a bona fide garage onto the house.

Wandering around the shop, I couldn't help but notice once again my growing collection of projects that has caused me to dub this place "The Someday Shop." I call them projects, but for now, they are simply items collecting dust. There is coming a "someday" when I will launch them into new life through various repairs, refits and renovations. The broken mower. The shorted lamp. The chair-in-pieces. The antique hand cultivator. These and many, many other items are presently idling away in the waiting room of the someday shop, straining to hear my voice calling to them; that their turn upon the project bench has finally come; that their number is at last called; that they are receiving the nod to move up to the big show; that "someday" is at last, today. Of course, I have good intentions of getting around to all of the projects, plus many more misfits that will certainly find their way through my shop door. It's just a matter of time. Always, it comes down to time.

The scripture that opens this reflection is really a prayer to God for direction in ordering my fleeting time. He gives me time as a tool to measure my days, but God himself stands above time, eternal and by very nature, timeless. The wisdom I need from him is for ordering my days, so I do not waste the gift that is plainly given to me one day at a time. It is indeed a tough mindset for me to embrace: I am created with an eternal spirit by which I will live forever, yet my pilgrimage here is limited and irretrievable, measured in units I can break into ever-finer measures: year, month, week, day, hour, minute, second. The someday projects may or may not get done, because there are always the weightier things of life that cannot be shelved. The wisdom to sort out the "somedays" from the "nows" is never complete: I need his constant leading and prompting, else the values could become strangely reversed and my days could drift into profitless shop-twiddles.

I'm learning the importance of numbering my days. Many things of life, and I do literally mean "things," just have to take the backseat. That's why they are still biding their time, on hold in the dusty space known as the someday shop. If I never get around to them, word has it they'll all burn up one day, anyway. Other things are valuable always, rightfully demanding large "chunks" of my time. These, by and large, seem to always center on the relationships of life. These make up the parts that are eternal, and their care and nurture cannot be shelved for a future, "convenient" time to revisit. And today? Today was a good day; a beneficial day. I did no typical "work," I never pulled a vehicle out of the drive, and I followed little that resembles my "everyday" routine. Yet, I took the time for what God values, and allowed myself the day to value it as well. Lord. Word. Family. Friends. Nation. Remembrance. Hospitality. Love. Rest.

Tomorrow comes, and his leading will be just as vital for my day. I desire to live in the day he gives me, fully engaged and profitably centered. It all comes down to my daily knowing him, asking him, and obeying him. That's a tradition I want to keep for all my days. I know I won't have his daily leading, if I daily opt to put him off until "someday."

And as I have come to realize, traditions can be very fulfilling things.

Wanderers in the wilderness...

But don't just listen to God's word. You must do what it says. Otherwise, you are only fooling yourselves.   James 1:22; NLT

We're closing in on a trip, Isaac and me. There is a rite of passage all of the Masters boys must complete with dear ol' Dad somewhere between their tenth birthday and asking for the car keys. The rite includes travel: by car, occasionally by plane, but always, always by foot. We're talking backcountry trekking—backpacking—and this isn't a walk for the fainthearted.

The female population of the household recoils in terror whenever I mention the possibility of them joining me on safari. There is something genetically going on that I cannot quite grasp. It is as if I have asked them to move to a curb in Calcutta, or raft in to homestead on the remotest of the Aleutian Islands. They question me pointedly about how anyone could enjoy being away from electricity, daily bathing, and routine hygiene. I tell them that on these trips, no one minds; we all stink equally. Then, they usually scream and run away.

The last big trip out was several years ago, with sons Ben and Jordan to Isle Royale. They survived nicely, and now we even occasionally talk. This year's trip with Isaac is centered at Pictured Rocks, and I am looking forward to introducing him to that spectacular Superior shoreline. We also have a friend accompanying us, just due to the fact he is a great brother in the Lord. It doesn't hurt that he can carry large unwieldy loads without tiring, but I assure you that this had nothing to do with his invitation. Mostly.

I had my introduction to backpacking at a time when it was neither trendy nor commercialized. In those grand days, our gear was shouldered on slightly altered versions of pack mule carriers—guaranteed to chafe you raw before the first sunset came to pass. No padded hip belts and sternum straps to balance the load, no sir. You cinched up the leather and waxed canvas, and didn't whine about minor inconveniences like, say, a cervical dislocation. Food was heavy, tinned and bulky. The only thing dehydrated was the backpacker—nothing a little iodine-treated creek water wouldn't soon relieve. Or start. My sleeping bag alone weighed more than a complete outfitting of gear today, even figuring the inclusion of the new Microlite® Camp Cupa-Cappuccino maker.

As I grew more experienced, or as I am apt to say, "Lived to tell about it," I began to organize my backpacking trips by neat lists and practical memos. This became the basic "bible" for my many trips north over the years. I had a lot of opportunity in those years to introduce several area youth to the adventure, spiritual refreshment and personal growth that a few days in the wild afforded. In preparing myself and other hikers for an expedition, we would go over these lists in detail, and I often used visual demonstrations to emphasize why it was extremely important to follow the backpacking "bible" to the letter. The teaching part was always followed by "shakedown" events; day hikes and overnighters where we could tweak ourselves, our gear and our knowledge to help insure a good trip when we were truly "out there" on the big excursion.

Still, some campers never quite got it. I have seen more than a few amazing departures from the "bible" by my backpacking disciples over the years. My insistence for well broken in boots was once met with a hiker showing up in sandals, his new boots not yet even laced in the box tucked under his arm. Another turned over his packing to Mom, which was a huge faux pas. I honestly could scarcely lift his pack. We had to unload it and cull the nonessentials after his mom, waving, rode off in the family wagon. Out came blue jeans, several sweat shirts and towels, two pairs of tennis shoes ("she said in case one got wet,") the obligatory mom-rule seven sets of underwear, socks and t-shirts, the largest tube of toothpaste I have seen to date, a huge multi D-cell flashlight, and for some reason still unknown to me, an AC radio and a small fan. He was mumbling something akin to an excuse, but I couldn't hear him much as my ears were ringing from the blood pressure surge. Knowing the code and ignoring it upon embarking is simply not an option. Accommodations and shortcuts quickly turn into disaster on the real trail, bringing down not only the hiker, but usually his entire group as well. All it takes is one freelancer, not following the book, and everyone eventually will experience some level of pain.

I find there is an apt parallel between my backpacking experiences and the life of a believer in this world. In the New Testament book that bears his name, James is writing to challenge Christians to always live out what they have professed to believe. All of one's armchair musing, public debate or directed teaching of the Word of God is only authenticated when mirrored by that life's consistent practice "on the trail." James should know that "say and do" shows genuine faith. As one vital in the early church, his was a life of sorting out the true faith from the passing culture, and then putting into practice what Christ—James' brother—had not only taught, but also modeled. As a "pillar" spokesman, James was (is) particularly concerned about Christians who flow with words but trickle in actions. If the life in Christ isn't practical and lived out on the street, James warns that we are play-acting, with nothing but judgment awaiting the curtain fall.

Every age including the present has its rough sections of trail. There are many who massage the basic tenets of faith, demanding of the Christian community a particular "righteous" response, especially when it suits an agenda and benefits their immediate need. No wonder Christ cautioned His followers as they embarked, to be as wise as serpents and gentle as doves (Matt. 10:16). To keep a foothold, being neither naive pawns nor the callous indifferent, one surely needs a constant preparation of the Spirit-led ear, eye, voice, foot and hand.

On the trail, there are also those who for a season walk alongside, but then halt in the journey. *They went out from us, but they were not really of us; for if they had been of us, they would have remained with us; but they went out, so that it would be shown that they all are not of us. But you have an anointing from the Holy One, and you all know* (1 John 2:19-20; NASU).There are myriad variations to this theme of leaving off the Lord one claimed to follow. A thru-hiker, that is, a true one set to complete the journey of the Christ-life, must employ several resources to remain steadfast. These are especially crucial to keep perspective and resolve when once-thought companions dry up by the roots (Matt. 13:20-22).

Such resources include a faith sustained by the Word and prayer, and a gracious accountability to like-minded partners, mutually being answerable with honesty and humility. If a drought of these occur, it is inevitable that casualties on the trail will mount.

Lastly, on the trail today, there is increasingly a burden upon me, much as a pack. Not every burden is evil, especially if the Lord grants it. I believe this burden should be felt by every one that truly names Jesus as Lord. That burden is the knowledge that the walk and talk of one life leaves a huge impression over others, either for good or evil. In effect, we are always "on," teaching in every day and every situation. There is no self deception that for even one day, I may choose simply to live and not be an example to others. And what we teach by our word, but more acutely by our example, can be either of the Lord or of ourselves. There is no neutral third arena. The idea of a Christian living an isolated life, concerned only with his or her trail, doing what pleases self, aloof to both the Christian community and the community apart from Christ is frankly, absurd. The deliberate public "show" is often dressed up in terms like witness or testimony, but I have come to believe that those who can compartmentalize and mentally choose when this mask is donned or removed are in the end no friend to Christ or His Church. Inconsistent actions treat others as dispensable, when we should be absorbed with getting others on the right path before it is too late. *Multitudes, multitudes in the valley of decision! For the day of the LORD is near in the valley of decision* (Joel 3:14; NASU).

So we prepare, Isaac and me. We read, compose our lists, pack and repack, rehearsing our trip. But you might now surmise that there's more to our preparation than talking about the hike. Strapped into packs holding weights, rocks, and anything to simulate what will be our load, we have taken to streets and area trails, putting to practice all we are gleaning from the hiker bible. The best instruction on the page means nothing until it is put to practice in the field. We intend to hike the length of Pictured Rocks, and there is only one path that will afford that destination. It is our heart to make good on what we have read, and practiced, until our last steps are taken and the packs can drop.

Like-minded. Trained on the same page. Encouraging each other when it gets tough. What a joy in the journey it is.

What a joy it should be.

The journey to backpack the Pictured Rocks National Lakeshore Trail is now just memory. The return to that great wilderness was an opportunity to record impressions from my hike that mirror in many ways my "walk" as a Christ-follower in this world. I have compiled here several stories, relating the collection of my thoughts from that time on the path that winds from Grand Marais to Munising, following the rugged Lake Superior shoreline.

Now after this the Lord appointed seventy others, and sent them in pairs ahead of Him to every city and place where He Himself was going to come. And He was saying to them, "The harvest is plentiful, but the laborers are few; therefore beseech the Lord of the harvest to send out laborers into His harvest. Go; behold, I send you out as lambs in the midst of wolves. Carry no money belt, no bag, no shoes; and greet no one on the way."

Luke 10:1-4; NASU

Traveling light. It seems incongruous in a land where the motto for getting away from it all seems to be, "Take it all with you." I've passed motor home after motor home, laden with goods, towing vehicles dinghy-like, also headed for the great outdoors up north.

Somehow, I feel naked. Exposed. Our gear has been reduced to what we can manage upon our own backs. A tiny collection that has left much empty space in the back of my station wagon. I find myself second-guessing what we've brought. Many items, though useful, were weeded out and left at home. We'll spend tonight in a motel, having one last comfortable rest before beginning the trek tomorrow morning. And tonight, before bed, we'll go through the equipment one more time. We'll pull out a few items, talk it over, and then agree to set them aside, last minute. This backpacking thing is really an art of ounces. Too many tiny exceptions to the rule, too many minute yet unnecessary "necessities" thrown in, and the whole trip can be jeopardized. Injury. Fatigue. Grim pack mule march. Unpleasant slog. And then the nagging questions that whirl like the stable flies and requisite mosquitoes will come. "What was I thinking?" "How did I talk myself into this?" "When will we ever get there?" "Whose idea was this?"

I reflect back to earlier days. I didn't always have the "traveling light" mentality. After all, those were younger days, stronger days. When your back is tough and you've things to prove, the big burdens appeal more to pride than common sense. And I've carried my share of packs that were insanely heavy. Those days are gone, thankfully. But I paid the price by trudging down trails I should have been enjoying.

I've attempted to pour that wisdom into Isaac, convincing him that he can learn from my mistakes and not have to repeat them all firsthand. He has responded well, and his pack will indeed be manageable. He's big for ten years, and has the frame to carry more. Yet I want him to take pleasure in the journey; not being blinded by weight on his shoulders clouding his perspective.

I find the parallel to my life in Christ most fitting. Jesus invites me to cast my burdens upon Him, in the everyday. *"Come to Me, all who are weary and heavy-laden, and I will give you rest. Take My yoke upon you and learn from Me, for I am gentle and humble in heart, and YOU WILL FIND REST FOR YOUR SOULS. For My yoke is easy and My burden is light"* (Matthew 11:28-30; NASU). When He becomes the focus, and my concern is for pleasing Him, how quickly the other encumbering things of life drop away.

Likewise, in the verses from Luke that begin this chapter, I receive direction from Him that unloads my "pack" of worldly burdens. To focus on sharing the good news, and being feet on that trail (Acts 10:15), it is plainly evident that things of life have to be laid aside. The world offers a lot of items that may be attractive, comfortable, and even sensible, but the Lord knows even good things can become the distracting main things very quickly to the traveler. And very soon the traveler can become the homesteader; too encumbered with the amassed collection to worry about mission.

So we hit the trail. Even with our gear whittled down to the barest of necessities, the packs were far from feather light. There was that back-of-the-mind nagging that we didn't have everything we wanted. But there was also a very present relief that we weren't carrying one ounce more. The hike was ahead, and we were looking forward to enjoying the trail. It would be awful to miss it over regretting the load.

Experience has taught me, it's best to keep it that way.

Can two people walk together without agreeing on the direction?
Amos 3:3; NLT

What type of journey are you on? For most of us, the question could be answered with multiple replies: "I'm on the journey of…"
- an education.
- a return to health.
- a flight from my past.
- seeking my purpose in life.
- recovery.
- my retirement years.
- a career.
- my emotional wellness.
- raising a family.
- a meandering, random life…

The journeys that frame a life, although numerous and often interwoven, usually share some common elements. They have a beginning point, a route to travel, and a destination. There are detours, setbacks, dropouts, and surprises at many points. Some journeys are often repeated, to either the betterment or detriment of the traveler. Some are anticipated, well planned, of limited duration, and pleasant. Others we are thrust upon, with little or no preparation, no finish in sight save death, and speak to us mainly about the virtues of simple faith and endurance. My travel to the Superior shoreline mirrored many of the same traits as that of my other journeys of life.

Our hiking trip was planned, but we knew that any number of issues along the way could literally wipe us off our feet. The great act of motoring up nearly 400 highway miles just to reach the trail-head was of itself no small step. All of our route planning, supply packing and preparation to be physically fit were now at the testing point. The transit bus dropped us where the pavement ended, and there, we simply began by taking the first step northward to our path. While on the trail, we had a custom to pause each morning as we broke camp and readied the packs. In prayer, we took turns asking the Lord for his guidance and protection. It was not an act of resignation, or a mindless ritual. We truly needed His hand upon us for the trail ahead, and the decisions that we would have to make as we moved forward. *Come now, you who say, "Today or tomorrow we will go to such and such a city, and spend a year there and engage in business and make a profit." Yet you do not know what your life will be like tomorrow. You are just a vapor that appears for a little while and then vanishes away. Instead, you ought to say, "If the Lord wills, we will live and also do this or that."* (James 4:13-15; NASU).

The realization we enjoyed of never walking alone is not a common element in every heart and mind. Not all have the presence of the Lord, though His invitation extends to all. *Now as Jesus was walking by the Sea of Galilee, He saw two brothers, Simon who was called Peter, and Andrew his brother, casting a net into the sea; for they were fishermen. And He said to them, "Follow Me, and I will make you fishers of men." Immediately they left their nets and followed Him. Going on from there He saw two other brothers, James the son of Zebedee, and John his brother, in the boat with Zebedee their father, mending their nets; and He called them. Immediately they left the boat and their father, and followed Him* (Matthew 4:18-22; NASU).

It is common knowledge among hikers that it is not wise to go it alone on the trail. Everything can change in one moment. Illness, injury, or a misjudged turn onto a wrong path can be devastating or deadly for the solo traveler. So it is in all of life as well. The reality of our northern journey was that a party of four, not three, made the trip. The Lord was with us, and is with us, whether in the busy hustle of village life or at those remote "end of the world" locations. Proximity is never the Lord's problem. When He is not near, it's because I've been keeping my distance.

Our time on the trail also was a good reminder to me about the importance of just being in the day the Lord gives. Reduced to the basics of one path, food, shelter, fellowship and commune with God, it was refreshing to breathe in life momentarily unfettered from the rush, noise and complexity of the usual pace "downstate."

"But seek first His kingdom and His righteousness, and all these things will be added to you. So do not worry about tomorrow; for tomorrow will care for itself. Each day has enough trouble of its own" (Matthew 6:33-34; NASU).

You might argue that removing oneself to a backcountry retreat is escapism from the real world, but I say it is more an encounter with what the real world—life in Christ—should be for me. I know many who are racing through their journey, missing out on all the beauty due to a focus on one illusive "finish line" after another. For me to miss out on traveling with the Lord would be comparable to my strapping on running shoes for a sprint down the length of the shoreline trail. I may get through it, fast, but to what purpose? What of all I've missed? Would any finish line really be worth it if I fail to enjoy the relationships and relish the experiences because of a self-directed bent to just race?

One last observance today. No one stood to greet us when we came to the end of the trail. It was just a path here on earth, at times pleasant and at times tough. We had no false expectations of crowds, or press, or reward of any type for all our effort in completing the path. The reward was what it was—our experiences and camaraderie along the way. There was great joy in the journey, and we knew the finish would be anticlimactic. The finish, you see, wasn't the focus.

The path of earthly life has an endpoint too. For those who travel the Lord's route, there is much anticipation. He has given us ample truth that the journey's end actually leads us to a new life, new paths, new everything. That finish is indeed the focus. And the crowd awaits us; yet One in particular whose face we long to see, whose greeting we desire more than any other to hear.

No other journey and no other finish on God's green earth would ever compare.

————————————

Thus says the LORD, "Stand by the ways and see and ask for the ancient paths, where the good way is, and walk in it; and you will find rest for your souls."

But they said, "We will not walk in it."   Jeremiah 6:16; NASU

The particular geography that is home to the Shoreline Trail at Pictured Rocks lends itself—directionally—to an uncomplicated hike. My journey in traversing a good portion of this upper Michigan trail made that truth plainly clear. Even a casual glance at the park service maps confirmed what was unmistakably obvious to our eye: If we kept the lake on our right shoulder, we would eventually get to our end-of-the-trail destination.

This fact became ingrained in Isaac's mind. The ten-year-old was very keen about learning compass skills and orienteering, and the path we had chosen lent itself nicely to his first experience at hands-on map reading and travel. Often throughout our days, as we stood at the cliffs or beaches, taking in one vista after another of Superior's magnificent offerings, I would turn to ask Isaac, "Which way are we going?" And his answer was always, "To the left!"

The path itself caused us to wonder concerning its age, and the various individuals that had, over many centuries, walked where we now had privilege to walk. Though rough, with numerous obstacles, roots, rocks, mud, bugs, steep inclines and descents, it was still an "improved" trail from what the forerunners had known. Often, we were greeted with crude but effective wooden steps to help us in tackling the steeper bits of a trail section. At numerous points, we were assisted by narrow but adequate bridges over deep ravines that filled as spillways, racing over the cliffs when the rains came hard. Many rivers were also spanned for us, affording a safe crossing and a vantage point to look and listen; each meeting their journey's end by joining the mighty lake in a final, unifying plunge of spectacular waterfall. Staying with the trail around to the next jutting point, we could look back and view these cascades. Superior swallows without any fuss the myriad gallons of water that join it in endless, freefalling procession.

The features we enjoyed to help us in our trail progress also served to underscore a simple truth about this path: there were many dangers lying within mere feet of the trail's edge. With sheer drops of fifty to two-hundred feet and more, caution was always in season on this hike. One misstep, one unguarded scramble for a better photo, or one moment of sheer inattention, and disaster would be quick, terrifying, and final. A fall from those heights, and no one simply dusts himself off and goes on. We were reminded of this fact at a grim trail encounter; obtrusive orange barricade fencing with block-lettered signs affixed. This particular bluff was closed to us hikers due to an ongoing criminal investigation; the murder of a woman thrown from this cliff by a hiking partner—her husband.

The analogy of a path in Northern Michigan to the path of life is almost too fittingly a comparison to meditate on. God's Word is littered with ample reference to staying on the right paths, avoiding the deadly trails, and relying on the Word as the true guide and compass for our journey here below. The truth of these similarities bears up well upon reflection: life is too short, precious and precarious to go at it without direction.

All around me, I see disaster upon disaster as mankind follows some "new path" purporting to offer spiritual enlightenment. It is somewhat baffling to me why spirituality is "in," yet simple faith in Christ is viewed as passé—"old path." The underlying new gods that are sought out are in reality nothing new. The chief deity moving the machinery behind the curtain still is ultimately revealed as "self," with a god and a system of religion conveniently fashioned to meet personal, cultural or political appetites, goals and ambitions. From watching the news or scanning the paper, I am all too aware that comfortable, expedient, relativistic gods abound, in my neck of the woods and all about this troubled globe.

Blame might need to be meted out. Perhaps we as the keepers of the Christian trail have not done our part to maintain the old path. Admittedly, there have been lapses, divisions, and outright destruction that can be laid at the feet of those of us who know Christ, but fumble badly, and often. Coupled with that, I cannot overlook the fact that there is also the recurrent beat of the sinful human heart described in the first chapter of the book of Romans: *Yes, they knew God, but they wouldn't worship him as God or even give him thanks. And they began to think up foolish ideas of what God was like. The result was that their minds became dark and confused. Claiming to be wise, they became utter fools instead* (Romans 1:21-22; NLT).

I am reminded that the Lord Jesus, in a time of testing as his public ministry began, faced two of his three challenges from Satan while standing upon the pinnacles (Matthew 4:1-11). For any of us, an unguarded trek upon the "heights" of life, with its present dangers of worldly thinking, amusement, speech, success and approval, can lead to a plummet. The fool that leaves off the good path will in his foolishness blaze a trail that ends at the cliffs of destruction.

Your word is a lamp to my feet, and a light to my path (Psalm 119:105; NASU).

It was important for us to adhere to the path snaking along the shore, and to keep alert for dangers, especially on the heights. Father God, give us resolve to keep on the old path. We'll do our part to maintain and improve it for the next generation of travelers, but guard our hearts that we never entertain, even for one step, the abandonment of it.

The floods have lifted up, O LORD, the floods have lifted up their voice, the floods lift up their pounding waves. More than the sounds of many waters, than the mighty breakers of the sea, the LORD on high is mighty. Psalm 93:3-4; NASU

Possibly, leaky hatches sent it to the bottom. In its day, it was considered one of the greatest. Measured against our modern vessels, it would seem puny. To Superior, we must be reminded, all comers are puny. It sank still smelling of newness, on only its second voyage.

In August of 2007, following a full century of mystery as to its location, the remains of the freighter Cyprus were at last discovered. Another permanent grave marker can be added to the greatest of the Great Lakes; these magnificent fresh water seas that devour the vessels of mere men. It was found just beyond the eastern terminus of the Lakeshore Trail we were upon, a few miles off the coast at the area known as Deer Park. There, the skeleton of this ship has lain in the quiet dark depths, covered by four hundred and sixty feet of water.

In our isolation, we had no way of knowing that the shipwreck find was unfolding in the same days encompassing our trail hike. Of more pressing concern than leaky hatches was our leaky tent, and whether it would even stay together through two wild nights of storms that ripped into our near-shore camp sites.

The LORD reigns, let the earth rejoice; let the many islands be glad. Clouds and thick darkness surround Him; righteousness and justice are the foundation of His throne. Fire goes before Him and burns up His adversaries round about. His lightnings lit up the world; the earth saw and trembled. The mountains melted like wax at the presence of the LORD, at the presence of the Lord of the whole earth. The heavens declare His righteousness, and all the peoples have seen His glory. Psalm 97:1-6; NASU

Now, looking back from the quiet comfort of my study, coffee on my electric mug-warmer and myself shower fresh, our nights of "riding the storm out" indeed have strong—very strong—comedic overtones. Scene one: My friend Jay and I; forty somethings, bleary and sleep deprived, wet, grossly uncomfortable, and compellingly awake. Scene two: Isaac; ten years old, in a sleep akin to that of a low-grade coma, blissful, relaxed in soggy relaxedness, unaware of any storm. He is unstirred even as lightning strobes the movements of Jay and I in our futile in-tent mop up operations. The thunder explodes all around, shaking the ground and breeding the forty-something's concerns about all the dead timber directly overhead in this remote, permit-only backcountry camp area. Scene three: flashback. I should have considered it an omen when I discovered my inflatable ground pad had a tag on it bearing the words, "U.S. Coast Guard Approved."

Can you lift up your voice to the clouds, so that an abundance of water will cover you? Can you send forth lightnings that they may go and say to you, "Here we are"? (Job 38:34-35; NASU)

To spend a night or two in a nylon womb while the storms rage is, for me, an inescapable reminder of God's awesome power. Not that I do it often, or plan to repeat it in the near future. Call me a fast learner. With the darkness came the storms, and the sudden hush before the rumbling took me back to childhood days of myriad westerns I had viewed on our trusty black and white Philco television. At their requisite camp fire, coffee pot steaming in the moon beams, silhouetted horses clustered all about, one good guy would comment about the stillness of the night, and another good guy would make that ominous rejoinder: "Yeah, Clem, almost too quiet." Then, all heck would break loose as the marauding bad guys attacked.

As I recollect, the cowboys always found a convenient cave to hide in when the storms were a-brewin'. We had lots of caves around us in our hiking area, but we figured most of them were inhabited by bears keeping vigil for some apnea-dulled hikers seeking dry digs. So we lay in our soggy tent; waiting for morning, electrocution, or a quick blow to the head from one of the barkless trees creaking nearby.

The upside to experiencing the storms lasted with us for the next couple of days. Upon waking (if we truly slept at all), there was a presence of constant sound: a deep, repetitive crash and thud that came up from the waterfront. In due time, we broke camp and made our way back to the trail that headed up along the bluffs. Superior was roiling, and the impact of the waves upon the sheer rock faces was spectacular. Underfoot, the vibration of those impacts could be felt, punctuated by loud "booms" as at various points the waves went into shoreline caverns and exploded on those interior walls deep below. Creation itself responded to the irresistible power of God, and we were privileged to be witnesses to this incredible show of force.

The next night, we set up camp, taking comfort as our damp gear dried even before supper was over. A brilliant full moon lit the night, and although cool, it was tranquil as the storms were now distant. Superior lay but a few steps away; it too was silent, waveless, and at peace.

I sat up again within our tent. Isaac's still, contented sleep reminded me that our strenuous days on this trail together were certainly worth the effort. I read more from God's Word, and pondered the last two nights we had experienced. Perhaps I need to rethink the lessons of my times in the storm. I am reminded that often my perception of God is too limited. The omnipotent One often fades from my consciousness as I wrestle with days and struggles that storm at me. The god of my imaginations is often impotent and distant; I heave and plod ahead, trying in my own strength to do that which I have convinced myself I must do on my own. How foolish.

After all, the same God who created and directs all, also delights to show Himself mighty in my unspectacular day to day. I caught a fresh glimpse again, at the cliffs of Superior. I am thankful too that God is not left on that deserted beach, abandoned from my life. He is over all, whether I am paying particular attention or not. God help me to keep my thoughts on You, storm or no storm.

O come, let us sing for joy to the LORD, let us shout joyfully to the rock of our salvation. Let us come before His presence with thanksgiving, let us shout joyfully to Him with psalms. For the LORD is a great God and a great King above all gods, in whose hand are the depths of the earth, the peaks of the mountains are His also. The sea is His, for it was He who made it, and His hands formed the dry land. Come, let us worship and bow down, let us kneel before the LORD our Maker. For He is our God, and we are the people of His pasture and the sheep of His hand. Psalm 95:1-7a; NASU

For a day in Your courts is better than a thousand outside. I would rather stand at the threshold of the house of my God than dwell in the tents of wickedness. Psalm 84:10; NASU

Selection and choice are all a big, normal part of my everyday world. I am accustomed to having many options for nearly every area of my life. Just the simplest of things, such as breakfast, can itself take many different forms depending on where I'm at, who's doing the cooking, and how much time I can devote. Other more complicated areas, like houses, investments, insurance, or my favorite vice—building my library—require that one decision after another be made. It takes just a moment of reflection for me to confirm the fact that all in all, I like having choices. Lots of choices.

The art of backpacking is centered mainly upon making many right choices before even setting out. Once you are "underway," the choices you have labored over in the preparation, planning and packing are choices you will have to live with for the duration of your hike. That, or at least until you can scrap it all and hitch a ride out of the boonies back to your vehicle and the world of choices. One admonition: The choice to pull the plug on your adventure does not always conveniently occur at an access road with a friendly motoring tourist, so it is best to make wise choices from the start.

In choosing our section of this Shoreline Trail, we had self-limited any room for non-essential gear. The "go" list of goods had left us with packs that were manageable, but by no means feather light. Much of the "fluff" that might have made our hike more convenient had never been considered at all. There were no large rain flies, cabin tents, 26-piece cook kits, extensive wardrobes, massive flashlights, 500 page books, chaise lounges or porta-potties, to name but a few. Even other truly practical items that we had placed on our pack list were eventually crossed off; when it all has to be shouldered, something has to give, or your back will. With very few exceptions, we had the basics and little more. The choices we had made were going to determine not only how we functioned during our days, but also whether we would have a good shot at success in finishing what we indeed were starting.

There is a lesson that I have relearned on this side of that successful finish. Reflecting on our trail days, aided by the photos Jay supplied and my nighttime notes penned from the tent floor, I think of how wonderful even the simple things became when there were no other "greater" things competing for our focus.

There, the meals we cooked were heartily consumed. Back home, our camp menu would never suffice. After all, the fridge bulges, the oven is hot, and we delight to exercise our refined taste in dining.

There, the morning and evening cup of instant coffee, with its slightly "off" flavor and whiff of white gas bouquet, varied in strength due to my pouring technique. It still was truly savored. Back home, those extra coffee packets unneeded for the trip will grow dusty on a pantry shelf, as I choose to grind a freshly roasted batch of beans and preheat my porcelain mug to receive that percolated, caffeinated elixir of the dawn.

There, the days were unhurried and simple. We had approximations of when we would get to the next camp, but there was ample time to enjoy the trek, stop when we liked, linger over a view, or just rest. I never wore a watch. Back home, the days are fleeting choreographies of times, appointments, and check lists. Having a day with the simple goal of living in it would never fly in this productive world downstate.

There, our evenings would consist of barefoot walks on rock or sand beaches, exploring the shore and listening to waves, wind, or at times nothing but vast silence. Back home, evenings are consumed with still more activities, pausing only to collapse into bed for a few fitful hours before arising to start it all again.

See the hiker upon the treadmill, not the trail...

Finding enjoyment by making, and then living with the simple choices. How much that needs to be my focus for more than a brief excursion to the hinterland once a year!

"Enter through the narrow gate; for the gate is wide and the way is broad that leads to destruction, and there are many who enter through it. For the gate is small and the way is narrow that leads to life, and there are few who find it" (Matthew 7:13-14; NASU).

There's more than a casual appeal to the idea of getting back to the basics of life in the Lord. Often times I wonder if I've even entered the reality of it at all. I meet many of God's people who like me, often seem absolutely distracted by this onslaught of a world mad with choices, buying into its bent for despising the little things; the simple things. *For consider your calling, brethren, that there*

215

were not many wise according to the flesh, not many mighty, not many noble; but God has chosen the foolish things of the world to shame the wise, and God has chosen the weak things of the world to shame the things which are strong, and the base things of the world and the despised God has chosen, the things that are not, so that He may nullify the things that are, so that no man may boast before God (1 Corinthians 1:26-29; NASU).

God, guard my mind and heart that I would delight to choose the simple things. As you demonstrate, sometimes the simplest is the best for me. And help me to not just tolerate the little things, but to delight in them as well. As you show me often, the little things sometimes turn out to be big things in the end.

"But as for you, Bethlehem Ephrathah, too little to be among the clans of Judah, from you One will go forth for Me to be ruler in Israel. His goings forth are from long ago, from the days of eterni-ty" (Micah 5:2; NASU).

Jesus walked this lonesome valley. He had to walk it by Himself; O, nobody else could walk it for Him, He had to walk it by Himself.*

And He withdrew from them about a stone's throw, and He knelt down and began to pray, saying, "Father, if You are willing, remove this cup from Me; yet not My will, but Yours be done." Now an angel from heaven appeared to Him, strengthening Him (Luke 22:41-43; NASU).

In my scripture reading and studies, I am prone to forget that I am a stranger wandering among the environments and cultures that the writers and actors of the Bible experienced firsthand. There was time on this hike to meditate about the isolation I was feeling, and imagine how those people I am familiar with on the printed page actually faced their days of terrains and governments that were often hostile and foreboding. Of all these, I pondered most how the Lord Jesus may have felt leaving His heavenly realm to come to this earth for a trail that knowingly would end upon a cross. Thankfully, my relationship with Him goes beyond the paper and ink of the Bible page, and blessedly beyond my own limited thoughts and imaginings. Still, I did conclude that there was a similarity in our respective trail journeys. I had willingly placed myself upon my path, as He too had readily and not reluctantly taken to His. There was however, a total breakdown in my comparison when it came to thinking about the scope of our travels. I walked on a trail that thousands had walked for simple pleasure, admittedly with no great mission or consequence. Jesus walked for the sin of the world. His person and destination uniquely and solely qualified Him for the mission, and the consequence of His pilgrimage had eternal ramifications for all of mankind.

We must walk this lonesome valley, We have to walk it by ourselves;
O, nobody else can walk it for us, We have to walk it by ourselves.*

The LORD is my shepherd, I shall not want. He makes me lie down in green pastures; He leads me beside quiet waters. He restores my soul; He guides me in the paths of righteousness for His name's sake. Even though I walk through the valley of the shadow of death, I fear no evil, for You are with me; Your rod and Your staff, they comfort me. You prepare a table before me in the presence of my enemies; You have anointed my head with oil; My cup overflows. Surely goodness and lovingkindness will follow me all the days of my life, And I will dwell in the house of the LORD forever (Psalm 23; NASU).

My meditation also focused on the paths of life that we all must face. Like my northern hike, not every segment of our earthly journey is as smooth as others. We had determined that there were "long" miles and "short" miles we were hiking; the topography determined the pace. While being careful not to race through our days on the Shoreline Trail, we still kept track of approximate distances and our relative "speed" in hiking. It was a sobering moment when we calculated our average of a whopping one-mile-per-hour. Given all the ascents, descents, obstacles, and points for caution, it came as no surprise. We could at times go no faster; what was important was to just keep moving ourselves forward to our next destination. Life likewise throws sections of "tough trail" at us. Similarly, it seems that at those times the important thing is to keep pressing on. Whatever miles the Lord has laid before us, it is a sure thing that we are to walk them all. It is comforting to know that the Lord is not waiting on the other side of the valley, but is very present, walking through even the "long" miles right by our side. Many poets have even painted in words the right notion that in His unfailing compassions, He lovingly carries us when our physical, emotional, mental and spiritual feet can step no more.

We observed that the Pictured Rocks tour boats came along with regularity as we wound up, down, in, and around the cliffs. The passengers could observe us, but they could do nothing to aid us in our trek. There was a distance that separated us, and the journey was truly ours to own. Oftentimes it seems to me that our hardest earthly struggles are not through our own suffering and pain, but through having to remain—like those boating tourists—removed "observers" when pain and suffering come to those who are near to us. Companionship is essential. Even the lake-bound passengers reached out; their exaggerated waves bringing us a sense of camaraderie. Though they had to remain in their place, it was good to know someone noticed and cared. But for those in my world enduring rough days, my empathy and fleeting presence seem so futile and impotent. I often pray that God would take their path and give it to me, if I could but free them from the pain. But I am limited, finite; no god at all. It gives me pause to consider that this is exactly what Jesus felt, but what He being God <u>did </u>accomplish, when He saw our need, took our pain, and secured our bright destination. *After you have suffered for a little while, the God of all grace, who called you to His eternal glory in Christ, will Himself perfect, confirm, strengthen and establish you. To Him be dominion forever and ever. Amen* (1 Peter 5:10-11; NASU).

Sometimes it's good to walk the lonely paths. It brings a clarity that the bustling highways often blur. Not all of life is a level march, and perspective is essential to keep one's footing when a bend in the path reveals a rough patch ahead. But above all, keep walking! Not in dread or resigned defeat, but confidently in the strength of the Lord. Remember, He walks with us, and bears all our burdens. Keep the Book open, and allow Him to speak to you from its pages. From His communication flows the assurance that our final destination will be worth every step of our journeys, even the miles we endure now as our "long" ones.

The lyrics of the spiritual I have included in this piece are certainly useful to us for reflection. It is sobering to contemplate what Jesus undertook to set us free. At the heart of the song, I believe I understand what the writer was saying. Yet the second stanza I've included pales when we come to realize this life-altering fact: Christian, you will never take even one step by yourself in any valley, lonesome or not.

Are you walking in this essential truth?

*Jesus Walked This Lonesome Valley. American Spiritual; anonymous

---

Therefore if anyone is in Christ, he is a new creature; the old things passed away; behold, new things have come. 2 Corinthians 5:17; NASU

I put it out of its misery last night. I had tried in vain to breathe life into it, but to no avail. It was time to face the undeniable fact that it was not coming back. And so, very unceremoniously, I tossed it into the metal recyclables carton in my shop. Sometime, in the years to come, it might enjoy a reincarnation and be something useful once again. I just knew that it was over; there had to be a severance. It would never boil another drop of water in the wilderness for me.

The backpacking camp stove had served me well, accumulating twenty-four years and dozens of trail trips as a dependable friend. A few months back, I had labored to restore it for my impending Lakeshore Trail hike. It had accompanied me on past excursions to that same destination, twice in high summer and once for a grim January slog that has come to be referred to in my traveler's tales as "The Great Snowshoe Fiasco." It was, as I discovered through an internet search, functionally obsolete. Parts to rebuild it would add up to more than a new model—imagine that, and in America too. In effort to save a buck and shore up my sense of manly-man ability, I skipped the new parts and tore into the relic, dismantling it, cleaning it up, and reassembling it for one more go. It worked fine on the shop bench.

Cue the ominous music.

Trying to "keep the old" was a mistake. In the end, mechanical tinkering ability and frugal mindset aside, my decision proved to be nearly disastrous. However, this truth did not become practical knowledge for me until we were deep into the second day of our journey out on the trail.

During dinner, several crucial seals on the stove began to leak. It might be helpful here to mention that when white gas is involved, you could pretty accurately say that every seal on a gas stove is crucial. Anyway, vaporized gas started escaping from various points on the stove, causing flames to emit from various points on the stove that were never supposed to emit flames variously. It was at once exciting and exhilarating. Images of the upcoming news story, *"Moron Torches North Woods,"* complete with my sans-eyebrows photo and lengthy analysis of my folly, burned in my mind. Emergency trail rebuilding of the stove proved somewhat unsatisfactory, given that I had a piece of wire, a chunk of tin foil, and some grossly ineffective cheap import multi tool knock-off composing my only repair kit. The function of the stove improved somewhat, but for the remainder of our hike, what little use the stove received was had in wide open areas, with very little fuel, and under the scrutiny of a man regretting he had not sprung for a new model. Isaac and Jay would stand some distance off, heads close together and whispering; probably rehearsing details so that their stories would corroborate when the authorities showed up to piece together the ground-zero scene of the detonation: "Now son, could you just show us one more time where the imbecile—I mean, your father—was standing when he lit the match?"

I would like to pause here and make it a matter of public record by putting into writing that the stove was the only item on this jaunt that should have been abandoned for newer things. While I would like to say that, the awful truth is that there were other problems with unfitting gear in addition to my stove-turned-flamethrower. I also endured a mummy-style sleeping bag that was made for a man pencil-necked, undernourished and absolutely not big-boned, or as my cardiologist likes to put it, weight appropriate to height. I lost several lash points on my ancient backpack that simply broke off; age playing havoc with the connectors and rendering them brittle. And finally, my old leaky tent, of which I have written unflattering words in this chapter, was consigned for children's backyard play duty immediately upon our return home. In its final stand, I think it held up for about sixteen minutes under the assault of my wife's brood. Funny, that still beats the last sofa record by a good four minutes.

So I've learned firsthand that oftentimes, the old things are not fitting. What had at one time been a collection of items useful to me became instead a collection of weights that almost became my undoing. I was relying on things that had lost their usefulness in my life. I had hung on to the old gear because memory told me that it was still of value. I had worked hard to own it at one time, when it was full of appeal, shiny and new. But times had changed; these items had lost their worth, and there was no returning to how it was back then.

It is for me a good mirror of my walk with the Lord as well. Paul isn't just penning a platitude when he gives the words that start out this story. There is a rebirth in coming to Jesus. His offer of salvation is not a dressing up of old things, but a complete newness taking in every part of my being. He offers much more than a rebuild of my life. The old ways are no longer fitting. The old gear won't suffice. He doesn't patch together something—anything—and try to make it hold up. Instead, He offers total freshness. A clean start. Out-of-the-box new gear, period.

I find perhaps the toughest part of the new life in Christ is appropriating the truth of it for myself. Old ways die hard; I had thought life in Christ wouldn't have so many struggles. The "old gear" of life apart from Him is hard to lay down; wasn't all this newness supposed to descend and transform me at once, for all?

This life in Him is much like being on the trail. You take one day at a time, and go with what the trail presents to you. There are constant choices to be made. Good choices, those exhibiting the newness of life in Him, yield the peaceable fruit of wisdom and faith. Bad choices, reflecting a desire to return to the "old gear," vary in their destructiveness and often limit the range of next choices available. On the trail, things once thought useful can turn into burdens, and need to be laid aside. While the new life He supplies offers fresh paths with new outlooks, these can only be enjoyed when the former paths are once and for all abandoned. There must be a steadfastness to be alert for dangers and distractions. There must be a concern and priority for your traveling companions. And above all, there must be a joy in the journey, though not every segment is easy.

Enjoy your hike. I'll see you along the trail, or at the finish.

I have observed something else in this world of ours. The fastest runner doesn't always win the race, and the strongest warrior doesn't always win the battle… Ecc. 9:11NLT

I've never been accused of having too much style.

I recall the winter Olympic games when Lindsey Jacobellis forfeited gold in Torino for having too much of it. While snowboarding the halfpipe demands showboating to build scores, snowboard cross is a different animal. All you need to do is get down the hill, and fast. Her showmanship board-grab with seconds to victory led to her fall, and collecting silver; second place. So much for out-of-place flash.

Speaking of style, I too have dabbled with winter sports. The closest I've come to Olympic grandeur however, was the shanty incident on Cranberry Lake.

Being the proud owner of a new collapsible ice coop, I couldn't wait for work to end so I could get to fishing. Having all my gear along and a permission note from my wife, I was set for a great evening of crappies and gills. There was a gentle breeze, but nothing-[ominous music]-nothing to be alarmed about. Gliding out on the lake with this sleek fish trap was a dream. My first shanty had weighed more than a hummer, because in those days everything was required to be overbuilt. But this? This was class. This was hip. This was style.

The first indication that something was wrong was very subtle. I had glanced up from my perimeter position setting a tip-up to notice my newly erected blue baby casually pulling away from camp. Immediately I broke into a lateral sprint. "Lateral sprint" is a writer's device to convey the image of a large guy fully clad in WWII Norwegian Special Ops military surplus gear with size thirteen Mickey Mouse boots lumbering madly across baby-butt smooth ice in an interceptor-line with a blue cube that seems to be wildly picking up speed.

I too was accelerating nicely at this point in my pursuit, and the shoreline was looming closer by the second. We met; the coop, the shoreline and the chunky guy, in a great tangle of blue tarp, sweaty outerwear, and aluminum quik-lok™ poles. I had inadvertently fell into and through my prized coop, and the ensuing slaughter of wax worms, mousies and Euro larvae that had been unwitting passengers in my cargo pockets was a carnage I still have trouble revisiting. The destruction was amazing. The death of style had never been more brutal.

On a happy note, the local outfitter got another sizeable sale from me that winter.

I wish Lindsey Jacobellis all the best in her career. I hope she flourishes and matures and finds herself a standout, representing Team USA again and again.

I see a few lessons for us all in Lindsey's story, and my experience too. Lessons good to remember for people, country and church. Focus on the team. The finish line is still the most important thing. Even while racing alone, you still represent the homeland. Style is nice, but substance gets the job done. Don't celebrate prematurely. Discipline will win the day. And from the life of Tanja Frieden, Lindsey's competitor that got the gold: Stay focused. Those out front may not be there when you look up.

And oh, yeah. Use the buddy system —you'll be glad you did, when the wind comes up.

Have you visited the treasuries of the snow?   Job 38:22a; NLT

Two men. Four snowshoes. One half-baked idea.

Here at the start, I use the term "men" but loosely. We were male. We had some initial, patchy stages of facial hair. We had trouble sustaining organized, complex thought. These three should certainly qualify us to bear that title, I do believe.

The half-baked part entailed a mad dash northward to meet the new year by snowshoeing in at Pictured Rocks National Lakeshore.

Lake Superior.

December thirty-first.

I share this tale of adventure today—a bright and balmy January afternoon—because I need the reminder that somewhere, right now, winter is happening. Yesterday I passed the golfers on my drive home, giddy that their season has extended beyond all wildest imaginations. New Year's Eve, I found flowers sprouting amid our perennial beds. This my friends, is passing. Global warming aside, do not be lulled into believing that winter will tiptoe by quietly.

My buddy and I made that trek north, using the finest arctic expedition equipment we could fashion in my dad's garage in about twenty minutes. We loaded the car with all the essentials: a slightly modified silo tarp, a chopped toboggan with attached machinery crate and a twenty-foot rope harness, and food—lots of frozen food from mom's freezer, including what must have been a four-pound chunk of goulash. And, to be sure, really great matching sets of Michigan style snowshoes, which we trained in rigorously for several moments while the car warmed up.

"Arriving at the lakeshore" is actually a bit of a misnomer. You don't get anywhere near the lakeshore at that time of year, but we found a wide spot where the plow had turned around, and parked our car. Just before departing due north to Superior, we wisely left a note on our car to set the park ranger's mind at ease. Little did we know that they didn't exactly make normal daily rounds in the dead of winter. By happy coincidence, on our way out several days later we would meet up with Mr. Ranger. We had seen more snowshoe tracks as we neared the vehicle, and sure enough, we met a rather red-faced man in Government Issue heavy winter wear. Red-faced Ranger informed us that we were a day late, he had been looking for traces of our whereabouts, the temperature had hit an actual minus 20 degrees the previous night, and that we were... (Here, he used descriptors that had my mother been along, she would've cuffed him upside the head). Anyway, back to my story.

I was accustomed to snow depths in my hometown never exceeding much over a foot. It was surprising to leave the parked car and walk up about four feet to get on top of the blanket that graced that area. Lugging a chopped toboggan with attached machinery crate holding perhaps 80 pounds of gear by a twenty-foot rope harness proved to be somewhat clumsy. If I stopped for a fraction of a second, the whole Conestoga started sinking out of site into the powdery whiteness. When I started up an incline, the law of gravity became painfully real as the rope chaffed even through the double layer gloves and down parka. Upon cresting the hill and heading down, I became eerily aware of a grinding sound increasing in volume. A quick backward glance revealed that this was the noise of the whole shooting match picking up speed as it raced toward me. I stepped out of the way, but seconds later was launched after the sled as the slack rope around my waist and in my hands sprang to tautness and drug me along to the valley floor. There we stopped, and I began methodically checking my extremities while the supply wagon disappeared, slowly going down into the snow. Then, grateful to be alive, I'd start the whole process again.

Camping out at Superior in the dawning of the new year is not tricky at all. To practice, just conduct all your normal business for a couple of days from within the comfort of your home's chest freezer. Relax in the luxurious splendor of a 20 mil black plastic tarp. While away those long evenings by breaking off the stalactites that have formed overhead from your breath's condensation, and see how far you can pitch them toward that crunching sound that menacingly circles your campsite in the bleak darkness. Keep your drinking water under your clothing, close to your skin. Even then, you'll have all the ice in that canteen that you could ever want. Try heating a four-pound brick of perma-frosted goulash over a ten-b.t.u. backpack stove using a cast iron fry pan. Blow on the flame constantly to simulate a driving wind. Fill your boot with some of that slushy water and count the hours it takes to warm it up with your campfire—you know, that fire that sank out of site into the snow at a rate equal to the pace you kept trying to add wood to it. Don't worry about actually drying the boot out; just get it flexible enough so you can put it back on again. Once you're away from the heat, it'll freeze back up and believe me, it isn't going anywhere now.

I did manage to squeeze in a lot of fun once the delirium set in and the fear of slow agonizing death faded somewhat. Exploring the Superior coast, with its ice caves formed over the bluffs and piled mountains of ice at the shoreline was stunningly beautiful and beyond anything I had ever experienced of the depth of winter. Blowholes form along the ravaged beach, caused by waves coursing under the ice and breaking through at a weak spot near the surface. The water heaves up with sand, freezing almost instantly and leaving huge, gopherish mounds that grow in height with each new wave's arrival and contribution. It was a world that I never knew existed, and yet I thought I knew what winter in Michigan was all about.

Who is the mother of the ice? Who gives birth to the frost from the heavens? For the water turns to ice as hard as rock, and the surface of the water freezes. Job 38:29-30; NLT

The last night there, January third, the snow quit falling. As the fire glowed its last, I sensed that all was well. Tomorrow would bring an easy morning's trek to be back at the car. The sled was nearly empty. The snowshoeing had found its rhythm. The promise of warmth, good food, and family was now very near to realization. In the stillness of that night, I decided to take one last walk; the few hundred yards from campsite to bluff, overlooking Superior in its frozen panorama.

The clouds had been clearing for some hours now, and although the temperature had dropped to where my snowshoes made a squeak instead of a crunch upon the snow, I had to linger and simply stare upward into the vastness of the winter's night.

From there I watched, as a million million stars appeared overhead, silent in the enormity of the universe and from my vantage point in that icy northern wilderness. The creator who hung the stars in space gave these heavenly markers, pointing out the seasons. And for that night, fresh in the new year, I sat, and enjoyed my creator's artistry, and power, and presence.

Can you hold back the movements of the stars? Are you able to restrain the Pleiades or Orion? Can you ensure the proper sequence of the seasons or guide the constellation of the Bear with her cubs across the heavens? Do you know the laws of the universe and how God rules the earth? Job 38:31-33; NLT

He is the God of the snows, and the God of the January mild or strong. Bless Him in all his variety and subtlety, for in every treasury of our senses and surroundings, God is God.

As the deer pants for the water brooks, so my soul pants for You, O God. Psalm 42:1; NASU

The psalmist observed it, and made the connection. I've known such a thirst for God, but have never seen the deer panting for water. I have, on the other hand, observed grown men and women panting after the deer, so perhaps that picture of desire is more fitting for my life and times.

But that picture is far from picturesque.

This is the season for the deer camp. From my deck at home, I am prone to draw in a breath of crisp air at some of these November sunrises, and think back to the days when I too had the privilege of joining the hunt. Lots of memories, and most of them somewhat pleasant.

I remember it was considered poor form to hunt down here, when what a real manly-man hunter did was go up. Grandpa said so. Way up. Over the bridge up. Dickinson County. Up, up, and away over near the Wisconsin border, where really great people really do talk that yooper way. We would leave Jackson County, on several occasions narrowly missing massive bucks leaping across the road by our house, to venture to a county full of two-tracks to nowhere, chasing an elusive herd of deer estimated by the local DNR office at 22 head, covering by foot nearly all of the 775 square miles of cedar swamp and faceless terrain we claimed as "prime buck country." It was called prime because all the bucks in the county added up to a prime number, namely, three.

As our all-male contingent neared the usual deer camp locale, I recall vividly the many campgrounds with water, electric, hot showers and other amenities that we would pass up. We all sneered great manly sneers at such soft digs as these. We were here to hunt, not to have pedicures and sip tea, for crying out loud. What would they come up with next—flush toilets? And so we would whiz by, winding eventually down increasingly narrow paths until we entered a lane marked by trees bearing traces of silvery aluminum from past years' encounters with the sides of our travel trailer. The shimmering effect was mesmerizing, as was the next three hour project of clearing our campsite. The local mill at Sagola could've run their particle board production for days on the volume of brush we cleared at our spot, making room for our man-den on wheels and the accompanying fleet of trucks and cars we drove flotilla-like to that destination. It always amazed me that every year, the brush had grown back, but twice as thick as the year before. Since Sagola wouldn't send a truck over, we instead would build a fire that for all intents and purposes was probably visible from the moon.

Then God blessed Noah and his sons and told them, "Be fruitful and multiply. Fill the earth. All the animals of the earth, all the birds of the sky, all the small animals that scurry along the ground, and all the fish in the sea will look on you with fear and terror. I have placed them in your power. I have given them to you for food, just as I have given you grain and vegetables." Genesis 9:1-3; NLT

I was a lousy hunter. Clad in my hand-me-down red and black checked outfit, the only thing I did well was sweat and chafe; neither a fit topic for mixed company in this readership. The 100%

wool apparel had a texture akin to a similar sounding item, steel wool. For fun at home, scrub two isolated regions of your body with these wools. Note how similar the resultant skin damage is as well. In hindsight, there were only a couple of reasons that I was ever included in the hunting party at all. First, I could cook somewhat, which helped since slogging through impenetrable forest from 4 am to 5 pm burns (in our careful estimation) around 20,000 calories per day. Second, I was really good at carrying—or more precisely—dragging heavy things.

I would rise and prepare a breakfast fit for thrashers around 3 am, having gotten at least 20 good minutes of sleep due to sounds from our trailer rivaling spring hatch night in some section of the Okefenokee Swamp. After night three, I would have preferred bunking in the swamp. Anyway, the real hunters, filled with breakfast and alert from pots of strong black coffee (no cream in man-camp, thank you very much) would slip off to their blinds, my brother leading the way, melting into the woods as stealthy and silent as a sniper on patrol. I would muddle around the camp perimeter for a few minutes, shouldering a .35 that was so heavy I still have a pronounced limp today. It was usually my lot to inadvertently step in a hole and fill one boot with slush water, rendering a foot numb as a club almost instantaneously. After about 30 minutes of enduring that, I would squish back to the trailer to start lunch preparations (today's special: cast iron surprise). The routine could change at any moment, as a three-round rifle volley was my signal to douse myself with Gold Bond, grab the drag rope, and head in the direction of shots fired.

Afternoons were spent in much the same pattern. I learned to dread the three shot volley at dusk. We never lost a deer, but there were some long nights bringing them in. Once, we even tagged for our own a second deer we came upon. No one came along to claim it, and we waited far too long into that night. *Lazy people don't even cook the game they catch, but the diligent make use of everything they find.* Proverbs 12:27; NLT

Venison always tastes better after the carcass has been drug through a cedar swamp, doused in two or three small icy streams, hung where it can enjoy a freeze/thaw cycle for a few days,

As I Was Saying . . .

strapped to a vehicle and coated along a 600-mile-route with road salt, diesel fumes and washer solvent, processed from a garage floor, and finally crock potted with cream of mushroom soup, don't you think?

And Lord help me, I enjoyed it all, so very much.

Jesus took with Him Peter and James and John his brother, and led them up on a high mountain by themselves. And He was transfigured before them; and His face shone like the sun, and His garments became as white as light. And behold, Moses and Elijah appeared to them, talking with Him. Peter said to Jesus, "Lord, it is good for us to be here; if You wish, I will make three tabernacles here, one for You, and one for Moses, and one for Elijah." While he was still speaking, a bright cloud overshadowed them, and behold, a voice out of the cloud said, "This is My beloved Son, with whom I am well-pleased; listen to Him!" When the disciples heard this, they fell face down to the ground and were terrified. And Jesus came to them and touched them and said, "Get up, and do not be afraid." And lifting up their eyes, they saw no one except Jesus Himself alone. Matthew 17:1b-8; NASU

We had pressed on, despite the rains, for six days. It had been for several in our group the make-or-break hike, and by every indication it was break. Ineptitude and lousy weather had teamed together to make a merciless coalition. Soggy clothing, blistered feet, slick steep trails and the gloom of mountains shrouded in clouds and echoing with thunder had taken their toll. The promise of a glorious lookout at the highest elevation in the park kept us moving forward. With each raging stream forded and mosquito-saturated night endured, the miles slowly clicked away. We would be there soon. The view would be worth it all.

We arrived at our pinnacle on a dreary Saturday mid-morning. The signs of civilization appeared for the first time that week. Our ascent had suddenly terminated into a parking area, where curious folk peeked out of Winnebago doorways and through foggy station wagon windows to behold this mud-encrusted troupe that they would have to endure—hopefully upwind—along a short route and brief climb to the observation deck. We followed the pathway, glorious in its smooth construction; amply equipped with benches, drinking fountains and signage. In a few minutes, it neatly transitioned into a gently graded corkscrewing ramp. Soon, we found ourselves leaning at the railing, staring into grey vastness. There was nothing to meet our straining eyes; nothing to take in but the swirl of cloud and its contents—cold, soaking mist. No reference points. No distant peaks to look down upon. Though it was right there, directly in front of us, our vision of that greatness was completely obscured.

We returned to the parking area, deciding to drop our packs and eat a bite before pressing on. One dear soul offered us the shelter of his trailer awning and a pot of hot coffee. We took the gift, even dragging a picnic table over to add to the alfresco charm, though I recall we ate in subdued silence. Later, we resumed our hike; a mostly descending path that would in two days expel us at the trail head where we had left one of our vehicles the week before.

The mist accompanied us continually.

That experience from years ago came back to me tonight as I read again this challenging passage from Matthew, who writes as one of the disciples who stayed at the base camp. The three who received the invite by Jesus to accompany him up the mountain had been acquainted with him for some time, but still could not see him for who he was. Even when the stunning brilliance of his glory was displayed visibly to them, the best Peter can offer in his fuddled mind is to pay homage by erecting little memorials, and that honor to be equally prepared for Jesus, Moses and Elijah.

Of course, the Father will have nothing to do with His Son receiving divided worship and honor, so He voices His displeasure and command through presence and speech that immediately causes the disciples to fall, faces to the earth.

And certainly, for me reading it today, it is all too clear. It all makes perfect sense. The disciples were slow. So slow in fact that Matthew often has to tell me when they are catching on, when it finally clicks, when they are at last just this side of clueless. I con-gratulate myself on my spiritual in-tuneness. And while I'm at it, I'll drop my pretense, face the facts, and walk back into my fog. Yes, it is all too common to have Jesus obscured to my eyes as well.

• When I get my vision fastened on all that is around me, how can I truthfully say that Jesus is my focus?
• When Jesus gets equal time and treatment alongside other "pri-ority" people, events, or activities, how can I claim to see Jesus as my Lord?
• When "doing" for Jesus replaces "being" in Jesus, what driving vision is really shaping my actions?
• When the swirling fog of my day arrests my attention: schedule, economy, health, politics, leisure—how can I claim to be "looking to Him?"
• When in fear of God's existence and voice I look away, what am I saying about His presence, His word and His will for my life? Am I afraid that God's will is bad? Or that His ways are too harsh? Or am I simply more suited to mirror-gazing, prideful and content to look upon myself and my works; that which is safe, comfortable, and attainable by my wits, schemes, biases and visions?
• Am I silent and obedient, quick to "Listen to Him!," or am I more at home speaking my mind, even when my words betray that there's not much happening up there to report on?

Thankfully, Jesus came to the three undone disciples, and with his touch, had them look up. He met their eyes, wide in the fear and awe and fog of their encounter. He calmed their anxious hearts, and assured them that all was well. Then, together, they set off down the mountain for further ministry that awaited them.

Their new vision of Jesus would challenge them, convict them, grow them, and remind them that He was indeed the Son of God. Was it a perfect understanding? No, but it would serve them well in the days just ahead, when night would veil both a garden betray-al and a fireside denial. It would also give them a candle of hope at a time when darkness would cover the land; the Father turning his eyes from the Son who became sin.

And ultimately, they would have their spiritual sight. He would indeed fill their vision. This is the one, as Peter would later recount, who has brought us *"out of darkness and into his marvelous light"* (1 Peter 2:9b).

And so I pray. May we be open to receive the vision that Jesus would grant us. May we be careful to walk in that vision, until the day when our faith becomes sight. The frequent clouds of our earthly walk will be lifted forever, when we stand in the brilliance of His presence. It will be worth the ascent; every cloud we have struggled through.

For you have been called to live in freedom, my brothers and sisters. But don't use your freedom to satisfy your sinful nature. Instead, use your freedom to serve one another in love. Galatians 5:13; NLT

Call it middle age, or just a bad case of the February "grumps." I am concerned about how soft this younger generation has become. It's not about electronics or video games per se, but they certainly figure into the equation. An abundance of teen transportation and lots of free time and money also play their role, but they are not the focus of my concern. What has got me thinking and steaming this evening is the fact that today was a day when school was called off, simply because it was…cold.

Today's youth know nothing about the cold, much as I heard in lectures from my elders when I was but a ruddy lad. Every generation was the toughest generation, so it seems. But the truth (as I remember it) is this: when I was a kid, school was not called off, period. The bigger the snow or the lower the temperature, my school relished the fact that students would enter the halls of academia all the quicker, just to escape from the nightmarish conditions outside. We once were threatened during the big freeze of '68 with outside recess if we didn't get our math work done. OK, I made that up. But you get the point—what was normal then is called hardship today. What was permissible and well within the boundaries of what we would do or not do then has very little in common with today's perspectives. Who moved the boundaries? And have we gotten better or worse for the shift?

A couple of Sundays ago, my class got me thinking about boundaries during our discussion of the temptation of Christ. The example I thought of applies to snow and cold days as well, and it concerns none other than the habits of our late family pet, a dog.

Our backyard was large and well stocked with trees, grass, tool sheds, picnic table, toys, shaded sandbox and swing set. It was framed by a sturdy fence, designed to keep youth safely contained for playtime. And believe me; we had a lot of youth to work with. My wife brought a lot of children into my marriage.

Within this backyard of wonders, our dog would roam. But rather than enjoy all there was to explore within the yard, the dog would spend her time running the very perimeter, eventually leaving a well-worn path at the base of the fence. Life for the dog always seemed to be about what lay out of reach, over the boundary on the other side of the fence. She expended all her energy for this life on the edge, rarely taking in anything that was available to her within the zone that was safe and pleasurable. Some dogs never learn.

How important it is for me to consider those borders, here on a cold February night. The kids are anxious tonight, bracing themselves for the possibility of school again tomorrow. Morning will determine if conditions cross the boundary, or if we are "on" for the day. Similarly, sometimes boundaries are clearly set for me as a believer. I have God's Word, his indwelling Spirit, and the counsel of godly friends to keep me "in the yard." Other areas are not so clearly fenced off; these are the times where personal conviction and preference had best line up with what I say I believe. I guess the bottom line is to focus on how close I can stay, not how far to the edge I may wander. I would suppose nothing brings dissatisfaction and discontent as quickly as a life bent on running the borderlands.

And as life in this world reaffirms, more freedoms do not strictly mean more enjoyment.

So maybe it was too cold today for kids to venture out and plod their way to the school or stand in line for the bus. I've had brush-es with frostbite and can attest that it's not a fun time. I can under-stand that boundary.

The girls have come downstairs with baskets of dirty clothes, loading up for the laundromat uptown. Megan is in gym shorts and a t-shirt. The wind chill is a brisk -20, according to the TV meteor-ologist gesturing wildly across his regional map. I try to inquire nonchalantly about this strange combination of arctic weather and tropical attire. The response is classic teenager, both in depth and foresight. I let it go.

She'll have a good story to tell when she's older. After all, her generation is the toughest, you know…

———————————————

As I ponder upon my bed...

Now to the one who works, his wage is not credited as a favor, but as what is due. But to the one who does not work, but believes in Him who justifies the ungodly, his faith is credited as righteousness... Romans 4:4-5; NASU

I heard an interesting bit on the radio during one of my drives home from the office. It seems that science has isolated a naturally occurring compound in our brains that can fend off the effects of sleepiness when given in concentrated doses. In the clinical trials conducted on certain lesser primates, it seems to work amazingly well.

Bob: "Hey Harry—that sure is one alert monkey!"

Harry: "Uh huh."

Outside of the obvious humor in wanting to secure such a product to spritz liberally on my children at sunrise, congregations at the worship hour, and myself just after supper, there are certain cautions to this "look what we can do" discovery. While there may certainly be some advantages to having such a product available on our store shelves in the coming years, I wonder if in the end it will be yet another chip off the ever-eroding foundation of our society—our work-enamored society.

Now, far be it from me to decry the importance of labor. Labor is biblical, American, and resident in my bloodstream. I comment at times about the lack of work ethic that plagues pockets of this land, and am as frustrated as the next person about the current dearth of life-sustainable jobs for the many, many who want nothing more than honest work, a quiet life, and a steady paycheck.

The advent of this new wonder drug that could fend off the effects of sleep deprivation might have its uses, but there may be more darkness than light about having, or needing to have, such a potion. Life lived at warp speed, needing more hours to our day to cram in more productivity, amusement, or myriad other activities, may in the end not be much of a life after all.

For all of our pouring ourselves into our work, there does not seem to be an increased output of happy, contented households. For all of the late hours spent in games, gambles and go-go-go, I am not seeing the steady rise of a population inspired toward personal integrity, mutual love, national pride or international unity. We may not be seeing much of lifestyles that guard our rest, but we certainly are seeing a lot more arrests, cardiac or otherwise.

Even the music of the present generations reveals, through its titles, a fast-paced search for that which defies discovery: Can't get no satisfaction. Still haven't found what I'm looking for. Workin' for the weekend. Nine to Five. Take this job…

I wonder how the marketing campaign will pan out for the marvel spritz that will give us more "productive" hours to our days. Given the present payoff surrounding us, why would anyone want to ante up in order to heap more hours and energy into something that has such a frustrating, emotionally negative payoff?

And of course, the question about spiritual emptiness begs to be asked.

So maybe, just maybe, it's a deeper core issue. One that can't be answered simply by trading off some hours of rest for additional hours of doing.

Maybe it's an issue of first, being.

Paul's words from Romans four should serve at bringing perspective to the child of God, laboring in this world. We are accepted because of Christ's work, not our own. No effort on our part, even if we gave it round-the-clock attention, could ever buy our way into His presence. We enter by faith, and we remain because His work was perfect.

The Word by which we receive that knowledge must be believed. Knowledge accepted by faith leads us to being. Being then transforms our doing. The order is indeed critical, else faith is shipwrecked by dead works; people attempting to be Christians by doing right things. The Lord will not receive these, come that day of accounting (Matt. 7:21-23).

If the Word informs me concerning eternity, I must also accept its authority for the days given me under the sun. In its pages, among all the guidance given, I learn about the importance of work, and rest, and balance in all things. This is more than simply God's "advice" to consider; as some "suggestions" given for man to weigh equally alongside other worldly counsels. The Creator has left us His instruction for how to approach this life, and enter the life to come. He knows. We must trust. And do.

It is from His principles that my mind is already made up concerning the spritz that is to come. I wouldn't even care if it was manufactured exclusively in Michigan as part of the new economy. It's a road I will not travel down.

Besides, caffeine's my spritz of choice, though I purposefully steer clear of it after the dinner hour. You know, after a day at work, I don't want it to interfere with my approaching nighttime rest.

It is useless for you to work so hard from early morning until late at night, anxiously working for food to eat; for God gives rest to his loved ones. Psalm 127:2; NLT

For there is no partiality with God. Romans 2:11; NASU

Sooner or later, it surfaces between siblings. Their birth order or age differences matter little; temperaments from fiery to tranquil all fall victim to this phenomenon as well. At some gathering or amid a conversation, they will recall together incidents from their childhoods, but each with their own selective version of special times, major purchases or biased attention that was lavished upon one of them as children. As the reminiscences flow, the accusations inevitably spill out, usually referencing either parents or near relatives at the center of the discussion.

"He (She, They) always did like you better."

At home, I believe that the rivalry behind this mentality normally hits its peak among the children of mainly my wife's doing somewhere around their tenth birthday. Up to that point, they demonstrate a steady underlying theme of competition, and a constant vying for attention. We as the adults reap awesome benefits from this scramble for parental favor. Paula gets unlimited foot rubs; I garner eager lawn care helpers. Unfortunately, there is a turning, or as I like to call it, "the shift," where with age, the children's other interests and opportunities phase out this competition from their priorities. Good luck trying to get a foot rubber or leaf raker then. Better have the candy open, or your wallet handy. Even then, there are limits.

Even with the "active" competition closing, the observations and opinions framed by the now-older children still tend toward seeing favoritism displayed by us, their extremely flawed and feet-of-clay parental units. Bake a cake, cook a meal, or attend an event—and someone's bound to dredge up in loud, public protest the time you forgot the quarter under their pillow or made them eat the stupid green beans.

One mom I recently overheard cleverly summed it up in a fashion that surely hushed up her squabbling gang of adult kids for a while. Responding to their standard charge and the "favoritism" line, she replied, "You people just don't get it. I don't like any of you!"

While it is admittedly fun to hear the stories from the kids' perspectives, our first tendency is to deny the charges outright. Of course we're not biased. Of course we are fair and even-handed, and distribute love and loving acts in exactingly equal fashion among the children. Right?

So maybe there is something to their case. After all, we have our moments where one of them does something we really like, while another is messing up big time. Love for loved ones may not be abandoned, but certainly "like" has its moments of flux, doesn't it? I am confirmed of my own bias when I see it all around me, experience it personally, and recognize that scripture is replete with examples from the lives of saints and sinners long since parted. From the preferential treatments of Isaac and Jacob, to the "privilege" of Peter, James and John, there truly is nothing new under the sun.

Paul's unfolding of the gospel by way of the letter to the Romans takes, at its start, a leveling look at preferential treatment from God's viewpoint. From that early section come the words that begin this story; words of assurance that God is neither impressed nor influenced by our scramble to curry favor by outwardly performing religiously while inwardly rejecting His revealed truths.

As I Was Saying . . .

Lines may be drawn and earthly distinctions may be formed in the minds of men, but God's standard is firm and His judgment is fixed, unbiased, and—above all—absolutely just. Paul is unmixed and admittedly even blunt in his summation of our standing before God. There is a level standard for judgment before the Lord God, and He plays no favorites in the final analysis. Those who are true believers are found to be in God's favor. Those duplicitous and self-serving are weighed and found wanting.

How refreshing!

How sobering.

Along with the encouragement received when reading God's Word, there is also this challenge: To gain knowledge from Him brings a resultant expectation from Him to be accountable with that knowledge. *For merely listening to the law doesn't make us right with God. It is obeying the law that makes us right in his sight* (Romans 2:13, NLT). Though perfect obedience would be the mark, perfection is unattainable. Still, "unattainable" is no excuse for leaving off every sober effort to progress in our walk under His revealed light.

I find that as I am living in self-confrontation by God's standard, I seek to point less, speak later, and endeavor to reserve more judgments for the Higher courts to come. There's enough to tend in my own garden to occupy my days. If I fumble badly in living the Christian life, there's nothing I could utter to convince the world at large that Christ makes any difference in any life. No wonder the Scriptures say, *"The Gentiles blaspheme the name of God because of you"* (Rom. 2:24; NLT).

Some days it is beyond me to even contemplate the wonder of His grace: He bestows faith to believe, hope to persevere, and assurance that His Word is true. And a person with a changed heart seeks praise from God, not from people (Romans 2:29c; NLT). He means what He says. He loves us, and has a plan for our lives. His lessons are taught to us as a lifelong class; we will grapple and stagger with deepening meaning and application, as we respond to His plan unfolding in us. Some of the lessons are tough, but it is still important to stay with His plan. He has loved us enough not to leave us as we were, and in His preferential love He will transform us.

Are you enjoying your preferential treatment?
It's not the miracle that God always did love you more.
The miracle is that God chose to love us at all.

...and to make it your ambition to lead a quiet life and attend to your own business and work with your hands, just as we commanded you, so that you will behave properly toward outsiders and not be in any need. 1 Thessalonians 4:11-12; NASU

I knew a man once who told me things that set me free. His world was a world of valued work, honor, morality and truth. His education was limited on paper but vast in the credentialing of living an examined life.

He was a powerful man, yet kind. He had a love for simple things, and lived out his days with unpolished speech and in careful labor. He had a proverbial style in conversation that touched me deeply. We met at the time when I needed him most; I, the naïve and restless, youthful in my thirst for purpose, disillusioned in my Quixote-quest for honorableness and affirmation of the existence of good and right.

Of all times, I remember especially our meeting on occasional winter mornings, standing together in the quiet of the pre-dawn. I would nod to his tales and musings, as breath and coffee steam swirled around our faces, a visual magnification of the chill in the air. How could one have such a zeal for life, to be "on" at that hour, and with such a constant drive?

We had some fleeting time to labor together on home projects, and I would value what he valued; the older models, the simpler tools, the satisfaction of a job well done. I stumbled over skills and words, never feeling like there was much I had to offer in the manly art of mechanical proficiency, or the main event of conversations beyond safe topics of sports, trucks or work. Still, he let me in, always patient, always telling and re-telling until he was sure that I got it.

He told me once that the right man could make a business just selling one commodity: honesty. People would one day rush to hire a man who with unwavering character could keep his word and perform exactly the task that he was hired for. Such a man would never need work, for integrity would always open doors.

He told me too, that though his was a life far from perfect and of some notable regret, he had peace with God through Christ.

There came a day when he fell ill, and the sickness was unto death. In my estimation, he was too young and too good, and he died too soon. Such it is always with all my summations of both mankind and God's hand: my own scale is faulty and my judgments are mingled. I, not being God, could not grasp how this could fit into His plan. And I, not being God, could do nothing in my power to prevent his going. I only knew my own hurt, and try as I might the words to bring him solace and comfort in his last days could only haltingly come through my thick lips.

I knew a man once, as he lay dying, who told me things that set me free. And this is what he said: He had come to believe that as bad as man was, there was still hope for him because God had looked down with pity and sent his son to take care of it. All would be made right one day, but it was important to live a clean and enduring life, because God wouldn't take kindly to people being linked to his name and living in the wrong. And even if it were all for naught in the end, he said, I still think the life I lived by faith has been the best life I could've chose to live.

And then he died.

If we have hoped in Christ in this life only, we are of all men most to be pitied. But now Christ has been raised from the dead, the first fruits of those who are asleep. 1 Corinthians 15:19-20; NASU

So, by the hand of God and in the great plan of His, I am still here today. I, too, like my long-gone friend, am trying my best to live in a way pleasing to God. Faith in God is evidenced in the life, not just the words. Truly, on some days the wear of life itself is for me a constant reminder to hope for heaven that cannot by now be that distant.

I have another hope, reserved for that age and place to come. My hope is for the occasional cool morning, in which I find I have a friend awaiting. And with him I long to stand and talk; to watch the swirl of crisp fresh air about his head as he breathes in and expels, joyous, never-ending conversation, punctuated often by his reminders that he had told me it would be this good. This very good.

"He who has found his life will lose it, and he who has lost his life for My sake will find it."   Matthew 10:39; NASU

It's been a whirl of a new year already, and the on again, off again winter makes me hope for the long days of summer all the more. I remember the admonitions of my youth, when I was often told by my elders that time would go by much faster as I grew older, becoming like them. They were of course, at perhaps 40 to 60 years old, all ancient in my clear, blue eyes.

And of course, with the sole exception of Michigan winters, they were correct.

Now being found within my self-defined category of "elder," I do tend to dwell more these days over the pace of this fast-forward life. The relentless advance of technology has multi-tasked us to the point of madness, and the notion of quality of life—that ethereal, whispy inner feeling of good at the end of the day, seems ever more elusive even amid all the "living" that we're purportedly doing. Frantic commuters; fractured families. Frustrated consumers; frayed faithful. Fast, futile living doesn't take long to lose its appeal—sort of like having the same ring tone for, say, more than three or four days.

Also reaffirmed at this point in life is that those who focus on the world's currency of more fame, more stuff, and more sway are really losing out. Seeing how life actually pans out for the "winners" of that lottery is evidence enough. Apparently, and contrary to all we've been told, having "everything" is no guarantee that one will enjoy a life that is indeed fulfilling.

Celebrities now "off" themselves with unswerving regularity. Many of the surviving are living out dead lives of charade and meaninglessness. It seems that the voyeuristic tendencies of our celebrity-cult nation, fed by an endless spew of paparazzi-prepared gruel, have added now a new obsession something akin to necrophilia. I cannot recommend loudly enough that it is prudent—very prudent—to once and for all, look away.

The clamor for "more" also leaves a wake of ruin, sweeping away new victims day by day. It is a very rare thing to discover a truly contented soul, even among those with a relationship to God. It seems that we are groomed for discontent, fed on want, and neutered to any concept of one handful, with rest.

The quest and resultant abuse of power has enjoyed continued popularity in light of the emerging global economy and our expanding culture of insider privilege, golden parachutes, buyouts, mergers, and hostile takeovers. While the multimillion dollar deals, arrests, asset seizures and trials occupy one end of the spectrum, the other is filled with the smaller power grabs at personal, familial, and community levels. All generate their own share of the disenfranchised and trampled.

And in my summations and to my credit (or blame), I haven't included even a mention of the examples that continually flow from government at every level.

Into my midlife pondering, I now address the words of Christ that begin this story. The Lord is not addressing the masses, warning them of the end that awaits a faithless life. It would be a great point to make on this comment from Him, but He gives other ample warnings to that end that hold up well in their own contexts. Here, the point to ponder is that He is addressing none other than His own. Upon that group of twelve rests the weight of the mission, the future of the gospel, and, by application, our very lives as well.

For me, the point is clear. With all of the teaching and miraculous happenings, the disciples were still given the prerogative to choose.

"It is your life," Jesus in effect says. "You may cling to it, use it for your own purposes, and walk the way of the world." "Or, you can surrender it all, for now. And find true life at the end of these days."

They did indeed choose, and their obedience included long seasons of sifting and polishing and refining and testing. The resurrection of Christ would lead to their remarkable filling, and eleven would continue on, bearing their crosses, fulfilling another's mission for their lives, accepting the paths He would put before them. Yes, one did walk away. There was too much to lose. The Fame. The Stuff. The Sway. And, truly enough, he did indeed receive what he thought would complete his life.

Fame, but as "the betrayer."

Thirty pieces of "stuff," but tossed away in his self-loathing.

Sway, but from a desolate rope in utter despair.

This afternoon, it's been another hard storm, and winter shows little sign of releasing its grip on us anytime soon. But I have hope. Spring always comes. This path of life has become familiar in its circuits, so I can relax, enjoy what I may of winter, and know that this wintry walk will last but a little longer.

Life in Him also demands a level head. The road varies in intensity, and the route I am to take is not necessarily the same route chosen for you. But given time, focus, obedience and allegiance to His plan, the roads will all converge when we one day will stand before Him, to begin what we have waited for all along.

Now, that's what I call livin'!

You threw me into the ocean depths, and I sank down to the heart of the sea. The mighty waters engulfed me; I was buried beneath your wild and stormy waves. Jonah 2:3; NLT

One more thing can be added to the list of attributes I'll never be remembered for. That one more thing is the art of swimming. I was a late swimmer to begin with, due to the fact that I did not come from a swimming family. I did the "Y" thing, but ended a long string of bus rides and pool classes with little more than belly-smacker rash and a strange chlorine-related sinus infection. While others thrived in otter-graceful fluidity; I stood dripping and alone as poster child for the Sinks-Like-A-Stone-Statue Club. Looking back, I suppose it was helpful for the water-rescue class to have a live target. One bright day in my tenth year of life, it was my grandfather who finally taught me the meager aquatic skills that I still possess today. It was probably only four or five feet of water, but when he threw me out of the boat with the instructive phrase, "Swim!" I did manage to stay afloat on what little water remained that I hadn't swallowed. Merry Lake, it was called. Oh, the irony of place-names.

My aversion to swimming is not truly my fault, for I have landlubber genes, you see. Genealogical traces have unearthed the fact that for generations back, my Irish-Franco-Germanic ancestors have long been hailed on the European Continent as The Wading Masters Clan. Add to that the present day annoyance that even when I do wade, marine mammal police boats arrive to affix straps about me to drag me back to the deep, while children on the beach flail water at me with their tiny sand buckets and imploringly cry, "No, Shamu, you shan't die! No! No!" It's no love affair between me and the water, at any exposure level.

OK, so that's silly, but the truth is, I doubt that I even own a swimsuit at present. As I recall, my wife retired my last one due to a hole in the knee, but that too is an old joke. I simply am not a swimmer. I can paddle if I absolutely have to, but a nerve-damaged left leg causes me to flail about with some serious drift to the port side. This "swimming" if I must use the term, strongly resembles a wounded fish in its surface death flutter, just prior to becoming gull filler. Granted, in my case, it would have to be one enormous gull, and not too picky at that.

By association, I read an article last week about the sport of free-diving. I will gladly add that activity as well to the list of things I'll never be remembered for. It is played out as simply as the name implies: dive down as deep as you can, and then surface. The "surface" part seems especially critical to me if you want to actually be alive and standing on the podium when the trophies are passed out. Incidentally, "passed out" is probably a poor term to use. Anyway, there are variations of freediving events (such as whether or not fins are used), but the truly amazing bits about this sport emerged after I read more by visiting a few web sites. For example, the current women's record (fins only) is 289 feet—use a football field to step that one off. Competitors train on dry land for enduring CO_2 saturation, as well as O_2 depravation. One current winner can hold her breath for six minutes and twenty-five seconds.

Six minutes and twenty-five seconds.

All of which leads me to some spiritual applications for the topic at hand. How does someone discover that they can hold their breath for six minutes and twenty-five seconds? My first impression would be that that knowledge does not come by stumbling upon a freediving competition site and deciding at whim to don some flippers and give it a whirl. There must instead be a dedicated and programmatic building of endurance, believing that one day such control and strength can be a reality. I also ponder the truth that the breath holding of a freediver occurs while under extreme physical exertion, not while they are meditatively curled up in a chair with mood music and soft lighting all about. The skill may be developed in the quiet, but it is only tested in the deep. So it is likewise, in the "strength training" of the disciple. As important as the study and mediation upon the Word is, the proof of the heart is only revealed by the next dive into life's ocean of trials.

It seems to me that a Christ-life in this world is also about coming to terms with the depths. Those who avoid the trials and flutter on the surface truly miss the wonder of the deep. The process of learning spiritual breathing through the descent and ascent of connected-to-God living is, like freediving, a focused and constant exercise. Learning how to receive the breath of God in the day-to-day of life is a faith experience comparable to the preparations these athletes build into their lives as well. If I am learning how to breathe in God for the "shallow" everyday, there is a steady endurance being built in my life for the certain times when I will be plunging into the depths that every life must encounter.

Note the breakdown of the similarities: a freediver can walk away from the sport, never to enter the depths again. The Christian, as with any other person on earth, has limited or no control over when the depth-challenges will next present themselves. Likewise, there are no truly tempting earthly rewards for enduring life's descents. The reward of the stoic to simply "bear up" may be a smug satisfaction with self, but that incentive proves hollow in the end. The Word teaches that there is great spiritual reward presently and great reward eventually for those who go God's way, even when that way leads to the very sea bottom of life's testings.

Breathe deep. Don't be afraid of the depths. The God who places you in the ocean of life is not himself a distant trainer safe on shore. He goes with us, every foot of the descent and for every minute of what to us may seem like a breathless testing.

Where can I go from Your Spirit? Or where can I flee from Your presence? If I ascend to heaven, You are there; If I make my bed in Sheol, behold, You are there. If I take the wings of the dawn, if I dwell in the remotest part of the sea, even there Your hand will lead me, and Your right hand will lay hold of me (Psalm 139:7-10; NASU).

He will not let you stumble and fall; the one who watches over you will not sleep.   Psalm 121:3; NLT

Thomas Alva Edison, Wizard of Menlo Park, I owe a lot to you. The electric light is so much a part of my world that it is hard for me to imagine life without it. On cloudless nights, I've looked down from 35,000 feet to vast expanses of the world that has yet to know the reach of the electric grid. Their night truly does cover the land like a curtain. Flying over the dense "broccoli" that comprises the bulk of the Bolivian landscape, the occasional glow from a gas lamp can often be seen after minutes of observing nothing but pitch-black jungle. My mind races as I wonder whom the lamp illuminates, living out there, secluded from enlightened civilization and perhaps living forever beyond the reach of an electrical network. What do they feel as the night approaches? At dusk, are they already anxious for the coming of the dawn? Only God knows.

Closer to home and most hearts, I've recently read that we have a notable history combining North American sports and the world of electric marvels. The first night football game was played on the 28th of September, 1892. One account states that the primitive lights were brought in and suspended on a pole in the middle of the playing field. Now that would lend itself to some interesting color commentary—"Smith takes the snap; handoff to Jones. Jones fakes left, breaks a tackle, pivots right and...oh no! He's knocked himself out on that new fangled light post…"

I'm not much of a night person myself. I have no firm statistics, but simple observation over these years leads me to believe that not much good ever happens after 10 pm in this world of mine. I believe that many lives would be on track and many problems would remedy themselves if folks would simply go to bed when it is evening, and then get up when it is first light. Benjamin Franklin, who never had the privilege of living in the glow of the electric marvel, penned his famous Poor Richard's line, "Early to bed and early to rise, makes a man healthy, wealthy and wise." I can only remember without reference one parallel that is played out as well, "Late to bed and early to rise, makes you stretch your blood shot eyes." I'm working on a good one for "late to bed and late to rise"—I imagine it'll have something about teens after the comma.

Now I know that there are many who must man the night watches, else all of our lives would be disrupted. Granted, many are taking to the streets and off to work just at the moment I'm calling it a day. The ones who should be calling it a day are the ones that need the exhortation.

To be sure, there was a time when I could go all day and half the night, then do it all over again. The energy needed to sustain such a life on scant sleep has long since vanished, though I still find my mind plays tricks on me, making me think I can still plug it out with the young bucks enjoying their twenty-plus hour days. Our usual descent into this thinking (for my wife also has these regressions to youth) involves our agreement for a "movie night" in our chamber, accompanied by an assortment of "healthy" snacks. The kids bring in a selection, we all pile on the bed, and the good times begin. Several hours later, wife and I awake with our glasses askew and extremely dry mouths. The kids have cleaned up the snacks and retired to their rooms, where they discuss the impending living arrangements for their party animal parents who never even finished viewing the opening titles downstairs. Of course, their discussion can go all night, because they're young…

In my defense, with a metabolism charting somewhere between "Serbian Pine" and "Igneous Rock" I need all of the nighttime rest I can make room for. For some years now I have been using a breathing machine to counter my sleep apnea. This condition is caused by one's airway collapsing and shutting off air movement, but I personally would rather relate it to my athletic physique and utter manly manliness even taking my own breath away... This little breathing machine is truly a three-fold blessing to my world. First, it gives me better odds of actually waking up every morning. Second, I have a lesser chance of nodding off during the day, which could be particularly distressing especially on a Sunday during my own message. Third, my wife, after laughing hysterically at me in my headgear, which resembles part of a Soyuz cosmonaut's emergency mission abort system, sleeps even more soundly herself. Yep, it's win-win all around in my world.

If I could only get in a little daytime rest, things would be even better. It is ironic and maddening to think that when I was an incredibly handsome and compliant toddler, I was absolutely opposed to the concept of the compulsory nap. Now, at an age when I would seriously consider making generous contributions to any gubernatorial candidate who would run on the platform of "mandatory naps for every taxpayer," I find there is simply no relaxing time for such a luxury. Poor Richard also said, "There will be sleeping enough in the grave." Poor Richard gets irritating on occasion, doesn't he?

There is comfort in the night, whether long or short, in simply knowing that God is there. The Word of God relates many incidents that were framed by night, including the stories of those who sought out Jesus and those who came to betray him. The one who has created the night has done so with purpose, for all of his created things need their time to repose and rejuvenate for the day ahead. Even Jesus slept. The Son of God, above all created things, still needed his rest as fully man yet fully God. He needed his rest as part of his preparation, to accomplish all that the Father required for his days.

There is also comfort in knowing that God never sleeps. While I can feel overwhelmed by the strength and stretch of evil in this world, it is reassuring to know that nothing escapes the eye of my Father. I needn't toss on a fitful bed, pondering whether God has seen the injustice of my day. Destruction is certain for those who try to hide their plans from the LORD, who try to keep him in the dark concerning what they do! *"The Lord can't see us," you say to yourselves. "He doesn't know what is going on!" How stupid can you be?* Isaiah 29:15-16a; NLT

More than ever before, I find that the night often grants me the quiet time that I need with my Lord. Usually when I am awakened in the middle of the night, it is for an appointment with the Lord. He ministers to my spirit the rest that I need as I wait upon Him in the still darkness. Oftentimes it is for prayer, other times for the reading of His Word. I find a notepad kept handy is often full of notes the following day that are the fuel not only for my personal devotions, but also for my teaching, messages and other writings. Such is this writing today.

Pleasant dreams, and may your nights be filled with His presence.

I will lie down in peace and sleep, for you alone, O LORD, will keep me safe. Psalm 4:8; NLT

The LORD is near to the brokenhearted, and saves those who are crushed in spirit. Psalm 34:18; NASU

It is the scent of this world, but a world away.

You'd think with over 10 trips—a cumulative hundred and twenty days—I'd have gotten over the fragrance. It's a particular blend of antiquity and calla lily, smoldering wood fire and hot tortilla, animal and human, roasting coffee bean, diesel fume, incense and bougainvillea. The bouquet varies by location, day, and particular additions, but these basic elements are the groundwork of its fragrant composition.

I know the scent. I know it the moment I awake to start another round of my day-consuming tasks in the hospital. My nose is true. It's Guatemala, again.

It has been a number of years since I first volunteered to be a part of the Michigan medical team to Guatemala. Their mission struck a chord in me, and though I am no doctor, even a medical team needs a chaplain and a cook, so the match was made. The team varies from year to year, some returning as regular as the seasons, others but a one-shot encounter in this land of the Maya. Myself, I cannot seem to walk away. The need of the people, physically and spiritually, leaves me humbled and resolved to do the February thing again. The barriers of language, culture and distance are not easily overcome, but thankfully there are some residing there who also share my heart. They know the languages, live in the cultures, and are continually present. I can do nothing more than assist and enhance their efforts, encourage them, and with the team do our part to show the compassion of Christ through hands skilled in medical process, and hearts that beat compassion where little compassion is known.

It has become for me much more than the "February thing" as well. There is a work God has done in my heart. I sense Christ's presence more fully, wherever I am in His world. He has shown me my advantage, and the resultant God-expectation to use that advantage to assist others. I have less need for the things of the world, though in my culture I am surrounded by everything that competes to supplant my need for Him alone. I find myself amazed at the wealth of care available to me, and how often I equate (to my shame) good health with God's blessing upon me.

I have met with the believers in the highlands of Guatemala. I have visited their dirt floor homes and worshipped in their tin-roof churches. I have witnessed their offerings of corn and eggs—the best they have, with great sacrifice—brought to the communion table and set before the Lord. I have heard their songs and listened to the translated testimonies they share. Stories of hardship, war, sickness, starvation, but always their assurance that the Lord was and is near, and that He alone is their salvation.

I find my own testimony weak by comparison. I have known little of their experience. I grumble when the waiting room is full. I bemoan the price of goods that I must have. I feel unblessed when the doctor's report is not what I want for my happy and content life. The scent of Guatemala for me is often the scent of Christ, removed from the trappings of the culture I know too well.

There comes a response from every North American participant in missions to those countries such as Guatemala who are now emerging. One such response could be a total disavowal to our lifestyle and privilege, jettisoning all that speaks of wealth, affluence and consumerism. One could choose poverty and service, the Mother Theresa approach to life, which certainly has its foundations, merits and place in this world. I would be quick to note that for those taking that vow, there are others in the wings motivated and organized to supply for the practical need of ministers operating at the street level. One cannot minister from an economic vacuum.

With some reflection however, I think a second and better approach is to recognize the summary teaching of Christ concerning the three servants. "To those who use well what they are given, even more will be given, and they will have an abundance" (Matt. 25:29a; NLT). The biblical view of wealth and opportunity as gifts from God to serve others is certainly what the Lord has impressed upon me in my service to Him. In this country, my income and social status are laughable by my peers, but I am comparatively rich beyond measure in resources and opportunity to my friends in Guatemala. With the right motivation and some true effort, I can use what God gives me to impact lives everywhere, whether in rugged, beautiful Central America, or the side roads and city streets of Jackson County, Michigan. It's really about perspective and priority, not prosperity.

May my life and yours exude with the scent of Christ.

"Do not worry then, saying, 'What will we eat?' or 'What will we drink?' or 'What will we wear for clothing?' For the Gentiles eagerly seek all these things; for your heavenly Father knows that you need all these things. But seek first His kingdom and His righteousness, and all these things will be added to you. So do not worry about tomorrow; for tomorrow will care for itself. Each day has

enough trouble of its own." Matthew 6:31-34; NASU

What are the stress points that invade your day? Are they runaway energy prices, sticker shock at the store, or the lead stories of greed, corruption, hypocrisy or terror often gracing the news? How are you bearing up under the current conditions of world, nation, state, market, schools, family, relationships, and even your own mortal being? Any spikes in blood pressure, restless nights, or migraines linked to these concerns lately?

Granted, whether scrambling for hides, scraping for hardtack, or scrimping for Mr. Ford's Innovation, every generation has had its economic challenges. Humanity seems to be rather adept at mixing Need and Want into a blur. In this, Scripture identifies mankind's constant theme of strife and unrest. As Need and Want clash, resultant wars of various intensities and durations have peppered this brief age of Adam.

It can be observed that through our centuries, the societal Need of humanity has often been addressed when the good have reigned, even amid populations that have not bowed their knee to Christ. Conversely, when evil and its drive for Want is at the helm, the Need of the masses is dismissed out of hand.

It is notable that oftentimes the Need or Want of humanity has spawned remarkable innovation and personal industriousness— usually commendable things. Sadly, lawlessness and recklessness are more frequently seen as its markers in today's present darkness. It seems that more and more, this blurring of Need and Want is casting a long and lingering shadow over mankind's path. For many in our own land, the Great American Dream has yielded instead to a nightmarish plight that is stark reality.

Personal health and well-being, either relationally or physically, is also a lingering source of stress for life these days.

On the relational side, disintegrations abound, even in a communication-saturated society. Through the miracle of the microchip, we now have numerous ways to spawn drivel by the megabyte and conduct impersonal and damaging e-mailing and text messaging. Phones are a boon to loose talk without end. "Much-talking" is in and of itself seen as having great value, when in reality it undermines the sacredness of speech, the value of discretion, and a core truth of healthy relationships: choose your words carefully; they cannot be taken back.

Focusing on our physical state, we increasingly demand greater wonders from our medical society. The "right" to restored health even after years of neglectful living and unstoppable aging (for we all are dying) has set the stage for undisciplined lifestyles, unrealistic expectations, and of course, innumerable lawsuits.

My reporting, in light of Jesus' words above, is not given to verify the "gentile" mindset. Looking around, Christians seem to readily model these same behaviors, and can be found possessing the resultant stresses as well. Want outstrips Need, to the detriment of self and others. Relationships-on-the-rocks are statistically keeping pace with the population without Christ. A gospel message of health and wealth packs the house, while Need still outpaces Aid. Many inoculate their conscience with what Jesus said, "The poor you will always have with you." Then it's time for more commerce—Vanity Fair being open 'til ten, or twenty-four-seven at the click of a mouse; a drive-through that never shuts down.

We seem to be doing well at picking up speed, even in light of losing direction.

Then Jesus takes his seat, and begins to speak to our need. Our true need. Certainly the masses that heard Him that day had known their own hard times. The task of trying to carve out a life within their unstable economy. The misery of having to exist under the rule of an occupying force. The droning of their party politicos, always benefiting the "haves" and asterisking their promises to meet the Need of the population. The human condition of illness and pride and greed and lust that tore apart families, forged swords by the million, and often turned even the most spirited to despondency and servile resignation.

The preacher sat upon the mountain, setting out the priorities of those who will serve God truly, follow Him unwaveringly and trust Him wholeheartedly. He chooses still today to shake us to our core with this, His word of challenge, priority, and comfort.

Am I leaning upon Him for the day-to-day? Am I living in light of His daily presence, or have I shut him away and decided I know best how to provide for my Need? Are my cravings of Want being checked in light of His counsel? Am I learning the blessing of asking, and then thanking Him for daily bread? In obedience, am I free to be an answer to another's prayer of need? When the worries of life come knocking, am I letting God answer the door?

Every word of God is tested; He is a shield to those who take refuge in Him. Do not add to His words or He will reprove you, and you will be proved a liar. Two things I asked of You, do not refuse me before I die: keep deception and lies far from me, give me neither poverty nor riches; feed me with the food that is my portion, that I not be full and deny You and say, "Who is the LORD?" Or that I not be in want and steal, and profane the name of my God (Proverbs 30:5-9; NASU).

He is teaching me this: far above just for a "rough season," a life that is focused on the blessing of knowing Him will truly be met by His provision. This is not only "one day" in the kingdom to come, but even in the day I now occupy.

Seek His ways. Experience His provision. Share your bread. This is the day.

Listen to me, dear brothers and sisters. Hasn't God chosen the poor in this world to be rich in faith? James 2:5, NLT.

On the northern frontier, there is a town where the rivers Madre de Dios and Beni converge. It is the home of rutted dust streets, incredibly dangerous river gold dredging, Brazil nut harvest operations, scores of "African Queen" homemade boats, and the fellowship of Pastor Elmer's church. We have entered Riberalta, Bolivia. Our team is invited to a gathering at "the church" as we are prone to call a building where Christians assemble. We arrive somewhat worn from the open truck that has heaved us along to this rougher side of a rough town. The church—the people, as you now know—welcome us in.

The building where the church meets is made of cane and tin. Windows are just wall openings that can be shuttered, though I can't imagine anything actually being prevented from entering that truly wanted to get inside. The floor is dirt, compacted nearly smooth. There are backless wooden benches, but far too few given our arrival. A table that wouldn't pass muster for even my shop projects graces the front, poised for rickety assistance in offerings or communion.

It is early evening, and a single gas lantern hoisted by a slender rope will provide our working light for the service. A man is in charge of this lantern, and there will be periodic pauses in our worship as lowering and pumping the lantern are done. The lamp will also provide the enticement for several insects-on-steroids famous to this region. They will conduct a wild worship of their own high overhead tonight.

We begin this blended worship of songs and faith stories in the real-time world of translation in Spanish and English. I am acutely aware of words. What I say must resonate with my translator so that he in turn can convey it accurately to our new friends. We have trained for these times. We have trained to talk of God and faith without mixing in references to our possessions and disparate lives in North America. We are deliberate to emphasize North since these too are Americans we are visiting this evening. To close the service, we present Bibles, and then an offering for construction of their future house of worship. We are informed that there has been a fellowship time planned.

There is no adjournment to a banquet hall. There is no microphone announcement and piped in music. There will be no whirl of dishes and microwaves and warming ovens and crock-pots. There simply are the women of the church and cloth covered baskets that have been sitting at the base of a wall. We are soon holding little empanada-like pastry pockets with various fillings. No dishes; we accept, munch and visit. I am aware of the many that have been and still are standing because there are not enough benches. We are honored guests, and we shall remain seated. To get up and request that others take our seats would be offensive, not mannerly in this culture.

Pastor Elmer and his wife hover, quietly giving orders to the women and their baskets. I get only fragments of their conversation as my Spanish is limited and halting. But I do glean this: with the empanadas distributed, it is now time for a drink.

More baskets appear, and a collection of cups now covers the wobbling table front and center. These are a varied lot, obviously having come from the church family homes for this occasion. There is no throwaway dining ware from MegaMart. There are vessels of glass, plastic, and pottery in many shapes and colors. I do not see any cup that has an identical mate. It is an odd assortment, but it is not only their best, it is their all. Pastor Elmer has discretely pointed out a cracked jar to his wife, who has delicately gathered the unfitting-for-company cup into a fold of her skirt and secreted it to a basket along the wall. I have seen it with my eyes.

Large bottles of Orange Crush are brought forth. These are worn from years of rough use and refill. The lettering is barely visible on most. These glass bottles, long gone upon our store shelves back home, are a staple of the bottling companies here. You see them everywhere: stacked in wood-sectioned crates, dusty and rattling by on open trucks, for sale in areas so remote I wonder how they arrive without roads. Some even double as fuel measures for "stations" that are little more than a barrel of gasoline and a sign guaranteeing to fix any flat. These bottles live rich lives, and on this round through South America, they have been (prayerfully) sterilized and refilled with soda for consumption on an evening such as this. The gas lantern is tended to, again.

Pastor Elmer oversees the distribution—an odd communion of sorts; empanada the body, Crush ("kroosh") the blood. We, the guests, are served. We sit and sip: little phrases of Spanish, polite smiles, interpreter-assisted dialogue. Mike, our missionary, guide, interpreter and culture-broker all in one, gives us a heads-up. We need to finish our Crush, now. We are a little slow on the uptake, for this is a region where clocks and schedules have no stranglehold. Is there truly a reason to hurry? Mike smiles and then brings light to us, his motley band of fifteen gringos. It's not about time. It's the cups. They need our cups, so they too may have a drink.

We finish. The cups are ingathered back to that frail table, refilled and redistributed among the church. This is done by that body without any fuss, drawing of attention, or reluctance—it is just what you do when you love others first. The fellowship continues until it is time—Mike knows—for our departure. A few more minutes of prayer, some photos, and we load back into our hired ride, the evening now ended. The sermon in life will never end for me.

It's fitting I should remember again what God impressed on my heart that night in the fellowship of Riberalta. In these days of construction and "happening" for our congregation and community, I am increasingly aware of what God is not impressed with as well. Buildings are wonderful tools, but people are the church. The church may be linked to a location, but it must be known by its love.

Forever, Pastor Elmer and the fellowship of Riberalta, I thank you for showing me Christ, living and loving in Bolivia. I pray He will be seen as clearly at our outpost in the Father's world, too.

As Jesus went on from there, He saw a man called Matthew, sitting in the tax collector's booth; and He said to him, "Follow Me!" And he got up and followed Him. Then it happened that as Jesus was reclining at the table in the house, behold, many tax collectors and sinners came and were dining with Jesus and His disciples. When the Pharisees saw this, they said to His disciples, "Why is your Teacher eating with the tax collectors and sinners?" But when Jesus heard this, He said, "It is not those who are healthy who need a physician, but those who are sick. But go and learn what this means: 'I DESIRE COMPASSION, AND NOT SACRIFICE,' for I did not come to call the righteous, but sinners." Matthew 9:9-13; NASU

How do you explain a man leaving all he knows to step out and follow another at merely a simple, direct command? We've all had bad days at work, where perhaps for sheer relief we could envision punching out and relocating, but what do we make of Matthew, moving down from a steady income to unemployed, following an itinerant teacher into unknown, uncharted territory? We often speak about the call of God on a life, and this has to be a pure example of it. It makes no immediate sense by any of the worlds' standards, yet it is logical and irresistible in the heart of the responding, fledgling disciple.

It is of little surprise that in the next breath of scripture, we are off to dinner. Scripture often includes descriptions of meals or food in its pages. Honest enough stuff, for meals are a mainstay and anchoring point common among friends, families, and groups small or large. It occurs to me that within every culture I have ever visited, meals are a chosen vehicle to facilitate social interactions; though the spread is vastly different, the desire for fellowship is unwaveringly the main course.

These days the food passages leap off the page, for I am trying to decrease the general heft of my church's current pastor. Something about the combination of observing another birthday, rounding another year, and my shadow taking on the appearance of an eclipse-in-process has given me incentive to shed a few. I know the Lord has told us that man doesn't live by bread alone, but as much as I agree heart-ward with this truth, it has been easier stated than lived within my world. I would like to blame it on my desire to have a lot of fellowship, but that's the easy way out. I have simply enjoyed it too much, and it's time for the change.

It doesn't take long for the religious folk to start grumbling about the company this Jesus is keeping. The NLT translation is even more graphic in stating their criticism: "Why does your teacher eat with such scum?" The critics sure sound like a fun bunch to hang around with over a salad and steak, eh? I feel something akin to an ulcer within, just knowing they're within earshot of the table.

The best rebuttals we ever encounter from the Lord are unswervingly aimed at the comfortable religious who after all, have their standards, their traditions, and are all about preserving decorum and the way things are supposed to be done. I reflect back on exit comments I've been given over many, many years. Often, "we're not comfortable with..." weighs heavily in the parting shots critique. Lord, help me from ever being comfortable in a religion. Walking in your light keeps me uncomfortable enough, uncomfortable enough to want less of me and more of you.

From everything we have presented to us, it seems that for most, there would never be a desire to reach out to outsiders, share a meal, and share some good news concerning hope in the One True God. It seems that a low opinion of those not fitting for their club, coupled with their high opinion of themselves, is a sure indicator of a private dining room—members only.

Jesus' summation of His dining preferences is certainly a model for every believer that comprises the church yet today. No doubt, we enjoy the meals we share with and within the family of God. It is imperative that we likewise enjoy reaching into our communities, seeking out opportunities such as meals to simply be there. In our common places, that common people like us frequent, we may well earn the right to share the news of uncommon joy. And that compassion, dear ones, is what Jesus is all about.

Friends tell friends about Him. It's not just a Sunday thing.

Sometimes, we even do it over lunch. And I'm always up for that.

...if there is no resurrection of the dead, not even Christ has been raised; and if Christ has not been raised, then our preaching is vain, your faith also is vain. Moreover we are even found to be false witnesses of God, because we testified against God that He raised Christ, whom He did not raise, if in fact the dead are not raised. For if the dead are not raised, not even Christ has been raised; and if Christ has not been raised, your faith is worthless; you are still in your sins. Then those also who have fallen asleep in Christ have perished. If we have hoped in Christ in this life only, we are of all men most to be pitied. 1 Corinthians 15:13-19; NASU

It's good to be back.

Not to make light of the matter, for the real situation is never funny or light. I'll ask in advance for your pardon while I poke a little fun at myself. It's all good and fitting today, for you need to understand that at this time yesterday, I was deceased. I know this for a fact; I read of it myself.

While at the office, sorting through Tuesday morning's e-mail, I came across a message sent from an old, out-of-town friend. It seemed a bit odd, that while it had arrived at my email address, it opened with a salutation to my wife, and not to me. Even more peculiar, as I began to read her mail (so sue me), was my friend's sudden pouring out of heartfelt sympathy for my darling and her children at their sudden loss of... me. With precious little detail further revealed, I hastily fired back a reply, wanting to find out how I had met my untimely demise. After all, Inquiring Minds Want to Know. I have to admit that for me, it was indeed a shock. I thought I had been feeling rather fit and healthy last week, but now, this. The hair thing is another issue, but health-wise, pretty much up to snuff for a chunky middle aged fellow of Germanic descent.

A couple of hours later, I received (as you might imagine) a fairly startled reply from my bereaved friend. My waterloo had come up in a conversation with other mutual friends. I hadn't lingered... it had been quick. Everybody had been shocked.

I sure know I was.

It's odd—I thought maybe someone would've sent flowers.

Anyway, apologies were proffered, and I was assured that all parties involved would be contacted with the important factual update. Thanks to the miracle of the internet, just one day later, I am known once again to be back among the living. My mind fled to the response of American author great Mark Twain, who once found himself in a similar situation in his slower-traveling news days: "The rumors of my death have been greatly exaggerated." Don't worry—I'll be watching my email a bit more closely for the next few weeks, just waiting to RE: and surprise the pants off of any correspondents typing out condolences.

"You've got mail...guess who!"

What a difference just one solitary day can make in a life. My life. Any life.

In this week of Resurrection, it seems fitting the Lord has allowed me the surprising and ironical glimpse at supposed death and the reality of continuing life. From man's perspective, death always seems so intrusive, so bleak, so very inappropriate and untimely, and so very final. As the opening passage of this story unfolds, Paul calls us to the reality of the resurrection, by first explaining that without a risen Savior, we could all pack it up and wait out our hopeless end.

Then, with a jolting sentence to return us to real reality, Paul puts our frail earth-bound feet back on the foundation stone that we have built our lives present and future upon:

But now Christ has been raised from the dead, the first fruits of those who are asleep (1 Corinthians 15:20; NASU).

It is not only a season in which to reflect on Resurrection, but it is an everyday truth for us to reflectively walk in. By necessity of living in a world where death still comes, it is important for believers to keep our heads in the game, realizing that death does not produce any finality to our eternal lives. True, one path—earthly—will end. Another, and a much superior walk at that, begins at once.

Someday, you may come to read or hear I am gone. Check the facts. This time the news of my passing may indeed be true. I choose "passing" as opposed to "death," for it better describes the change that I will experience in that moment. All of what has been me here, will be traded off in a breath for what I am to be, there. That is all. No wandering or suspension or isolation or degrees of crossing. I will trade places, and life will go on, yet also finally begin as it was meant to be. Forget the flowers. Sing for joy.

The Resurrection: Far from rumor; demonstrated in presence and power.

The Christ: Fulfillment of all that was, and is, and is to come.

The Gospel: Power for living, and power for dying—whatever "dying" can honestly mean to those who truly are living, and will live, forever.

Now I make known to you, brethren, the gospel which I preached to you, which also you received, in which also you stand, by which also you are saved, if you hold fast the word which I preached to you, unless you believed in vain. For I delivered to you as of first importance what I also received, that Christ died for our sins according to the Scriptures, and that He was buried, and that He was raised on the third day according to the Scriptures...
1 Corinthians 15:1-4; NASU